T0385856

GRIDLOCK

GRIDLOCK

LABOR, MIGRATION, AND

HUMAN TRAFFICKING IN DUBAI

PARDIS MAHDAVI

STANFORD UNIVERSITY PRESS ▪ STANFORD, CALIFORNIA

Stanford University Press
Stanford, California

Printed in the United States of America on acid-free, archival-quality paper

Library of Congress Cataloging-in-Publication Data

Mahdavi, Pardis, 1978- author.
  Gridlock : labor, migration, and human trafficking in Dubai / Pardis Mahdavi.
    pages cm
  Includes bibliographical references and index.
  ISBN 978-0-8047-7220-4 (cloth : alk. paper)
  1. Foreign workers--United Arab Emirates--Dubayy (Emirate) 2. Forced labor--United Arab Emirates--Dubayy (Emirate) 3. Human trafficking--United Arab Emirates--Dubayy (Emirate) 4. Dubayy (United Arab Emirates : Emirate)--Emigration and immigration--Economic aspects. I. Title.
  HD8666.Z8D836 2011
  331.6'2095357--dc22   2011003618

Typeset by Bruce Lundquist in 10/14 Minion

For my parents, Fereshteh and Mahmood Mahdavi

CONTENTS

GRIDLOCK

PROLOGUE

"**ONBOARD THIS AIRCRAFT** the following languages are spoken by our crew: Arabic, English, Tagalog, French, Italian, German, Amharic, Hindi, Urdu, Pashtu, Dari, Singalese, Mandarin, and Thai. We hope this will further assist you in having a pleasant flight," said the milky-smooth voice over the loudspeaker. I am a passenger today onboard Emirates Air, which is flying me from London Heathrow to Dubai (or DXB, as the locals refer to it). A Malaysian flight attendant comes to my row and kneels down to hand me and my rowmates a series of menus delineating cuisine from different parts of Asia. I know the flight attendant is Malaysian because her name tag states her country just below her name, Sumitra. She catches me looking and smiles at me shyly.

"She forgot to tell passengers that we also speak Malay onboard," she says, offering us pens for making our food selections on the menu.

The woman to my left tosses the menu into the seat pocket in front of her.

"I'm having the Halal meal, which isn't on here," she announces. She adjusts her head scarf, which seems to be perpetually falling around her shoulders.

I smile and glance at the woman to my right, who has just told me she is traveling to Dubai for the first time. She is from the Philippines and was routed through London for some unexplained reason. The woman is busy with the in-flight entertainment unit that makes flying on Emirates such a treat: over 150 films, and a nice-sized screen makes any long flight more bearable.

"I've been looking forward to this part of the trip," she tells me, referring to the video screen.

"Me too," I confess, smiling.

Instead of focusing on my own in-flight unit, however, I am obsessed with watching my neighbor as she scrolls through the seemingly endless list of blockbusters that I have been (not so secretly) wanting to see. After passing through *He's Just Not that Into You, Marley and Me,* and *Revolutionary Road,* she pauses on *Taken* and begins reading the summary. I lean over and say to her, "That film is about the supposed phenomenon of trafficking. It looks terrible, I can't even bear it."

The woman looks at me, puzzled. "Trafficking?" she asks, which catches the attention of my other seatmate who has stopped readjusting her head scarf and is now looking at the two of us. "I don't even know what that means, is it like street traffic?"

The woman on my left rushes to answer. "No, it's like human slavery. It's like when they kidnap women and make them their sex slaves," she says, her accent a mixture of Arabic and British.

"Oh," says the woman to my right, looking a bit embarrassed and concerned at the same time.

"Well, no," I say, "that's just what people *think* trafficking is, but it's more complicated than that." I sit straighter in my seat, aware that my voice has taken on that "I'm a professor" tone that my brother always mocks.

"Yeah, I'll tell you what makes it complicated," says the woman on my left, who later tells me her name is Mona and that she is from Syria but now works as a teacher in Dubai. "All these dumb movies like *Taken*, which I saw, by the way, on my flight over to London, all these dumb movies—at the end the bad guys, the villains, are always the Arabs. The trafficking takes place in Europe or the U.S., but inevitably the Arabs are behind it. What a load of nonsense. It really pisses me off." Mona crosses her arms over her chest and looks away from us.

"Yeah, these movies and all the media representations are really biased," I say, "but they are also problematic because they make it seem like all trafficking is about kidnapping women for sex work." I am ever eager to talk about my research.

"Problematic?" asks the woman to my right; her name, she later tells me, is Lola. "Trafficking? Problematic? I don't think I understand what you are saying. What is trafficking? What are these words?" she asks. Her eyebrows draw together as she squints at the screen playing the preview for *Taken*.

I'm not sure what to tell her; do I begin by saying that there are many contested interpretations of the term *trafficking* within academic and activist circles? That I struggle with the arbitrary labels of *migrant, tourist,* and *trafficked victim* that are infused with moral judgments? As I contemplate what to say next we all sit in silence, Lola's question hanging in the air: What *is* trafficking?

"What would you do if your daughter was taken from you?" booms the deep voice of the preview narrator. "Taken far away, to a place you don't know. Ripped away from you and taken by smugglers?" Images of a young girl and her father (played by Liam Neeson) flash on the screen. The father is chasing her from one country to the next while his daughter's screams echo through his mind. I am disturbed by the strategic sensationalism of this portrayal, in which age, gender, and race are used as devices to gain viewer sympathy in relating to the age of the young woman and her helplessness as she is taken from one place to another by her heavily accented, dark-skinned captors.

Lola looks at me, confused. "I'm someone's daughter. I've been taken away from my parents. I have to go far away to a place called Dubai, a place where they don't know," she tells me. "But I'm an overseas worker. Is that trafficking?"

. . .

This moment has stayed with me, one of several events transpiring in the summer of 2009 that helped shape the contours of my thinking about this book. I continue to brood over Lola's questions as well as Mona's anger about the global portrayal of trafficking. I was incredulous that in this quick, ten-minute conversation the essence of my research had been explored by two total strangers. Mona, the Syrian teacher, had touched on the racism implied in the rhetoric about trafficking (one aspect of my research), while Lola, the Filipina migrant, put her finger on the problematic discourses about the term *trafficking* and the confusion caused by labels such as *trafficked victim* versus *migrant* versus *traveler.* A few weeks later I found myself in a situation where I had to choose a label for myself, when the police were awaiting an answer to their questions of "What are you? Why are you here?" At that crucial moment I was unable to speak, partially out of fear, but mostly because I did not know how to pick a category.

The day had started out on a positive note, mostly because we didn't get lost driving to our first destination. I had set out with my research assistant, Chris, to visit Dubai Humanitarian City (DHC), the part of Dubai that was sectioned off for "humanitarian offices." Dubai, itself one of seven administrative regions, or emirates, of the United Arab Emirates (UAE), was divided into cities based on industry. We were living in Dubai Media City, which housed the television, radio, and print media staff in the UAE. Just next to us was Dubai Internet City, the area, as the name would suggest, containing the dot-coms. Next to that was Dubai Knowledge City, playing host to most of the schools in the area, and so on and so forth.

We had decided to visit Dubai Humanitarian City in order to get a better idea of the types of outreach the different humanitarian groups were providing in the UAE. One of the chief complaints of the migrant workers we had spoken with up to that point was the lack of formalized social services and support. Later on we would discover the thriving informal civil society efforts that had coalesced around the issue of migration, but at that point we were still trying to locate members of formal civil society. Many people lamented the scarcity of social services and that most of the social support came from ad hoc groups seeking to be formalized. On this note, we felt that a visit to DHC was necessary in order to better understand the workings of the groups there and how potential ties could be built between the formal and informal members of civil society.

When we drove up to DHC we wondered if we were in the wrong place. We had arrived twenty minutes early, having allotted ourselves an extra thirty minutes as we were perpetually getting lost, stuck in traffic, or both. DHC appeared to be comprised of several large, blue warehouses with only a few small office buildings, surrounded by a series of menacing fences topped with barbed wire. Security guards were stationed at each entryway, so we drove up to the first guard we encountered and told him our names. "The person you are meeting with has not yet arrived, so I can't let you in," said the guard apologetically.

We parked on the side of the road, directly under the sun, and waited. Over the guard's shoulder I read the sign "United Nations High Commissioner for Refugees." "Huh. This place is like Fort Knox. What would you do if you really needed help or were a refugee?" I asked Chris.

She nodded, wiping sweat from her brow for the fourth time in four minutes. "Dubai *Humanitarian* City isn't so friendly," she said.

Things started falling into place twenty minutes later when Patricia, the British woman who was the director of the organization we were meeting with, drove up and instructed the guard to allow us permission to enter.

Once inside DHC, I asked Patricia to tell us about the work she does in the UAE.

"Oh, don't you know?" she trilled in her high-pitched voice. "None of the organizations here actually does work in the UAE," she said matter-of-factly.

Chris and I weren't sure we were hearing correctly. Patricia read the confused looks on our faces and added, "No, no, we are all just logistics hubs here. None of the social service–type work is done here."

"Logistics hub?" I asked.

"Yes, meaning that we only have offices here so that we can buy supplies like blankets and water and trucks and that sort of thing. None of us do actual NGO work in-country." Hence the warehouses. Suddenly it all made sense. We *were* in the wrong place, we decided, gathering up our things. After talking with Patricia a bit more and meeting other folks in DHC who were all busy buying and selling various goods, we thanked her and decided to make our way back home.

Murphy's Law of Dubai, at least for us, was that if we got lost on the way to our destination, getting back would be simple. If, however, we managed to find our destination easily, that meant trouble on the way home, which was our case that day.

The roads of Dubai are like a tangled mess of spaghetti. Highways and streets, all spiraling around one another with no signage, combine with the constant presence of construction to render maps and other navigational tools useless. The congested traffic as well as the speed of passing vehicles can strike fear into the heart of even the most skilled driver. Add to this the fact that the population of Dubai is made up of over seventy nationalities, seventy different driving styles and rules that make predicting a driver's next move impossible. Needless to say, driving in Dubai is frustrating at best and nerve wracking and frightening at worst.

On our way back from DHC we veered off the main highway that we had become accustomed to, Sheikh Zayed Road, named for the visionary "father" of Dubai whose smiling face gazes down on the passing cars. The family resemblance is remarkable between the now deceased Sheikh Zayed and his son, Sheikh Mohammed, often referred to as Sheikh Mo by residents of Dubai. On this particular afternoon we decided to try our luck at navigating the back roads, as neither of us was interested in sitting in traffic in the high-noon sun.

"OK, I think I know how to get home, you'll just have to drive through one of those big scary roundabouts," cautions Chris. She is referring to the large, four-lane circles that render traffic lights useless and that for the unaccustomed driver can be as scary as walking a tightrope over a deep canyon.

I take a deep breath and merge into the roundabout, choosing to stay in the outer lane, the slow lane, because to me it feels safer. "Phew, this isn't that bad," I say to Chris as I merge into the oncoming traffic.

I should not have spoken so soon. After getting halfway around the circle our little Toyota starts to shake violently, the right side of it crumpling like paper as a large pickup truck merges into us. I am trembling, but decide to pull off the roundabout for fear of getting hit by other cars whose drivers have not so much as slowed down upon seeing our accident: mistake number one. I later learned that in Dubai one must never move the car from the site of an accident (though like other rules, one never finds this out until it's too late). As was explained to me condescendingly at the police station a few hours later, one must wait at the scene until the police arrive, regardless of whether this action might result in even more accidents.

As I pulled off the road and into a parking lot, the driver of the offending vehicle that had merged into my little egg-shaped Toyota Yaris, followed me and quickly got out of his car. "I'm so, so sorry Madam," said the driver. "I didn't see you, I'm sorry."

"I understand, it's no problem, but you'll have to pay to get my car fixed," I replied, still shaking from the accident. Just then a red Mercedes Benz drove up and a man in a police uniform got out of the car. "Where did he come from?" asked Chris as I shrugged in confusion.

The driver who had hit me ran up to the police officer and began speaking in rapid Arabic that we couldn't follow. The policeman and driver kept looking at us as they spoke. After about three minutes, the policeman walked up to me, hands on his hips.

"Yes, I knew it, it was your fault, that accident," he told me.

"My fault?!" I said in disbelief. "But you just apologized to me, you acknowledged it was your fault," I said to the driver. He was silent.

"What are you anyway, what are you doing here? That's a rental car, right?" asked the policeman.

I just looked at him, dumbfounded. I was still trying to process the chain of events, let alone his difficult questions about who and what I was, when he decided to haul Chris and me off to the police station.

When we got there things went from bad to worse. For starters, it seemed that everyone in the police station was male; their eyes continuously followed us because we weren't dressed in an *abaya* like the local women. My dark hair, dark skin, and the religious symbol of Allah that I wore around my neck caused further confusion. Where was I from? What was I doing here? If I was Muslim, why wasn't I covered? If I was a tourist, what was I doing driving a car? Needless to say we were stared at the entire time we were there.

"I feel like I could vomit," Chris said, cradling her head in her hands. "I almost wish they had a separate office for women."

I nodded, fighting back tears. We were both afraid, not because we had done anything wrong, but because the police station was a frightening place. We kept getting shuffled from one room to another by angry policemen, and no one explained to us why we were there, how long we would be staying, or what we needed to do to get out. I clutched my cell phone tightly in my hand in case I would need to call one of my lawyer friends in town whose numbers I had programmed into my phone the moment I arrived.

I couldn't believe how uncomfortable and downright terrified I felt. I suddenly realized that if I—a woman with a relatively strong sense of self who speaks English, Farsi, and some Arabic—was feeling so vulnerable in the police station, how much more frightening it would be for a migrant worker who had run away from his or her employer, didn't speak the language, and was uncomfortable around law enforcement in general. What would it be like for a woman who had been randomly picked up off the streets by a policeman who assumed she was a sex worker or "trafficked victim"? How would a man who had abandoned his job after months of working without pay be treated when the policemen realized he had outstayed his visa? How would anyone without a strong understanding of the complicated laws in the UAE stand up to the type of policemen who were now staring suspiciously at us?

After an hour or so of being yelled at by different officers for repeatedly sitting in the wrong area (we never did find the appropriate place for women to wait), I suddenly remembered that one of the Iranian sex workers I had become friends with had joked that she was grateful that many of the policemen in Dubai spoke Persian.

I looked around the room and decided to take my chances with the angry-looking officer sitting a few feet away from us. "Excuse me sir, could you please tell me why I am here?" I managed to squeak this out in Persian, biting my lower lip so that he would not see the trembling.

"Oh, you are Iranian," responded the officer in accented Persian.

I wasn't sure, but it seemed like I could detect a note of relief in his voice at finally having figured out at least part of "my story," the answer to the lingering question, "What are you?" I nodded, hesitantly.

"You're here on vacation then, and that's your friend?" He asked me, as if explaining it to himself and his colleagues.

I nodded again, wringing my hands, hoping he wouldn't start speaking to Chris in Persian. Luckily, she had wandered away at that exact moment, so for now we were safe. "When can I leave? Why am I being held here?" I asked the officer, in the most polite tone I could muster.

"Calm down, calm down, there's no problem," he said, laughing for the first time that afternoon.

"Well, I didn't do anything wrong and I'd like to leave," I said.

His laugh quickly faded and he became serious. "I'd watch that tone," he said. "You are in police headquarters. You have obviously done something wrong, so you're going to have to sit here and wait your turn. Someone will come and decide your punishment soon enough." The color drained from my face and I returned to my seat.

When Chris came back from her wandering, her previous look of fear had been replaced by anger. "What's wrong?" I asked her.

"The two cops over there have spotted your wedding ring," said Chris, motioning with her head to the other side of the room where we had been sitting earlier.

"So?" I said. I tried to avoid eye contact with the officers who were, in fact, staring at my left hand.

"So they are sitting there making snide remarks about why your husband would have let you drive, let alone let you leave the country without him," she responded, trying to contain her anger.

I stood up, outraged. Who did they think they were? I was a staunch defender of the people of the UAE, insisting that the UAE is different from Iran, that it isn't a place where human rights are violated, that the citizens care about their international reputation, that the country had gotten a bad rap for being a trafficking hotbed despite circumstances having been created by the intervention of the West. All of that rational thinking went out the window as I began marching over to the other side of the room, ready to unload my frustrations on the snickering policemen in the corner.

Luckily, Chris caught me before I made it very far, spun me around, and took me back to my seat. "It's not worth it," she said quietly, forcing me to sit back down. But the officers across the room had seen the anger in my face, and they all left their desks only to return ten minutes later with the officer who had brought us down to the police station in the first place, sandwich in hand. "Great, that's why we've been stuck here this long, because our cop wanted to go grab lunch?" remarked Chris. The officer motioned us toward his desk, tucking the remnants of his sandwich into a drawer.

"You have violated several rules, and you will have to pay," began the officer. Chris put her hand on my lap to calm me down. I sat silently, staring at the officer, waiting for him to continue. "First of all, you shouldn't move your car when you get into an accident, you are supposed to wait there until the police arrive," he said.

"But, that would have caused more accidents, that would have been unsafe!" I protested, trying to control my voice, which was rising notably.

"You were wrong. And you were driving recklessly, that's what caused that accident, so you will have to pay," he finished. He took out a piece of paper and scribbled a series of numbers onto it. I could only presume he was totaling up my fine.

"That's just not fair," I muttered, under my breath, shaking my head. "Can we go now?" I asked.

He shook his head. "Give me your passport first, we are going to keep it for a few days."

Give over my passport? Not a chance in hell, I thought. I had no desire to end up like so many others, stranded without my most valuable possession.

"I don't have it," I stated truthfully, which seemed to anger him.

"Why not?" he asked, making an effort to keep his voice low.

"Because I was always taught to keep it locked in my hotel when I travel," I said quickly, deciding right then and there that I was going to play the innocent tourist.

"Well then give me your driver's license, I'm keeping it for a while," he said. He reached across the table and took my license (which he had previously used to write my ticket) out of my hands.

"California, huh?" he laughed. "What are you doing here anyway?" he asked. "Two young girls, tourists I gather. But two girls alone. Driving. A rental car. On that side of town? You are lucky that you are only getting a fine," he said. He pocketed my license and retreated from the office.

I I I

Experiences such as these are reflective of my own schizophrenia when thinking about the UAE. At times I am sympathetic toward its citizens, the Emiratis, and frustrated by the anti-Islam and anti-Arab sentiments implied in some media depictions, as well as by reports and policies that paint nationals of the Gulf countries as noncompliant in addressing a trafficking "problem" that has its roots in the aftereffects of rapid globalization. At other moments I would become angered by small details such as the fact that Dubai Humanitarian City was merely a "logistics hub," or that a car accident would immediately be the fault of the person with less agency vis-à-vis the police, or that the police could arbitrarily decide punishment for an uncommitted crime based on their assumption of the answer to the ever lingering question, "What are you?" Throughout my time in the UAE, I struggled with that problematic question, which seems to create so much anxiety in a country where most of the population is from somewhere else (over 80 percent according to the UAE embassy). I could never place myself in a single category, a struggle shared by many migrants I encountered. Their experiences and stories rarely fit neatly into the categories constructed in policies and media depictions of trafficking and migration. The arbitrariness of labels such as *migrant, tourist,* and *trafficked victim* within the global rhetoric and policies on trafficking and migration continue to bother me, as does the inability of the international community to recognize how policies about trafficking are biased by race, class, and gender.

Many aspects of my research continue to unsettle me. How to write about trafficking and migration without reproducing the same caricatures of which I am critical? How to talk about sex work in a way that does not glamorize or victimize the experience and those in the industry? How to avoid the "politics of pity" or "politics of risk" portrayals when it comes to trafficking?[1] How to talk about conditions of migration when each migrant story is so unique, and when these very differences offer the most interesting and important gaps in our understanding of forced labor and migration.

Throughout this book I have tried to let my interviewees narrate their own stories while I provide the framework for a critical analysis of the issues. Any shortcomings in their stories are attributable to my inadequate translations and representations of their narratives. I continue to brood over their words and the global caricatures, stereotypes, and oversimplified sketches of trafficking, and I ask for readers' forgiveness when I find myself stuck in the "gridlock" of my subject.

1

TRAFFICKING *TRAFFICKING*

AT THE HEART OF THIS BOOK lies a question: How do popular discourses and policies about human trafficking and migration, hammered out in EuroAmerica (principally Washington D.C.), reflect and impact life in countries with different political and social topographies? Using qualitatively based, on-the-ground research in the United Arab Emirates (UAE), among the largest migrant-receiving countries in the world today, this work examines the uneasy marriage of policy, paradigms, and reality; namely, how policies conceived elsewhere affect the lived experience of migration, forced labor, and trafficking. Dialogue about human trafficking has itself been "trafficked" or taken over by innumerous policymakers, advocates, and lobbyists, and the resulting implementation of policies and laws on trafficking inevitably shortchanges the intended beneficiaries: persons undergoing situations of abuse or rights violations. Thus examining migrants' experiences is vital for understanding how policies on trafficking, designed to reduce abuse and rights violations, have in their implementation had just the opposite effect on the lives of many migrants in the Gulf. Once we grasp the contrast between policy/discourse and lived experience, policies that truly serve to protect the rights of migrant workers can be designed and more effectively implemented.

Added to the question of policy is the question of discourse: How do global conversations about trafficking (and media and journalistic representations such as *Taken* or MTV's EXIT program) create an image of the experiences of migration, forced labor, and sex work in the minds of the public?

How do these global stereotypes and caricatures affect policy at the global and local levels in places such as Dubai and Abu Dhabi? And in turn, how do these policies, as well as the global conversations informing them, affect the lives of migrants and trafficked persons? If we look at trafficking as an issue of migration or labor gone awry,[1] we can see the need to frame the concept within the conversations about migration and forced labor. Moreover, it is time to move away from the criminalization framework of current policies and toward reconceptualizing trafficking as a human rights issue.

Given the ways in which trafficking and migration in the Gulf have been castigated in recent policy and discourse, the UAE provides an ideal spot for studying the contrasts between discourse and experience. Between 2004 and 2009 I made several extended trips to the UAE to interview men and women working in various service industries such as domestic work, construction work, and sex work, who came from such diverse places as the Philippines, Iran, Ethiopia, India, Pakistan, Sri Lanka, Bangladesh, and Indonesia. I also spent several months interviewing government officials in the UAE about labor, migration, and trafficking policies as well as members of the U.S. State department involved in trafficking policy.[2] Overall, I interviewed 60 migrant workers, 30 social service providers, and 20 policymakers, bringing my interviewee total to 110. The research was conducted primarily over the course of four summers, and I was fortunate to benefit from the assistance of three students from the Claremont Colleges (where I teach) throughout my time in the field. One student in particular, Christine (Chris) Sargent (introduced in the Prologue), assisted me throughout the project, accompanying me to several interviews in the field and helping with research and analysis when we returned to the United States. When the term "we" is used throughout the text, I am referring to interviews and experiences shared with Chris.

Sarah Burgess and Abby DiCarlo provided administrative and occasional research assistance in the field. Our research team, consisting of myself and these three students, employed anthropological research methods of participant observation (immersion in a field setting to observe the population of interest) and in-depth interviews with migrant workers, informal service providers, and officials working on forced labor and migration issues in the UAE.[3] For the sake of confidentiality I have changed the names of all the interviewees in this book. In general, I have retained institutional names in order to reflect interviewees' desires to provide exposure of their organizations' work. Throughout the book I draw on the experiences of my interviewees, not to generalize from my small sample, but rather to show examples of lived experience and examine the disconnect between migrant narratives and policies written about them. I do not mean to imply that all migrant workers undergo the same challenges, nor do I believe that my small sample of activists is representative of all who are involved in building civil society or establishing policy. This sample, gathered over the course of my fieldwork, is comprised of migrant workers, activists, and policymakers I engaged with in the field. While not comprehensive or representative, I believe that these narratives show important disconnects in our understandings of forced labor, migration, and "human trafficking."

▪ ▪ ▪

Throughout my fieldwork, and also in my review of policy documents, I observed that policymakers, activists, and opinion leaders place various labels on certain migrant groups, labels that are often not only inaccurate and arbitrary but also gendered, raced, classed, and sexualized. For example, the word *trafficked*, a contested term that at once claims too much and too little, has grown (in popular discourse) to refer to the experience of all women who migrate primarily into the sex industry.[4] The legal definition refers to abuse characterized by the elements of force, fraud, and/or coercion. Though it stems from a desire to protect the rights of human beings from abuse and exploitation, the discourse around human trafficking in the U. S. that has been constructed through the lens of activism and media sensationalism tends to refer only to women migrating into sex work, while excluding women and men outside the sex industry. The misconception is thus perpetuated that human trafficking refers primarily to a woman, often young, who has been duped or forced into sex work. This construction of trafficking that hinges primarily on the sex industry has shaped the implementation of policies (at least in the UAE) over the past decade. The current disconnect—between the broad legal definition that embraces any worker who experiences force, fraud, or coercion, and the narrow latitude of activist and policy discussions that focuses on sex work—offers uncomfortable insight into how gender and sexuality permeate popular understandings of victimhood, vulnerability, and power.

While the term *trafficked* is mistakenly used mostly to refer to women, usually in the sex industry, *migrant*, especially in the Gulf, has a masculine and class-based connotation. In the UAE it refers typically to unskilled, low-wage male workers,[5] as does *laborer*. Unskilled female workers are referred to as housemaids (*khaddamah*) or nannies, or simply as "the help," even though they work in a wide range of industries beyond domestic and care work. Interestingly, migrant workers of Western backgrounds in the UAE are exclusively referred to as expatriates. Thus *migrant, laborer,* and *trafficked* tend to be loaded, gendered terms applied to unskilled or semi-skilled workers, while *expat* implies highly skilled, Western guest workers in the Gulf and can be applied to both genders of a certain class and of certain countries of origin.

While doing my fieldwork, and even in presenting the results of my research when I returned, I was struck repeatedly by the desire of audience members, policymakers, and persons I encountered in the UAE to place my interviewees into these artificially reified categories. The conflation of these terms, both in policy and discourse, has made me increasingly uncomfortable. This tension is even more frustrating because in order to deconstruct and untangle the terms I am critical of, I must invoke these same labels and phrases in my work.

A Note on Agency and Discourse

In presenting the stories and lived experiences of the migrant workers that form the basis of this study, throughout the book I draw on a series of concepts, debates and policy recommendations. A closer look at the labels and mislabeling arising from these concepts, as well as at the conceptual umbrella itself, follows.

I use the concept of *agency* throughout the text to refer to an individual's capacity, desire, and potential to make choices and decisions about his or her own life, trajectories, and future. Agency is the ability to act as an individual and to determine one's own fate. It is often thought to be limited by the concept of *structure*, the term used to refer to institutions or conditions that might support or restrict agency.[6] Structures can include systems such as education, employment sector, and state regulations, or socially constructed categories such as class, race, gender, ethnicity, nationality, and group identity. Individuals often find and exercise agency even within the structures that seek to limit them.

Throughout the book I use migrants' stories and show how migrants find pockets of agency in situations of oppression and repression. I draw on the concept of agency in order to move beyond the traditional view of migrant workers as victims solely of their circumstances, to point to the deliberate choices they make as enterprising and courageous persons seeking to make a better life for themselves and their families, to move into one industry or another, and to leave their home country in search of work in the UAE.

The concept of agency is also particularly useful in talking about and understanding the nature of sex work. I opt to use the term *sex work* to recognize the agency of persons involved in this industry, specifically those who view sex work as a job (rather than a defining identity).[7] In defining sex work, it is useful to look to the United Nations' definition embedded in the language of the report from the Division for the Advancement of Women (DAW):

> The term "sex work" or "commercial sex work" is generally understood to include a wide range of behaviors and venues, and includes, but is not limited to, street prostitution, brothel prostitution, exotic dancing, paid domination, and sexual massage. Many people who engage in sex work or commercial sex identify what they do as sex work, but it is also important to acknowledge that many other people who engage in informal and occasional sexual transactions may not incorporate this experience as an important part of their personal identity.

Use of the term *sex work* thus attempts to situate the industry within a framework of labor so that those involved in it can access the rights and protections afforded to other laborers. It also acknowledges the agency of sex workers, recognizing that not all persons engaging in sex work are victims or have been tricked or trafficked into this type of work.

I have also relied heavily on the concept of *discourse*. Discourse, in the Foucaultian tradition, refers to the production of conversations, ideas, language, and the way of talking about a subject that becomes regularized or institutionalized through repeated use.[8] People often use this term to refer to socially agreed-upon or mainstream imaginings of an issue. By default, because discourse is defined as the majority viewpoint, other views that may not fit within the dominant version of the conversation may be excluded. The constructed nature of discourse must be underscored. Discourses can become paradigms, reflective of a certain moment that defines the mainstream. The concept is particularly useful for reminding us that dominant versions of an issue are not always the unobstructed truth. In the following pages, I use the concept of discourse to refer to the dominant paradigms about human trafficking, sex work, and labor migration, particularly as they pertain to populations in the UAE. I also look at how discourse regarding trafficking has been produced through mainstream media, journalistic representation of the issues, and policy and political documentations. *Metadiscourse* consists of policy, media and journalistic representations, and popularized paradigms about a topic. These paradigms feed policy, as well as the implementation of policies, which then becomes a part of discourse. Thus I look at the effect of mainstream discourse on forming policies about trafficking and migration, and point to ways in which both discourse and policies not only differ from the actual experiences and trajectories of migrants and trafficked persons, but also impact them negatively and exacerbate the situation of forced laborers and migrants in need.

The Trafficking Discourse

The concept of discourse is particularly useful when looking at the way in which conversations, policies, and portrayals of trafficking align or disconnect with the definition of human trafficking (as outlined by the United Nations) and narratives of persons who have been labeled trafficked. The official definition of trafficking as stated in Article 3, paragraph (a) of the *Protocol to Prevent, Suppress and Punish Trafficking in Persons Especially Women and Children* prepared by the United Nations Office on Drugs and Crime (note the disjuncture in the UN agency designated to monitor human trafficking, an agency dedicated to organized crime and drug trafficking rather than the human rights arm of the UN) is as follows:

> the recruitment, transportation, transfer, harbouring or receipt of persons, by means of the threat or use of force or other forms of coercion, of abduction, of fraud, of deception, of the abuse of power or of a position of vulnerability or of the giving or receiving of payments or benefits to achieve the consent of a person having control over another person, for the purpose of exploitation. Exploitation shall include, at a minimum, the exploitation of the prostitution of others or other forms of sexual exploitation, forced labour or services, slavery or practices similar to slavery, servitude or the removal of organs . . . The consent of a victim of trafficking in persons to the intended exploitation set forth [above] shall be irrelevant where any of the means set forth [above] have been used.

On the basis of the definition of trafficking given in this protocol, it is evident that trafficking in persons has three constituent elements; (1) the act (what is done); namely, recruitment, transportation, transfer, harboring, or receipt of persons, (2) the means (how it is done), including the threat or use of force, coercion, abduction, fraud, deception, abuse of power or vulnerability, or giving payments or benefits to a person in control of the victim, and (3) the purpose (why it is done); possible categories include exploiting the prostitution of others, sexual exploitation, forced labor, slavery or similar practices, and the removal of organs.

As the agreed-upon definition of trafficking in the international community, this description is broad enough to encapsulate a number of abuses to migrants in many sectors; yet the functional definition of the term, as produced and perpetuated by the discourse, has focused solely on sex work. While the broad brush of this UN definition would seem to include the legal definition of trafficking given earlier—referring to persons who have experienced force, fraud, or coercion—policies and discourse seek to connect sex work (rather than forced labor or migration) with trafficking to the exclusion of migrants in other labor sectors who experience abuse. Moreover, each state has subtle nuances in the definition of trafficking and, more prominently, in deciding who counts as a trafficked person. It is useful to assess U.S. domestic and international policies on trafficking, as these have played a major role in structuring the discourse on trafficking and can also be read as products of discourse and debates about trafficking, migration, and sex work.

In the year 2000, President Bill Clinton signed into effect the Trafficking Victims Protection Act (TVPA; HR-244), part of the larger Public Law 106–386, Victims of Trafficking and Violence Protection Act. The bill (and its subsequent reauthorizations in 2003, 2005, 2007, and 2008) comprises the United States' most comprehensive response to human trafficking to date, and the consequences of its mandates have reverberated across the globe.[9] The stated aim of the TVPA is: "to combat trafficking in persons, a contemporary manifestation of slavery whose victims are predominantly women and children, to ensure just and effective punishment of traffickers, and to protect their victims."[10] Beyond this description, the words, ideas, and values endorsed in this legislation become increasingly contentious. The law addresses not only the issue of human trafficking, but also questions of migration, immigration, and security with which trafficking is indivisibly connected. The obvious tension within the Act to respond to the needs of victims and to address the violation of boundaries that trafficking involves is highlighted in the section "Authority to Permit Continued Presence in the United States," which states:

> Federal law enforcement officials may permit an alien individual's continued presence in the United States if, after an assessment, it is determined that the individual is a victim of a severe form of trafficking and a potential witness

to such trafficking, in order to effectuate prosecution of those responsible, and such officials in investigating and prosecuting traffickers shall protect the safety of trafficking victims, including taking measures to protect trafficked persons and their family members from intimidation, threats of reprisals, and reprisals from traffickers and their associates.[11]

As prominent trafficking scholar Denise Brennan has noted, while the provisions of the TVPA indicate that up to 5,000 T-visas (visas that allow trafficked persons to remain in the United States under protection) can be distributed per year, to date—ten years after the passage of this act—only 3,000 such visas have been issued. The numbers are significant and prompt the inquiry as to why, if an estimated 20,000 persons are trafficked into the United States every year,[12] the quota of 5,000 was established,[13] and why less than a tenth of a possible 50,000 T-visas have been issued to date. Some point to the stigma of associating T-visas with sex trafficking as the reason for their sparse distribution.

The TVPA makes an important distinction between trafficking and *severe* trafficking, which determines who has access to which protections and services. Primarily victims of the latter qualify for the TVPA's most developed services and resources. Severe trafficking refers to:

(A) sex trafficking in which a commercial sex act is induced by force, fraud, or coercion, or in which the person induced to perform such act has not attained 18 years of age; or (B) the recruitment, harboring, transportation, provision, or obtaining of a person for labor or services, through the use of force, fraud, or coercion for the purpose of subjection to involuntary servitude, peonage, debt bondage, or slavery.[14]

Here we can see the clear ways in which the legislation on trafficking has anti-prostitution undertones.

That the TVPA and the larger trafficking discourse focus so much attention on the issue of sex work and sex trafficking has generated a lot of debate within feminist circles. Moreover, the continued emphasis on "women and children" (as can be evidenced in the title of the UN Protocol) has generated much uproar among scholars, who have expressed frustration at the hyperscrutiny on women, specifically women in the sex industry.[15] These scholars note, and the ethnographic data in this book support these assertions, that there are women and men in the sex industry who have not necessarily been trafficked, *and* there are many instances of abuse inflicted on both men and women outside the sex industry.

Paramount in the TVPA's mission has been the creation of the Office to Monitor and Combat Trafficking in Persons (a division of the U.S. Department of State), responsible for the annual report on international trafficking that has rocked the foundations of trafficking policy worldwide. The Trafficking in Persons (TIP) report essentially functions as a global scorecard that ranks nations in a three-tiered system based on the perceived severity of human trafficking within state boundaries and the perceived adequacy of responding domestic policies. Up until 2010, nearly a decade after the passage of the TVPA, the United States itself remained conspicuously absent from these rankings.[16]

Countries that have achieved Tier 1 status (such as Italy, Sweden, and the United Kingdom) have been deemed to possess satisfactory countertrafficking measures, including effective anti-trafficking laws and well-developed outreach programs within civil society. Countries that have historically received this designation are located primarily in the developed world, principally in the West, New Zealand, and Australia. Tier 2 countries (such as Israel, Mexico, and Thailand) are those deemed not in full compliance with U.S. international anti-trafficking criteria, but considered to be making significant efforts to do so. Between Tiers 2 and 3 lies the category of "Tier 2 Watch List," which consists of countries (such as Argentina, the Philippines, and Russia) that are not making "significant enough" efforts to combat trafficking but do not yet merit the heavily stigmatized designation of Tier 3.

Countries currently placed in the bottom tier of the TIP report, those that do not comply with U.S.-designated standards to combat trafficking (such as Iran, Malaysia, and Syria), are subject to public shaming in the international community as well as sanctions in the form of the removal of nonhumanitarian aid, subject to presidential mandate. Failure to make the grade within the TIP can result in strained economic relations between the United States and the offending country, an important issue for a country such as the UAE which is the United States' largest export market in the Arab world (according to the UAE Embassy). Some government officials in the UAE noted that U.S. officials used the UAE's watch list status to strong-arm the UAE into bilateral agreements operating in the United States' favor.[17] Not coincidentally, countries placed in Tier 3 or the Tier 2 watch list are mostly Muslim countries (with the exception of Cuba and North Korea), while countries in Tier 1 are mostly Western. A critical look at the ranking system of the TIP reveals more about the current state of U.S. foreign relations priorities than about actual global human trafficking trends and flows.

TABLE 1   Trafficking in Persons (TIP) Report, 2009 Sample Tier Rankings

Tier 1

Australia	Denmark	Lithuania	Norway
Austria	England	Luxembourg	Poland
Colombia	Germany	The Netherlands	Sweden
Croatia	Italy	New Zealand	Switzerland

Tier 2

Afghanistan	El Salvador	Laos	Romania
Albania	Estonia	Liberia	Rwanda
Antigua & Barbuda	Ethiopia	Macau	Serbia
Armenia	The Gambia	Madagascar	Sierra Leone
The Bahamas	Greece	Malawi	Singapore

Tier 2 Watch List

Algeria	China (PRC)	Libya	Uzbekistan
Angola	Congo, Rep. of	Nicaragua	Venezuela
Bahrain	India	Pakistan	Yemen
Bangladesh	Lebanon	United Arab Emirates	

Tier 3

Burma	Kuwait	North Korea	Syria
Cuba	Malaysia	Saudi Arabia	
Iran	Niger	Sudan	

SOURCE: Trafficking in Persons Report 2009, http://www.state.gov/g/tip/rls/tiprpt/2009/123132.htm

Trafficking Globally

Critics within the United States and beyond have protested these rankings and the criteria used to determine them, citing a lack of transparency in compiling the report as well as prejudice and differential treatment based on the racial and religious composition of a given country.[18] Some point to the use of the TIP as a tool of American hegemony, and a way for the United States to further paint its adversaries in a negative light. Scholars such as Kathleen Frydl, a historian of the "wars on drugs" in the United States, point to the similarity in the use of American rhetoric about drug trafficking that was used to demonize

China during the early years of the twentieth century when the threat of communism loomed large.[19] The negative castigation of Muslim countries by the TIP may speak more to the climate of Islamophobia and Orientalism, couched in rhetoric about the "clash of civilizations," than about actual trafficking issues in watch-listed countries.[20]

Numerous scholars and UAE government officials with whom I spoke underscored the haphazard construction of the tiered rankings, emphasizing their speculative nature and basis in rumor rather than in-country research. Officials responsible for writing the TIP report typically spend no more than a few days in each country and surmise the "trafficking situation" based on a few conversations.[21] Critics also point out that U.S. foreign policy considerations and conflicts influence tier designations, further compromising the integrity of the reports. Tier 3 countries such as Cuba and North Korea have been included into this ranking arguably as a form of punishment for political hostilities, with the negative castigation mandated by this ranking providing a further mechanism for diplomatic leverage and pressure.

One example of subjective ranking is seen in the contrast between Iran (Tier 3) and France (Tier 1). Iran is deemed to have a severe trafficking problem and inadequate responses to the issue, which has earned it the lowest ranking by the TIP. Iran is a minor receiving country of migrants due to its lack of employment opportunities, poor economic situation, and tight borders, nor has it been a major sending country of migrants to the developed world, yet it has made significant efforts to set up shelters and NGOs to address the needs of its relatively small migrant population according to research I conducted in Iran between 2000 and 2007. A member of the TIP office noted in conversation her bewilderment regarding Iran's Tier 3 designation and acknowledged that her office did not have sufficiently strong sources inside Iran to provide reliable information about the "trafficking situation." By contrast, France, a country with a long history of involvement in informal migration and sometimes exploitative conditions for migrants, is ranked in Tier 1. In recent years, numerous examples of policies enacted by the French government have carried anti-immigrant undertones, and efforts to create organizations responding to the needs of trafficked persons have been insufficient.[22] France nonetheless continues to be classified as a Tier 1 country. These types of discrepancies undermine the integrity of the TIP and were pointed to several times by officials in the Middle East to refer to the arbitrariness of TIP rankings and the report's inherent weakness.[23]

Trajectory of the TIP

By looking at the trajectory of TIP rankings of the UAE over time, we can assess trafficking policy representations of the region as well as USA-UAE relations. In their variability from year to year, these rankings also reveal the prevailing political climate at the time each report was written and the glaring politicization of the issue of human trafficking both locally and globally.

The UAE started out on shaky footing with a Tier 3 classification in the first two TIP reports, issued in 2001 and 2002, in which it was cited as "a destination country for trafficked persons." These reports focused on two main populations of interest to the TIP authors: "boys . . . trafficked from Pakistan and Bangladesh for use as camel jockeys in UAE's camel racing industry," and "women . . . trafficked from the New Independent States, Africa, Iran, and Eastern Europe for sexual exploitation." In 2003, however, the UAE inexplicably rose to Tier 1 status, earning disgruntled responses from migrants' rights activists around the world who had been pushing for recognition of the abuses taking place in the UAE against migrant workers. Some advocates felt that the UAE was getting a "free pass" because of its financial relationship with the United States, and they argued for a demotion in future reports. The 2003 TIP report, the only year of the UAE's Tier 1 ranking, noted that "the government provides assistance and protection to victims; they are not detained, jailed or deported."

The following year the UAE's ranking dropped back down to Tier 2, a demotion related to "the lack of evidence of appreciable progress in addressing trafficking for *sexual* exploitation" (emphasis mine). This report, as well as those that preceded and followed it, was critical of the UAE's handling of sex trafficking. The 2004 TIP recommended that the UAE take "more vigorous steps to identify and rescue trafficking victims among the thousands of foreign prostitutes in the U.A.E."

In 2005, the UAE reverted to Tier 3 status. The justifications included an increase in sex trafficking and child slave labor. This report focused largely on the number of young boys trafficked into the UAE for the purpose of camel jockeying, a major concern despite the fact that the UAE had been commended in previous reports for its efforts to address the issue. The 2005 TIP also highlighted the UAE's lack of official shelters or outreach centers to meet the needs of trafficked persons (despite the fact that many informal migrants' rights groups did exist and were providing services to persons who had experienced force, fraud, or coercion). This report prompted state involvement in the issue and led to the creation of multiple government-sponsored shelters that did not begin functioning until 2008. In addition, Federal Law 51 was passed in the UAE, which promoted prosecution of those involved in human trafficking.[24]

In 2006 the country was moved up a notch to the Tier 2 Watch List. The authors noted that the UAE did not qualify for Tier 2 ranking because it showed insufficient effort to "combat trafficking over the past year, particularly in its efforts to address the large-scale trafficking of foreign girls and women for commercial sexual exploitation." Thus the 2005 focus on child trafficking was replaced in the 2006 report by a focus on sex trafficking.

In the 2007 TIP report the UAE remained on the Tier 2 Watch List as "a destination country for men and women trafficked for the purpose of involuntary servitude and commercial sexual exploitation." It was again castigated for its failure to take appropriate measures to address the issue of sex trafficking within its borders, a condition that was slightly remedied in 2008 when in-country authorities created the government-sponsored shelters that will be introduced in the following chapters. The creation of these shelters earned the UAE a place on the Tier 2 ranking in the 2008 TIP report, which applauded the UAE for its success in establishing shelters and an "anti-trafficking" task squad. The UAE's efforts in addressing the issue of sex trafficking provided the impetus for the upgrade to Tier 2, though the country's inattention to labor trafficking challenges is noted.

The 2009 report represents a turning point in the history of the report and is among the most comprehensive of the TIPs to date. The UAE was downgraded to the Tier 2 Watch List in 2009, but in contrast to previous years the report features a focus on labor trafficking and domestic workers, citing that the "trafficking of domestic workers is facilitated by the fact that the normal protections provided to workers under UAE labor law do not apply to domestic workers, leaving them more vulnerable to abuse." This report makes no mention of boys trafficked for the purpose of camel jockeying, and it highlights the issue of male laborers in its discussion of trafficked persons, which include women who "reportedly are trafficked to the UAE for commercial sexual exploitation." Within this most recent TIP report, the UAE is once again applauded for its efforts to combat sex trafficking, but it is also encouraged to address the issues of forced labor and migrant work conditions. Though these recommendations are steps in the right direction, the UAE's tier ranking still hinges on its perceived response to the sex trafficking issue, rather than broadening the scope to address trafficking within a context of forced labor or migrants' rights.

Responding to TIP

The TIP report rankings seem arbitrary both to casual observers and to officials within the emirate with whom I spoke. Many felt that a country's ranking had nothing to do with its labor situation or efforts to address the needs of trafficked persons and everything to do with how the United States perceived the country.[25] Some activists in the UAE with whom I spoke felt that as long as the UAE was profitable for the United States it would be ranked no lower than Tier 2, with the hope of being upgraded to Tier 1 dangled before it. When the economy began to crash, two activists said, the UAE was no longer considered a friend.

Officials and citizens in the UAE were frustrated and embarrassed when the UAE was moved to the Tier 3 or Tier 2 Watch List level. The official public response to the TIP reports of 2008 and 2009 was the issuance of statements from the office of the Sheikhs publicly denouncing sex trafficking, the passage of Federal Law 51, an increase in media coverage in outlets such as *Gulf News*, and a temporary increase in brothel raids. Just a few short days after the 2009 TIP report was released, stories appeared in the major UAE newspapers such as *Gulf News* about the arrest and prosecution of a number of "traffickers," who were immediately jailed and some deported without trial. A series of stories also appeared about brothel raids and the deportation of a number of sex workers who were also convicted and deported without trial. These types of stories faded within weeks, and it is not known whether further raids and arrests were conducted. What is known is that in 2008, ten persons were prosecuted for crimes related to trafficking, and in 2009 this number doubled to twenty, though it is not clear the exact nature of their crimes.[26]

Domestically, citizen response ranged from outrage at American imperialism veiled in a humanitarian report, to denial of the charges implied in the report. Most responses, however, reflected frustration and confusion. "No one really knows how or why that happened," explained one UAE state official in response to the 2009 UAE TIP ranking. "We think it's because the U.S. wanted to sign a bilateral agreement about nuclear energy with the Emiratis (the "123 Agreement"), and so they moved us down to get a better deal, to make us feel worse and give the U.S. leveraging power, but we're not really sure what that even means." One activist who works on trafficking became very angry and emotional when discussing the TIP rankings:

> Tier 3, Tier 2, we're not sure how who gets where! Plus, it's all propaganda any-ways. I mean, the U.S. wanted something from the UAE, maybe a better deal in trading, so they held it, they held it over [our] heads, they said you have a bad human rights track record and we know this, and we see this, and we [the Americans] know how to fix it. You, you, Arabs, you Muslims don't under-stand, and you need us. It pisses me off, it does! "You Muslims" are backward? I mean, give me a break, you think trafficking doesn't happen in the U.S.? You bet it does, but when it happens in the Arab world, Islam is blamed.

It is understandable why people in the Gulf become defensive about the issue. The rankings of the TIP Report are perceived as anti-Arab and anti-Islam. One government official opined, "They were OK with us being Mus-lim and doing what we wanted while we were making money for them, but as soon as the economic crisis hit, we became 'bad Muslims' again." Many perceive the ranking as a deliberate effort to reinforce a preexisting image of Muslims and Islam within the Western consciousness, an image of depravity, acceptance of violence, and indifference to suffering. Furthermore, many in the Gulf feel that they are given outside mandates that are not culturally or historically contextualized or aware. One Emirati academic was very articu-late on this matter:

> Yes, in the TIP report they say that we are supposed to increase the police. That's right, more police, that's just what we need. But do they know that we import our police from Bangladesh? That they aren't trained? That they are sometimes the abusers? Why are we supposed to spend our money on more police? Why not create a shelter? Hold the Red Crescent to their promise, help people. More police? Please. No thank you.

Others similarly reiterated feelings of injustice due to heightened scrutiny on sex trafficking in the Muslim world in particular. Another journalist em-phasized that most of the Tier 3–ranked countries were Muslim-majority countries. She expressed frustration toward both the standards to which they (Emiratis) were being held and the shortsightedness of TIP recommendations (such as increasing funding for police, as opposed to putting money into shel-ters) that they saw as unhelpful and unrealistic.

A series of recommendations accompanies the TIP tier rankings, with the idea that countries must comply or strive to meet these recommendations in order to improve or maintain their ranking. Countries such as the UAE that are vested in improving their image and TIP compliance record must respond to mandates drawn up in Washington D.C., which often miss the mark where context is concerned. The recommendations made to the UAE in the 2009 TIP report read in part as follows:

> Recommendations for the UAE: continue to increase law enforcement efforts to identify, prosecute and punish acts of sex trafficking.

Misguided and vague, such recommendations lead countries such as the UAE down a difficult path, in this case with its emphasis on sex trafficking that obscures attention from the larger issue of migrants' rights, and its emphasis on law enforcement to the exclusion of involvement by civil society.

Currently, the largest challenge facing migrant workers in the UAE is the structure of the *kefala*, or sponsorship system, that provides the legal framework for all documented migrants working in the formal economy in the UAE. This system works in favor of employers and has led to poor working conditions in the cases of many migrant workers. The *kefala* system is in desperate need of reform, as it is often the exploitative conditions of labor created under this system that lead migrants into situations of trafficking. In 2004 and 2005, inspired by the example of their neighbors in Bahrain who have recently repealed the *kefala* system and worked to provide more protections for laborers,[27] government officials in the UAE were beginning to work with migrants' rights groups to reform the *kefala* system. With the Tier 3 ranking of 2005, however, attention was redirected from *kefala* toward the issue of policing sex work. In addition, according to members of the UAE's National Committee to Combat Human Trafficking, several anti-prostitution activist groups from the United States began travelling to Dubai in order to train this group to combat trafficking by addressing the issue of commercial sex work. Furthermore, according to a State Department officer I spoke with in 2009, the UAE was given a low ranking in part because of a lack of civil society efforts to address the problems. The TIP report ignores the many informal groups that do exist in the UAE and that work on issues of migrants' rights within the UAE and the region. The fact that these efforts have been overlooked presents a direct challenge to those who have worked so hard to build this type of momentum.

Trafficking the Trafficking Debate

The major forces of activism currently structuring the debate and discourse on human trafficking are divided according to their stance on commercial sex work. Sex work is the central coalescing factor in the current constructions of policies and conversations around the topic of human trafficking. During its inception, strong, morally based anti-prostitution undertones formed the underpinnings and legislative aims of the TVPA and consequently the TIP. On one side of the negotiations involved in the legislative development of the TVPA were the "abolitionist" feminists, who give voice to the larger debates about prostitution and human trafficking and endorse the belief that "prostitution is a violation of human rights . . . 'an extreme expression of sexual violence' [and] trafficking is seen to be caused by prostitution, making the best way to fight trafficking the abolition of 'prostitution.'"[28] Abolitionist feminists such as Kathleen Barry argue that prostitution "reduces women to a body" and is therefore necessarily harmful, regardless of questions of consent or choice.[29]

This group of abolitionists, or anti-prostitution feminists, has monopolized—or trafficked—the legislative and popular discourses regarding human trafficking through two powerful and dangerous conflations: equating human trafficking with sex trafficking, and equating migration for/engagement in commercial sex work with sex trafficking and forced prostitution. The resulting trafficking framework is harmful to both migrants and sex workers.[30]

On the other side of the debate, feminists and public health officials who advocate for principles of harm reduction and sex workers' rights provide a counterargument to abolitionist feminist ideology.[31] This group believes that prostitution must be viewed in the context of wage earning. They emphasize that it is a choice women make in order to improve their living conditions, and a choice that should earn them respect rather than stigmatization.[32] They believe that the conceptual boundary between consensual and forced sex work marks a critical distinction in policies dealing directly and indirectly with commercial sex work, a distinction that the TVPA and the TIP fail to acknowledge. Furthermore, the sex workers' rights approach incorporates the narratives and participation of sex workers themselves into their platform and advocacy. The very different views of these two feminist camps regarding sex work has defined their approaches to the issue of human trafficking and the relationships they have pursued with different lobby groups and constituencies.

The fundamental point of contention within most debates on sex work centers on accepted interpretations or understandings of choice and coercion. According to one report, "the debate on transnational sex work has become mired in disagreements between those who focus on trafficking for the purposes of sexual exploitation versus those focusing on labor migration for the purpose of sex work."[33] It is important to recognize that the globalized, restructured economy depends increasingly on imported migrant labor, which has led to an increase in immigration and migration for employment worldwide. Migration is an age-old survival strategy requiring courage, strength, and a strong sense of agency. As research has suggested, migrant workers end up in situations of force, fraud, or coercion not because they are passive victims but precisely because they are courageous agents who migrate for a wide variety of reasons, including the need to improve their economic situations, a desire to travel, or to seek out love or other types of opportunities abroad.[34] We must also recognize that there is no universal reason for entering into transactional sex. To universalize meanings and values that different individuals ascribe to sexual labor would be to silence and deny the diversity of voices worldwide articulating manifold and sometimes contradictory reasons for entering into commercial sex work.

Trafficking narratives have also taken on specifically racialized, or perhaps ethnicized, dimensions in addressing at-risk populations of women in the developing world, who are often seen as uneducated and duped into trafficking. These undertones are especially present within the popular discourse on trafficking in the Gulf context and are keenly felt by migrant workers from developing countries. In a recent lecture about sex trafficking around the world held at Scripps College, an abolitionist activist problematically noted that "trafficking occurs because of the ignorance of Third World women."[35] Kemala Kempadoo astutely points out that racism within and about commercial sex work takes two forms: that of "racisms embedded in structures and desires within specific local industries (i.e. the fact that the demand for sex workers for example in Dubai is based on their race/ethnicity) and that of cultural imperialism refracted through international discourses on prostitution."[36] Kempadoo and Mohanty go on to note that the latter form of racism is less obvious yet more dangerous, as it has become embedded in certain feminist discourses about non-Western women who are, according to Kathleen Barry, in desperate need of "saving."[37] Barry, and other feminists who support her assertions, as Kempadoo notes, frequently paint a picture of non-Western women as being in distress and needing guidance or help. The depictions of these women contrast with those of Western women, who are referred to in the discourse as modern and in control of their sexuality and economic potential, and thus in a position to "save" the Third World women.[38]

Non-Western women who migrate, possibly to engage in sex work, or who employ transactional sex as a survival or supplemental strategy, and who may or may not be exploited or trafficked, are thus depicted as unmodern and lacking agency. Absent from this image is any self-representation by women from the developing world, which is taken as evidence of their helplessness and inferiority in comparison to their Western female counterparts.

The dominant discourse on trafficking functions to exclude narratives that do not conform to a simplistic idea in which migrants who have faced abuse as a result of force, fraud, or coercion deserve assistance and recognition, and those who face abuse but have exercised free will in choosing to engage in sex work are less deserving. This polarized framework negates the exploitation and violation of rights that many workers face in situations to which they have "consented," supposedly bringing their misfortunes upon themselves. The dominant trafficking discourses, consciously or not, reinforce the idea of a real, merited distinction between "'innocent victims' (who are forced and coerced as deserving pity and the criminalization of those who have abused her) versus the willing 'whore' who has sacrificed her right to social protection through her degraded behavior."[39] The insistence on this dichotomy functions nicely to simplify an incredibly complex reality, and to silence and deny the narratives that challenge the dominant discourse. It also limits who counts as a victim and who does not meet the criteria, as only those seen as innocent or deserving merit defense and outreach afforded by the trafficking discourse. In this way, assistance becomes predicated on perceived guilt.

Building Responses

A U.S.-based anti-trafficking coalition has been instrumental in outlining the "3 P's" (prevention, protection, and prosecution) and "3 R's" (rescue, rehabilitation, and reintegration) approach to trafficking, embedded in the language of both the TVPA and the TIP. Within this framework, the focus in anti-trafficking campaigns led by organizations such as the Coalition Against Trafficking in Women (CATW) or the International Justice Mission (IJM), is on the "rescue" of the women involved and prosecution of the traffickers.[40] As Gretchen

Sodurlund has noted in her article titled "Running from the Rescuers," rescue efforts can often seem more like arrest, abuse, and deportation. Furthermore, many women who are subject to "saving" campaigns have no desire to be rescued or deported and often seek out a way to return to the sex industry.[41] Activist campaigns and the TIP top-down approach that focuses on rescuing women in the sex industry also obscures the needs of migrants and trafficked persons who face abuse and need assistance in the form of legal counsel or in reclaiming lost wages. Importantly, the focus on rescuing trafficked "victims" avoids the question of systemic inequalities and diverts our attention away from working toward improving labor standards for migrants in all employment sectors.

The 3-P *prosecution* component overshadows the other two, a fact that is evident in the U.S. allocation of funds to organizations such as the CATW or the International Justice Mission (IJM), which heavily favor prosecution efforts (note that money spent on investigation and prosecution is seven times that spent on prevention).[42] Though convictions of traffickers have not noticeably increased since the passage of the TVPA, within this framework it becomes evident that trafficked persons themselves are somewhat seen as criminals. Their act of transgression (being undocumented or working in an illegal employment sector) is seen as a violation of state laws and thus neutralizes their status as victims. Consequently, efforts to protect trafficking victims take a back seat to prosecution and criminalization–based strategies.

Criminalization exacerbates the power inequalities already prevalent in human trafficking. Favoring prosecution and criminalization as the main U.S. strategy to combat trafficking tips the scales toward law enforcement personnel, which rarely increases the safety of those who have been trafficked, and diminishes the power and resources of social workers and service providers. Formerly trafficked persons across the globe have noted that law enforcement personnel are often undertrained at best, and abusive at worst.[43] Basu and Dutta, in their dialogue with a group of sex workers who have organized in India to promote the sex workers' rights approach, note that "sex workers . . . described themselves as being harassed and exploited. They pointed to social constructions and social evaluations depicting them as lowly and incapable individuals."[44] Police are typically subject to these constructions and value judgments and often work to solidify them further. Thus the specific recommendation for the UAE to increase police is problematic.

The TVPA's current criminalization framework views protection within the context of prosecution, and state protection of victims is increasingly contingent upon their willingness to testify against their offending traffickers. Yet so-called traffickers (also referred to as recruiters or brokers) seldom fit the stereotypes. Rather than members of organized crime or nefarious smugglers,[45] the persons facilitating migration can include members of an individual's family, friends, other coethnics, or members of the diaspora. Moreover, many sex workers end up in abusive situations not because of a specific trafficker but because the conditions of their labor and the systems in place in the host country lead them to instances of being trafficked. The requirement to testify against a particular person thus leaves abused people in a precarious situation. Migrants who have been abused by a specific person may fear the social and cultural repercussions of testifying even if their physical safety is not an issue. TVPA "policy is another way of regulating and possessing control over a woman's body through the withholding of services unless a woman can assist in the 'war against trafficking.'"[46] Such legislation puts far more effort into controlling women than facilitating the necessary economic and social equalities that would ultimately provide both protection and prevention.

Throwing Out the Baby with the Bathwater?

While it is tempting to argue that the term *trafficking* should be discarded altogether from discourse and policy, such an eventuality is highly unlikely given the force with which it has taken hold in the last decade. A more productive pursuit would be to reconceptualize human trafficking as one particular form of abusive practices found along a continuum of diverse experiences (which is implied in the legal UN definition of the term, but not in popular discourse). We must disengage from the notion that trafficking is rooted in a rising global demand for commercial sex, and confront the problem as yet another component of a massive response to severe global economic inequalities.

Migrants do not end up in the potentially abusive spaces they inhabit because they are ignorant persons. They may be ignorant of the actual conditions and problems they will face in migration, yet they are making decisions based on a series of individual and macro forces structuring their circumstances. This book aims to show the many different trajectories migrants follow regarding their decision to migrate as well as their experiences within migration. By examining caricatures about sex workers versus their experiences, and by understanding the challenges migrants face and their coping strategies, we begin to expose their agency and capacity as active agents.

Simplistic ideas and arbitrary labels about migrants and trafficked persons have masked the glaring reality that their lives are complex. The challenges they face are often exacerbated by the implementation of labor laws that are intended to protect them, as well as global rhetoric that has led to a clampdown on migration but has neither reduced demand for cheap labor nor provided incentives for people to stay in their home countries. Moreover, informal efforts toward reforming the sponsorship system and pushing for labor unions and rights have been eclipsed by international policies that focus on sex trafficking to the exclusion of other forms of abuse within migration.

ı ı ı

Currently, policies such as the TIP tend to work against those they are designed to protect because they fail to acknowledge the larger macro-social forces that shape migrants' individual decision-making processes. A cyclical problem is created, for example, by the fact that the United States can and will block countries that have not made the grade within the TIP from receiving aid from the IMF and World Bank. Many migrants have been faced with the difficult choice to leave their home countries in search of work elsewhere precisely due to the fallout of Structural Adjustment Programs imposed by the IMF or World Bank that have led to high unemployment in home countries.

While trafficking policies are currently operating to the detriment of those they are designed to protect, the TIP could change this. Since the installation of Luis C. deBaca as the new ambassador on Trafficking in the United States, a move toward separating the concept of *trafficking* from that of *sex work* has begun. While the popular understanding of the definition of trafficking currently encompasses all sex work, it must ultimately be both narrowed to exclude sex workers who are not under threat of force, fraud, or coercion *and* broadened to include all types of migrant laborers who have experienced conditions of abuse. The TIP and U.S. trafficking policies must be viewed as being interconnected with the issue of migrants' rights and forced labor. Reversing the current emphasis on criminalization measures over preservation of rights and creating a genuine labor rights context would transform the TIP into a meaningful tool for addressing the myriad instances of force, fraud, and coercion faced by migrants around the world.

The stories I present in this book are all examples of migrants employed in a variety of sectors who live and work in the UAE and have experienced some form of force, fraud, or coercion. Not all migrants are trafficked, and this study is based on a limited sample, but I hope to make the case that the majority of migrant workers who do face instances of abuse in the Gulf work in industries outside of sex work. Indeed, many of the most harrowing tales of abuse came from those working in industries such as construction work, domestic work, or other types of service employment.

Furthermore, a conceptualization of sex work as labor allows us to look at trafficking as an issue of forced labor. While not all migrants are trafficked, for those who are, we need to address the challenges they face within a human rights framework without hinging assistance on their occupation or perceived guilt or complicity. Also, recognizing that migrant workers make choices based on macro social factors helps to remove blame from the equation. In other words, a female domestic worker or sex worker in Dubai who consented to migrating is as deserving of assistance and social support if she is undergoing any form of abuse as a nonconsenting trafficked worker. Her consent and the industry into which she chose to migrate do not alter the fact that she may be forced, frauded, or coerced and in need of services. Moreover, migrants' legal or illegal status should not alter their eligibility for services and assistance (as is currently the case in the interpretation and implementation of policies such as those promoted in the TIP). The dominant discourse on trafficking and the practice of filtering policies through the EuroAmerican anti-trafficking lens has skewed our perceptions of trafficking. The stories in this book aim to problematize the narrow concept of trafficking and assistance that is focused on sex work and perceived guilt.

Creating a labor and migrants' rights framework would alleviate many of the challenges migrants face and help avert further instances of force, fraud, and coercion. At the very least, the TIP could play a role in breaking the cycles of structural violence that I introduce throughout the text. Reforming the *kefala* system in the UAE, educating members of law enforcement, and providing official support infrastructures to the many noncitizens who inhabit the Emirates would be steps in the right direction. As long as the trafficking discourse remains focused on sex work and operates within a criminalization framework, a human rights approach is untenable. Lived experience and the historical, economic, and social contexts of places like the UAE must be recognized in order to understand and curb the damage currently being inflicted by trafficking policy and discourse.

2

DUBAI INC.

June 5, 2009

*It is only 8 a.m. and already 108 degrees on this balmy Dubai morning. As
we walk outside our apartment building, located in the newer area of Dubai
in the southern part of town, Chris and I squint to avoid the dust from the
surrounding construction sites. Even though Dubai is suffering from the world
economic crisis, many construction projects still forge ahead at full force.
The smells of the Gulf, coupled with the desert sand that has been kicked up
overnight and the dust surrounding the construction cranes that litter the
Marina skyline, overwhelm me. A few palm trees sway in the wind, and I
look out at the mostly empty houses and apartment buildings on the Palm,
the signature collection of man-made islands that have added thousands of
feet of waterfront property to Dubai's real estate market. Most of the houses
and apartment buildings on the Palm sit empty, giving the impression of a
ghost town; skeletons of housing developments and wide, empty roads contrast
sharply with the crowded housing projects in the northern part of town that play
host to the migrant workers who built these houses.*

*"I don't even understand what the point is of having it shaped like a palm,"
Chris had said to me the night before as we drove to the Atlantis Hotel at the tip
of the Palm. We had decided to take a night off to celebrate getting my driver's
license back after I had paid the necessary fees and waited the obligatory ten
days that had been my punishment after our car accident. She broke the silence
that had blanketed us in unease as we drove the empty streets of the islands.*

PHOTO 1   Dubai Marina—southern part of town. Courtesy of Abby DiCarlo.

"I mean, you can't see that it's a palm, you just see land and water, why did it have to be shaped that way? What is the point?"

"You can see it from the air," I told her.

"So what? Who gets to see it from the air?" Chris stopped mid-sentence. "Oh yeah, I forgot, these Sheikh guys travel by helicopter, so they can see it," she said, answering her own question.

We both yawn as we get into our little Toyota Yaris to begin the trip from the economically privileged, shiny, newer part of town (the southern end, Dubai Marina) to the oldest neighborhood of Dubai in the northern part of town, which has in recent years become known as a working-class neighborhood. In southern Dubai and the Marina, the wide streets—where gleaming skyscrapers are often miles apart, allowing for breathtaking views of the Gulf, the Palm, and the Marina—contrast sharply with the narrow winding streets of Old Dubai in the north, which is home to the neighborhoods of Deira, Bur Dubai, and our destination this morning, the Bastakiya (or old fishing village) quarter. When making the drive from the south to the north, drivers can observe the wide open spaces between buildings gradually narrowing as they progress north. As

we merge onto Sheikh Zayed Road (the main highway running through the
Emirates), I see Chris nervously fumbling with the map of Dubai I had handed
her. I realize that playing navigator to my stressful driving is not easy, especially
after our car accident. We are both anxious because driving into Old Dubai is
terrifying. The narrow, winding streets and heavy population density create
many opportunities for accidents, not to mention the ubiquitous traffic jams that
keep drivers in a gridlock. Though Old Dubai offers more conveniences in terms
of being slightly more walkable than our part of town, where sidewalks were
an afterthought and end abruptly in highway entrances rather than leading to
enticing cafés, we chose to live in the Marina because it felt calmer and because

PHOTO 2 Bur Dubai—northern part of town. Courtesy of Abby DiCarlo.

the economic crisis allowed us to get a good rate on an apartment. Chris is eerily quiet and I realize she probably needs coffee.

"Should I stop at the Coffee Bean?" I ask her, hoping she will perk up.

"Well, we could, but that's on the other side of the road and I have no idea how to get there," she says. We both roll our eyes.

I nod and rest my forehead on the steering wheel as we pull up to a stoplight. "Dubai is not a very livable city," I had written to my parents the night before, and I was reminded of this fact again this morning. While one's destination might be just across the road, or maybe a few meters south or north, getting there is not so easy. There are no pedestrian bridges, and gated fences separate lanes of traffic so that one often has to drive ten minutes south or north in order to make a U-turn to get to the other side of the street. A few nights earlier I had gone to visit a friend in the financial district of Dubai in the center of town. Arriving early, I decided to stop at the Emirates Towers building next door before walking over to her apartment; from a distance the buildings appeared to be next door to each other. I parked at the Emirates Towers before realizing there was no way to walk from one building to the next. It took me twenty minutes in the car to go probably twenty meters.

"At least there is a Coffee Bean; helps with feeling homesick," I tell Chris as she nods, her head buried in the map. We decide to forego our caffeine pit stop in favor of concentrating on getting to our destination, the Sheikh Mohammed Center for Cultural Understanding, located in the heart of our biggest driving challenge yet: Old Dubai.

As we drive along Sheikh Zayed Road, I take advantage of its relative emptiness to take in the scenery. That morning it seemed that we were among the few people to venture onto the highway, or perhaps we were feeling the effects of the mass exodus of expatriates who had been leaving in droves as their companies collapsed due to the global economic downturn. The only people we saw were the masses of male migrant workers in blue uniforms that dotted the ordinarily golden brown horizon of the desert. Contrasting sharply against the backdrop of beige, pink, brown, white, and gold buildings, as well as the sand, the laborers in their dark uniforms always caught my eye. I told Chris for the hundredth time that I couldn't imagine working long hours in the hot sun wearing those uniforms, and she nodded in agreement. "At least the government has passed a law that they can't work between noon and 4 p.m.," I said, reflecting on a law that had just taken effect. The speedy implementation of legislation in the UAE was something we repeatedly marveled at.

"Yeah, I mean, I think they're trying; the government is trying to make things better," Chris said.

"I think it's just growing pains," I replied, knowing that Dubai had grown up virtually overnight. The tiny emirate had developed rapidly economically into a center of commerce and finance. It was now trying to develop a social infrastructure to keep pace with the booming economy that grew out of the vision of Sheikhs Rashed, Zayed, and now Mohammad, as well as the capital and investments of corporations around the world. "I think Dubai gets a bad rap," I said to Chris, who looked at me and shrugged. "No, seriously, I think that a lot of things could be improved here, not just the labor laws, but I think the government is trying, and they need support rather than constant criticism." Chris nodded thoughtfully, indicating our shared ambivalence toward our host city.

Some days I was angry with the UAE for its lack of social infrastructure and its laws that changed on an almost daily basis, and critical of the fact that it had become a symbol of capitalist excess. Other days, annoyed by worn-out tropes about Dubai being a city of glamour and glitz, or capitalism gone wrong, I wanted to defend the Emirates. From fishing village to financial hub, Dubai has always been a center of commerce and merchants have been key in its development. Seeing the bad publicity that followed the economic crisis, when headlines such as "The Dark Side of Dubai"[1] alluded to the fact that organized crime and perversion were responsible for Dubai's former reputation as a party town for the rich and famous, I wanted to inform people that the government was working on creating a social infrastructure, that it wanted to change things and needed support rather than constant scrutiny. Rather than continuing this conversation with Chris we both decided to turn our attention to the map so that we would find our destination swiftly before being caught up in the massive traffic flow of Old Dubai.

■ ■ ■

After forty-five minutes of uneventful driving, we made it our destination. We had come to the Sheikh Mohammed Center for Cultural Understanding to take part in a "cultural breakfast" and tour of the Center, located in one of the oldest homes in Dubai in the Bastakiya quarter, one of the earliest settled areas of Dubai that was home to Persian and Indian merchants in the early part of the twentieth century. Chris's attention to the map paid off, and for the first time in a while we didn't get lost as we drove into the Old Quarter and parked next to an oversized statue of an Arabian horse. The statue was painted a deep navy *blue, and beautiful Arabic script lined its legs and neck. "Do you think this is really an old house? Or is it just Arab kitsch?" asked Chris as we walked into the center. Two women greeted us and led us into the courtyard that was "air-conditioned for our comfort," as we were told.*

"Feel free to look around, learn about our history, enjoy his highness's photographs," said one of the women, handing us brochures and directing us toward photographs of Sheikh Mohammed, the current ruler of Dubai. We grinned as we looked at yet another photograph of Sheikh Mo'.

It's hard to avoid Sheikh Mohammed's smiling face, which looks down from photographs that line the highways, buildings, and inside restaurants and cafés. We made our way past the photographs to the narrow stairway leading to the rooftop deck of the house. As we climbed the stairs we saw a wind tower at the opposite side of the house, and I was reminded of the old homes in Iran that featured this same type of architecture of mud brick walls, small windows, and ornately carved towers supported by wooden poles that jut out to the sides. "I think this really is an old house," I said to Chris as we continued up the winding stairway.

"That would be a first. It sometimes seems like nothing in this city is older than a few decades," she remarked. When we got to the roof the classic Dubai skyline greeted us. In the foreground, the somewhat older buildings of the Bastakiya and their wind towers are visible against the backdrop of glistening high-rise buildings, each one more uniquely designed than the next, that tower over the area that was once a fishing village. "The old and the new," Chris said as I took yet another photograph of the skyline.

After taking in the view for a few more moments, we returned back to the courtyard area to enjoy the breakfast. Zahra, our hostess at the Sheikh Mohammed Center for Cultural Understanding, was waiting patiently to begin her lecture as a few more visitors strolled in. "Welcome to the Center, I am pleased to share with you some of our local culture. We will begin with the local food," she trilled in a high-pitched voice. Zahra told us she was born and raised in Dubai, but had gone to the United States to pursue undergraduate education before returning to the UAE to be with her family. She now lives in Dubai with her husband and three children. "The main point of this breakfast, though, is really to introduce you to our culture, Emirati culture," she emphasized, her English carrying no trace of an Arabic accent. If she had not been wearing an abaya and hejab, I would not have recognized her as Emirati.[2]

"People love to use clichés when they talk about Dubai or Emiratis," continued Zahra. "There are many rumors going around expat circles; people

*think they understand Dubai and Emirati culture, but they don't. That's why
I am here, so we can talk openly about your assumptions and I can clarify,"
she continued, walking over and offering us tea and dates. After taking a date
from her tray I lay back on the cushions that were placed around the circular
tablecloth that had been set out on the floor in the center of the courtyard. The
food was in the center of the circle and piles of pillows were in every corner.*

*That morning, we were among the dozen or so visitors to the Center. The
other guests were from the USA, Germany, Spain, and Australia. "So, the whole
point is, let's talk openly. You all have a set of assumptions about us Emiratis,
and I am here to clarify," Zahra said again. The room fell silent as we all looked
at one another, trying to figure out what to say next. "Come on!" coaxed Zahra.
"There are so many rumors about us, stereotypes about us, and just so you
know, we don't like any of them," she said.*

*The British woman that had been sitting to my right spoke up. "How do you
treat your servants?" she asked. I nearly choked on my tea. How could she be so
direct? My surprise was quickly subdued when the questioner followed up with
an explanation. "I mean, I'm not sure what to do with mine, do you give them
a cell phone? Do you give them days off? What do you do?" she asked. Chris
looked like she was going to be sick.*

*Zahra just smiled and sat next to the British woman. "We treat our servants
like our second hands," she began. "Well, more like they are our children,
and as children they need to be minded," she explained. I gritted my teeth in
frustration. Zahra was getting on my nerves.*

"Like children!?" I blurted out, but Zahra took my question the wrong way.

*"Well, yes of course. They are like children. You can't let them go out alone,
out of the house, I mean. You can't give them a cell phone, and you have to know
where they are at all times," she said. I felt my pulse quicken. Zahra must have
read something in my face because she quickly added, "but we Emiratis, we treat
our servants very well, I challenge you to find one Emirati family that doesn't
treat their servants with extreme care." I caught Chris's eye as we each reflected
on some of the stories from domestic workers we had heard in recent weeks that
would challenge Zahra's statement. At this point, I was getting fed up with the
cultural breakfast, but realized that leaving would be quite rude. I settled myself
back on the cushions and told myself it was good anthropological practice to be
around people who challenged one's viewpoints.*

*Through the next series of questions, however, I began to feel sorry for
Zahra and realized where her anti-foreigner sentiment, which she later openly*

revealed, must have come from. The Spanish couple to my left asked about the traditional dress of the abaya for women and jallabiya for men. "Did they just ask her why she is wearing a veil?!" Chris whispered to me. I nodded, catching Zahra's exasperated expression.

"We wear this because it is a symbol of our culture and religion," Zahra began, trying unsuccessfully to conceal her frustration.

"But could we wear it as a costume? Like for a costume party?" interrupted the Spanish woman. I almost lost it. How could people be so insensitive? But that wasn't the worst of it.

"How come the men have so many wives? We always see the Emirati guys walking around the mall with lots of women, like their harem or something," asked a woman from Texas in her southern drawl. Chris rolled her eyes and slumped back on the cushion.

"People always ask about the wives, but it's not like that," Zahra explained, this time more patiently. "When you go to the mall and you see a man with a lot of women, those aren't always his wives, a lot of time it's his one wife with his mother and sisters or sisters-in-law. It isn't always a harem," she said. Chris passed me a note: "CAN WE LEAVE?!" I folded the note back up and shook my head. I took out a piece of paper and wrote back, "I FEEL SORRY FOR THIS WOMAN." Chris nodded and continued eating her dates. Desperate to shift the conversation away from the ethnocentric tone it had clearly taken, I raised my hand to ask a question about the opening of the Guggenheim in the UAE and followed up with a question about health care. Zahra explained that the Emiratis were proud of their efforts to open the museum and were working on improving their health care so that all migrants would have access, not just the Emiratis.

The German man spoke up and asked about the recreational activities of Emiratis. Zahra smiled and continued her lecture. "We love to do all kinds of things, not just going to the mall. We like to go to the outdoors, like we like to go hiking and walking in the caves and mountains that surround Dubai," she began. "But we are respectful of our nature. When we go places, we pick up after ourselves and we leave the place how we found it, not like the foreigners," she said wryly.

"She hates nonlocals," I whispered to Chris.

"But can you blame her? I mean look at the crop we have here," she whispered back. Zahra had begun her diatribe about foreigners and it did not stop there.

"How would you feel?" she asked, her voice rising sharply. "How would you feel living in your home country and feeling like an outsider? Feeling like those who have come to your home don't respect it? You know, it used to be that

twenty years ago people would come here and they would walk into a bank, and at least they would try to speak some Arabic, or try to converse with the people here, and try to follow our rules," she said. Beads of sweat began to form around her otherwise flawless face. "But now, people walk into a bank or grocery store and they are mad if everyone doesn't speak English. They don't even try to follow our customs! At first we wanted to be open, to be okay with everyone, to make people feel at home here, but then we saw that our culture was under attack, and in our own home!" Silence filled the room.

Finally the British woman spoke up, "Is that why that couple who was kissing on the beach was arrested? Because they were violating your culture?" she asked, timidly.

"Yes," Zahra breathed, trying to regain her composure. "Look, we have to have some rules here, otherwise it will be chaos. There are people from all around the world here, and they are here, in our home, so they should respect our rules. Things just happened so fast. My grandfather was living a simple nomadic life, and now Dubai is overrun with all types of people and growing so fast, we are trying to adjust; we don't mean any harm, we are just trying to keep our culture intact." I was speechless. I could understand where Zahra was coming from, but at the same time was filled with ambivalence. Some of what she said I agreed with, but other aspects of her lecture unsettled me. Zahra then concluded our breakfast with one last tidbit.

We love our culture, and we want to make others respect it. If we see someone violating the rules, we love to call the police or the government on that person. Sheikh Zayed taught us well, we are all the secret police enforcement of this country. If someone does something wrong, like drives too fast, or is disrespecting us, we will call the authorities and have that person dealt with. Makes sense?

I was thoroughly confused. I was shaken by her statement about everyone being secret police, but at the same time, I was trying to understand her perspective. As I got up to leave, I thanked Zahra for her time. "I hope you came away from this with a deeper understanding of Emiratis," she said. I told her I wasn't sure I had, that she had raised more questions for me than she had answered.

Questions are good. Try not to oversimplify things. We aren't just a country for the rich and famous, and we aren't a place that likes to violate human rights, cultural norms, or anything like that. We are a people, and we are trying to build a nation that reflects our values but that can be a part of the globalizing world. I will leave you with that.

"CITY OF CONTRADICTIONS," "city of merchants," "from bikinis to burqas," "city of gold"; these are just some of the catchphrases referred to by Zahra that are often used to describe the emirate of Dubai, arguably the fastest-growing city in the Middle East in the last half-century. Boasting the tallest building in the world, the largest mall in the world, and a series of man-made islands in the shape of the world, Dubai has succeeded in making its brand name known to people around the globe. This small nation-state features economic development more rapid than that of China while attracting more annual tourists than India. The ultimate symbol of capitalism, Dubai has exploded onto the financial market, while its social development has struggled to keep up.

Dubai is seen as a place where people can come to reinvent themselves, so it is not surprising that it has become a center of migration. Relatively lax visa standards and abundant employment opportunities make it a major draw for migrants from around the world. Home to several universities, it also attracts many members of the intelligentsia of the Middle East, while some migrants from other parts of Asia and Africa see Dubai as a stepping-stone or gateway to gain experience that will allow them to migrate to EuroAmerica. As a major tourist destination in the Middle East, the emirate also attracts tourists from around the region and around the world.

The reality of lived experience in Dubai is different for each resident and cannot be captured by a single catchphrase or stereotype. Placing Dubai in context historically, economically, and socially, however, helps to understand migrant workers' experiences. It is important to move beyond the overly simplistic and sometimes sensationalized tropes about Dubai as a model of stability in the Middle East, or a city of contradictions, or a city of gold built on the backs of slave labor. Paradigms and stereotypes about the UAE have shifted in recent years from a sense of Orientalist intrigue at the rapid development of a "cosmopolitan nation" in the Middle East and role model for stability in the region, to the more recent critical lens applied to the Emirates wherein criticism of loose labor laws or harsh laws on social behavior characterizes global rhetoric about the Emirates (for a pop culture example, reflect on the blockbuster *Sex and the City 2* released in 2010 that was set in Abu Dhabi). During the 1990s and up until 2005, most articles about Dubai focused on the city as a destination for the rich and famous, attracting the likes of Tiger Woods, Brad Pitt, and Madonna. When development of the ecologically unfriendly World Islands project began, wealthy businessmen such as

Richard Bransen (of the Virgin conglomerate) rushed to purchase homes and beachfront property. The UAE had branded itself as a must-visit destination for the wealthy and adventurous.

Following the global economic downturn, however, the paradigms about Dubai shifted to an assessment of the "dark side" of Dubai.[3] Suddenly, a series of articles began to appear in the popular presses condemning Dubai for developing too rapidly on the backs of "slave labor." People pointed to the emirate as a case of "capitalism gone wrong" and started fixating on human rights violations, trafficking, and the sense of superiority or entitlement that made it okay for Emiratis to violate rights of migrants from around the world for their own development. EuroAmerican journalists, not employing any self-reflexivity or looking inward at their own countries (much less the role that Western capitalists played in creating the "dark side") began harshly scrutinizing Dubai. In doing so, they have stirred up a sense of cultural panic, fueling the Islamophobia that has become further entrenched in places such as the United States since 9/11.

Dubai has a long history of migrant and merchant involvement in its social and economic development. The emirate is struggling to catch up socially to the economic developments that have taken place in the last three decades. The condemnatory discourses recently put forth by more critical writings on Dubai are counterproductive; indeed, they are an oversimplification of a complex development process. Recent history in the UAE and Dubai points to the role of merchants in the development of this nation-state. Dubai's high-speed ascendance to the top is due in large part to the vision of the Sheikhs, as well as the economic vacuum left open by previous superpowers like Iran. As the region began looking for a free trading post and financial center, Dubai consistently stepped up to the challenge during the last two centuries. The UAE has historically been an important link along the silk and spice routes, helping ensure routes of access and trade to places like China and India. It has even acted as a virtual Arab Switzerland, interceding during times of war or conflict to act as a free port, supplying arms or basic necessities.

Why Dubai?

It is not surprising that a study of migration would find Dubai a suitable home; the population of the UAE is made up mostly of migrants, while in Dubai, migrants make up 92 percent of the city's population.[4] Dubai typifies the way in which many Gulf cities have developed over the past two hundred years. Thus, while Dubai is my primary case study, the history of the region and the context of the Gulf Cooperation Council (GCC) countries play an important role in shaping the modern-day UAE. Therefore, many of my findings can be applied to other GCC countries such as Qatar and Kuwait, which share the same type of social, political, and economic development as the UAE; have the same types of labor laws (based on the sponsorship or *kefala* system); and also contend with high migrant populations. Dubai provides an interesting case study, however, as it hosts the largest migrant population of any city in the region and is trying to develop and adjust laws and infrastructure to meet the needs of its heterogeneous population.

Dubai in Historical Context

The UAE consists of seven emirates (states); from largest to smallest: Abu Dhabi, Dubai, Sharjah, Ras al-Khaimah, Fujairah, Umm al-Qaiwain, and Ajman. Before the UAE established its independence from Britain in 1971, these lands were known as the Trucial States. The formation of the Trucial States constituted the end product of a series of agreements between various individual sheikhdoms in the Gulf and Great Britain, which was keen to secure its trading routes with India during the nineteenth century.[5] Prior to these agreements, the region's power dynamics were characterized by fluid and dynamic struggles between different tribes and tribal alliances. However, beginning in the early 1800s the region was changed forever through its neocolonial encounters with the English East India Company.[6]

The UAE's historical relationship with India is significant, as "British relationships with the Gulf polities were first directed by the provincial government of Bombay, then after 1873 by the colonial government of India, and after Indian and Pakistani independence in 1947 by the British Foreign Office."[7] The British government, concerned with the threat that Wahhabi militant Islamic forces and ideology posed to their commercial ventures, felt it necessary to remain involved in the Trucial States' internal affairs. For their willingness to cooperate and work so closely with the British, the ruling families were rewarded with support for their regimes and economies.[8]

Dubai has been a center for trade and commerce for centuries, dating back to the sixth century, B.C., when trade with Mesopotamia began in the region, and remains a primary trading port to this day.[9] Migrants, primarily merchants in the early part of the twentieth century, have long played a major role in constructing the emirate of Dubai. Before the discovery of oil, pearl diving constituted the area's main industry, and Dubai was a major site for the buying and selling of pearls to populations worldwide. Merchants became active participants not just in building the economy of the emirate, but also in creating infrastructure, building a sense of culture and heritage, and participating in advancing the image of Dubai throughout the region.[10] Dubai also served as a stopover for boats heading to and from Persia, India, China, and East Africa in the nineteenth and twentieth centuries. Thus, as a result of its strategic location at the mouth of the Gulf, its opportune harbor, and its position on the trade route between Europe and Asia, Dubai rightfully earned its nickname as the "city of merchants."

In 1833, the tribal Maktum family, which continues to rule successfully to this day, took over Dubai with the support of the British. 1833 was also significant for the waves of migrants that began flooding the city that year, creating settlements in the Bastakiya and Shindagha neighborhoods and starting a trend that would continue for years to come. Despite these and other developments, Dubai has enjoyed 175 years of relative stability (all the Maktum family rulers have died of natural causes), setting Dubai apart from the other emirates, which have experienced times of harsh unrest.

The period between 1900 and 1929 was characterized by two main developments: the growth of the pearl trade and the emergence of Dubai in 1903 as the main port of the Trucial coast. When the Persian imposition of high taxes began in 1903, its former trading center, Linagh, declined economically, resulting in many merchants relocating to Dubai and bringing with them their experiences and craft skills. By 1904, Dubai was declared a free port and British and German merchandise became abundant.[11] Within a few years, over 10,000 Persian merchants had settled there, bringing their businesses and trade routes with them. This would be the first of many times Dubai profited from Iran's mistakes. As journalist and Dubai expert Jim Krane has noted, "since the 1920s, Iran's cascading missteps have showered Dubai with wave upon wave of Iranian entrepreneurs and their savings."[12] In the 1970s, with the Iranian revolution and the rise of import taxes to 40 percent, thousands of Iranians migrated to Dubai. Today the Iranian population outnumbers Emiratis in Dubai by a ratio of 3 to 1, and Dubai remains Iran's largest trading partner to date.

The ruler of Dubai in the early 1900s, Sheikh Maktum, took many measures to stimulate local businesses and attract foreign trade. In particular, he abolished taxes, which helped to draw more merchants from across the Gulf. He also often turned to these merchants for financial assistance, giving them the unique position of involvement in governance. The Majlis, the highest central authority in Dubai, was made up of many merchants and tribal chiefs who then began acting as an ad hoc government, speaking out on behalf of the population's grievances.

The Dubai merchants were greatly influenced in their political thinking by world developments. The opening of the Suez Canal connected the Gulf with Egypt, and the advent of modern communication and increased trade routes became an important factor in the development of Dubai. During this time, the districts of Bastakiya and Shindagha began to develop as merchants started to indulge in extravagant lifestyles, erecting homes made of earth and clay as opposed to traditional palm sticks. However, the period between 1920 and 1959 witnessed some major economic changes; namely, the collapse of the pearling industry, the emergence of the oil industry, and air travel. In 1934, Britain chose Dubai to accommodate an airbase, and royalties began to pour into the ruling Sheikh's treasury due to oil exploration. This was one of the first major steps toward Maktum's independence from the merchants, which he gained through the reform movement of 1938 by dissolving the new Majlis, which he believed directly challenged his authority.

World War II was a time of decline for the Persian Gulf, though Dubai did take advantage of the political instability of other parts of the region during this period (as it would during the Iran-Iraq war and other conflicts) by working as a supplier of services, consumer goods, foodstuffs, and equipment. For instance, the unrest in the sultanate of Muscat in 1915 blocked the roads between Muscat and Matrah, which enabled the merchants of Dubai to supply inner Oman with provisions. In a strategy that still continues today, the merchants and rulers of Dubai focused their energies on diversifying the economy, which effectively locked Dubai in as the financial center of the Middle East.

The economies of the Trucial States were largely directed by rentier structures controlled by the British and major concessions granted by Trucial States rulers, while the majority of residents enjoyed little economic success prior to the petroboom.[13] In 1958, however, oil was discovered in Abu Dhabi, having a truly unimaginable effect on the future of the Trucial States. In 1971 Great Britain withdrew from its governing role and the federation of the UAE was formed, though the seven emirates did not adopt a permanent constitution until a quarter-century later, in 1996.

Dubai, from the UAE's inception, worked to fashion itself as the business-friendly emirate. Never as oil-rich as Abu Dhabi, Dubai has been vested in developing alternative economic resources, focusing on tourism and financial service.[14] Business and politics have always been closely intertwined in Dubai, where much of the infrastructural development was taken up by private-sector merchants.[15] Dubai's political structure reflects its historic and cultural traditions of tribalism: "There are no democratically elected institutions or political parties. There are no general elections; however, citizens may express their concerns directly to their leaders through traditional consultative mechanisms, such as the open Majlis, or council."[16]

Dubai has pursued multinationalism and diversity as one of its main strategies of advancement, and its resulting demographic makeup distinguishes it from most other countries of the region.[17] Migration from around the world into the UAE and neighboring countries is a relatively recent phenomenon and is directly tied to the post-petrodollars economic boom.[18] Estimates of Dubai's noncitizen population range from 80 to 92 percent. Some statisticians and researchers claim that in recent years nationals account for roughly 4 percent of the population.[19] Within the labor force, noncitizens comprise up to 98 percent of the workforce of the private sector, working mainly as unskilled and semiskilled laborers in the construction, domestic work, and service industries.[20] Yet one aspect of the Gulf that makes it unique is that all migration is for work and rarely, if ever, leads to permanent settlement, hence *immigrant* and *immigration* are moot concepts, as both terms connote an intention to settle permanently. While many migrants stay in the Gulf for several years, repeatedly renewing their contracts, permanent settlement and the attainment of citizenship is legally not an option.

Labor and Law

The extremely large foreign population and heavy dependency on foreign migrant workers has created serious problems for the UAE. Dubai is widely cited as a place with deep labor rights violations and gender inequality. Those who work on these problems confront a significant lack of data regarding actual numbers and the demographic makeup of migrants in the region.[21] Though the statistics about numbers of female migrants in particular and the industries into which they migrate suffer from a lack of accuracy and transparency, current statistical estimates show a dramatic increase in numbers of female migrants in the last three decades.[22] It is believed that "fifty to seventy-five percent of the legal migrants leaving Indonesia, the Philippines, and Sri Lanka are women, most of them hoping to earn money as domestic workers in the Middle East and other parts of Asia. The International Labor Organization (ILO) estimates there are more girls under age sixteen employed in domestic service than in any other form of child labor."[23]

Migrant labor in Dubai is structured by a *kefala*, or labor sponsorship system. Those migrating into the formal economy must operate on the basis of their contracts and work with a sponsor. This system is unique to the GCC countries and structures the lived experience of migrant work in the formal economy. Under the *kefala* system, each migrant worker is tied to a sponsor, or *kafeel*, who also functions as his/her employer. Residence and legal working papers for the migrant depend on the relationship with the sponsor. In the case of disputes with the sponsor-employer, migrant workers can be left without legal permits to remain in the UAE.[24]

As Andrew Gardner has noted in his thorough study of male migrant workers in Bahrain and later Qatar, the *kefala* system renders extreme variability in the experiences of workers in that the governance of the individual depends entirely on the sponsor. While some sponsors are quite accommodating and vested in protecting their laborers, others are exploitative and abusive.[25] Migrant workers often report that while their sponsors are sympathetic and have taken their complaints seriously, communication with them is not always easy, as middlemen can present barriers in accessing help from the sponsors. Within the *kefala* system, sponsors often confiscate employees' passports (though this is now technically against UAE law, our interviews revealed that it is still common practice), effectively restricting their mobility and their ability to pursue other employment opportunities. Thus, while in theory either party can break the contract at any time, doing so forces workers to pay for their return tickets, often a restrictive price further augmented by the debts that many migrants undertake in order to migrate.[26] Many workers who choose to break employment contracts attempt to stay in the country as illegal aliens, a better option for them than returning home empty-handed. Certain labor laws allow workers to take employers to court for the violation of labor contracts, yet during the proceedings workers become and remain undocumented and are often forced into the informal economy to make ends meet.[27] Additionally, according to the 1959 Residency Law, an alien can be deported as a result of a judicial or administrative decision if "the alien has been convicted and the court has recommended deportation, if he/she has no means of sustenance, (or) if the Ministry of the Interior objects to his or her presence on national territory for 'security or moral reasons.'"[28] Indeed, collapsing employer and sponsor into a single category may be the root of the problem. Migrants have no place to turn because the law is written to protect the employers rather than the migrant workers. In fact, the Ministry of Interior in Kuwait has written that confiscating workers' passports is "considered an effective crime-prevention measure, as they will not be able to leave the country to escape prosecution."[29] The language of this law is problematic in portraying migrants as potential criminals, while virtually ignoring the possibility that employers/sponsors could be guilty of crimes against their employees.

Several articles of the UAE's Labor Provisions law as detailed by the UAE Ministry of Labor are worth mentioning, especially as they reveal inherent contrasts between the language of the law and the lived experiences of migrant labor. According to Article 2 of the General Provisions:

> Arabic shall be the language to be used in all records, contracts, files, data, etc. . . . provided for in this Law or in any orders or regulations issues in implementation thereof. Arabic shall also be used in instructions and circulars issues to employees by their employer.[30]

The challenge presented by this law is that neither employees nor those who seek to provide them with informal social services typically have a strong enough command of Arabic to decipher the contracts. Though middlemen in home countries may purport to be well-versed in the ways of the host country, they frequently mislead their recruits regarding the contracts, which seldom acknowledge the rights of the workers.[31] Other aspects of the General Provisions that structure the lived experiences of migration include Article 3, which states that "the provisions of this law shall not apply to the following categories . . . domestic servants employed in private households, and the like . . . farming and grazing workers," and later under Article 72, seafarers are added to the list of migrant workers not protected by any labor laws.[32]

Under Article 37 of the law, the probation period for any migrant worker can be up to six months, during which employers do not have to grant sick leave and will not pay for a return ticket if the relationship with the migrant is not up to their standards. To this end, Article 84 states that migrants are not eligible for wages during their sick leave if it can be shown that the illness is a result of "misconduct" as decided by the employer. Article 155 specifies that if a dispute arises between the employer and the employee, both parties are responsible for submitting their complaints *in writing*, presumably in Arabic. This can prove challenging to the illiterate migrant, or to migrants who do not speak the same language as their employers.

While I argue that the articles of the law outlined above need serious revision, there are, in fact, a series of articles that in theory protect laborers' rights, but lack enforcement. Articles 65–73 outline appropriate working hours and the need to give workers time off at regular intervals. Similarly, Articles 80–90 outline a long list of occupational hazards and diseases that the employer must provide treatment for, both in the short and long term. These laws protect migrants' time and health, but are often not adhered to due to the lack of inspectors. According to a Human Rights Watch Report, "though a decree in 2006 asked for at least 2000 new labor inspectors, the number currently stands at just 48."[33]

The 1990 U.N. Convention on the Protection of the Rights of All Migrant Workers and Members of Their Families has not been signed by the UAE, and this convention is the only available international instrument able to protect domestic workers, since even the ILO Convention excludes contract workers recruited under the *kefala* system.[34] Migrants in the domestic work industry and those employed in the agricultural sector in the Gulf are unprotected by the labor laws. The legal domain of domestic work remains a highly contested issue across the globe, and in the Gulf the fact that this type of labor is outside the system of labor laws has been problematic. Working within the private homes of citizens, any dispute between domestic workers and their employers are viewed as "private matters" or "matters of the home" and not to be solved in a court of law.[35]

Many migrant workers and scholars with whom I spoke while in the field emphasized the need to reform the *kefala* system to make it more favorable to employees. This reform includes the need to provide rights and benefits for domestic workers and other migrant workers who are subject to rules of kefala without enjoying its attendant benefits. Indeed, it is the potentially exploitative situations caused by the system's structure that render many workers vulnerable to situations of trafficking whereby wages are withheld and abuse can occur. It is for this reason that activist groups within the region have been pushing for a reform of the system and have been frustrated at the international community's focus on sex trafficking without contextualizing trafficking within the broader frame of migration.

The UAE is a member of the International Labor Organization and the

Arab Labor Organization, and has ratified the Convention on the Rights of the Child, CEDAW, and the United Nations Protocol to Prevent, Suppress, and Punish Trafficking in Persons, Especially Women and Children. While the Emirates is working toward improved labor standards, human trafficking, with a focus on sex work has taken center stage. In a statement responding to the 2009 TIP, Minister Gargash, head of the UAE's National Committee to Combat Human Trafficking (NCCHT) formed in 2007, said, "it is incongruous to equate alleged labor rights violations, which are critical but a separate issue, to the coercive and unacceptable sexual exploitation of women for profit. This report lumps all of these issues together in a manner that is generalized and unconstructive."[36]

Health and Human Rights

Inequalities in health care are official policy in the UAE. While citizens can seek out health care largely for free, noncitizens must pay often considerable fees. In particular, while an HIV-positive citizen will be provided with all the medical support he or she requires, a noncitizen who tests positive will be deported. Though the current number of HIV-infected noncitizens is relatively low, this punitive immigration policy has the potential for serious health repercussions. With large numbers of migrant men and a growing commercial sex industry, the potential for a sexual-health crisis is troubling. Dubai's unique combination of underdeveloped political and civil infrastructure for noncitizens and a highly developed (albeit uneven) economy, contribute to a grim picture for foreign labor.

These contradictory characteristics of Dubai society have had serious implications for health and human rights research projects in the emirate. While it is easy to gain entrance to Dubai, particularly from a Western country, ethnographic research once within the borders is far more difficult. The contradictions are baffling, such as lax visa standards for entering the Emirates versus stringent laws against settlement, and the high demand for migrant labor versus the lack of infrastructure for migrant laborers. The *kefala* system also presents challenges in that migrants who are unhappy with their employers have no avenue of recourse other than absconding and becoming illegal, undocumented workers. Shifting visa regulations make it difficult to keep up with visa renewals and lead many legal migrants to become illegal as they wait for their paperwork, which can take months or years. Their illegal status then makes them more vulnerable to abuse and exploitation, conditions that mimic problems of trafficking. Lack of governmental transparency and cooperation (often due to absence and silence rather than official denial of information or requests), limited freedom of speech, employees' fear of their employers, and the prospect of deportation are all aspects of the challenges structuring the lived experience of migration for many of my interviewees.

Gender, Race, Space, Place

During my fieldwork I was repeatedly struck by the organization of social and physical space in Dubai; specifically, the ways in which the social topography and spatial access was affected by race, class, and gender. The physical spatialization of migrant workers hinges on local and locally produced discourses about race and produces distinct categories and income-generating potential for laborers in the Emirates. Deploying the term *race* in this context is complex, especially because locals used the word to describe nationality and were not always conscious of the social production of race and racism. In the UAE (and many other Gulf states) where migrants make up a majority of the population, country-of-migrant-origin (labeled as "race" by locals) determines social status and often income-earning potential, which leads to a problematic racial hierarchy for residents of the Emirates. For example, the lowest-wage earners in Dubai typically come from Ethiopia and Nigeria and are racialized as "black" according to perceived skin color, followed by unskilled and semiskilled workers migrating from South Asia who are classified as "brown." The pay scale increases according to the lightness of the employee's skin color[37]; "white" expats hold the highest income-earning potential, after citizens. Indeed, many interviewees from South and Southeast Asia expressed frustration at being paid less than their white counterparts, despite holding the same job. Though race is socially constructed and not necessarily tied to nationality, country of origin, or ethnic group, many of my interviewees continued to use the term *race* to refer to nationality or country of origin of migrant workers.

Gender also affects spatial organization in the UAE, and male-dominated spaces prevail by far in the public sphere of Dubai. On several occasions I commented with discomfort in my field notes or to Chris that we seemed to be the only women in a certain part of town or a certain space (such as in the bazaar, the police station, or while driving on back streets east or west of the main road). Though gender and racial segregation are not official policies in the UAE, people either self-select or are encouraged in some manner to occupy

PHOTO 3   The male-dominated space of the bazaar. Courtesy of Abby DiCarlo.

or not occupy specific spaces, and transgression of certain spaces by certain minority groups tends to result in general discomfort among all concerned.

Various social divisions or boundaries act to separate populations in Dubai; some of these are physical, others linguistic. Physically, noncitizens are separated from citizens and from other nationalities according to country of origin in the geospatial ordering of the city. Citizens tend to live more inland, away from the water, and have large homes typically surrounded by walls. They have also moved from the more crowded northern part of town to the southeastern section. Notably, most Emiratis do not occupy, and do not wish to occupy, apartments in the new high-rise developments that continue to dot the Dubai skyline. These expensive edifices are intended to attract EuroAmerican noncitizens and wealthier migrants from parts of Asia and the Middle East. EuroAmerican migrants, or expats, tend to live in specific apartment complexes typically populated by fellow countrymen. Less advantaged migrant workers live in Satwa (mostly Filipino and Southeast Asian) or Bur Dubai (in the north), while male construction workers often live in labor camps, now referred to as villages, on the outskirts of town.

The question of "public" space has become contentious in terms of who has access to which areas in Dubai.[38] The beach has unofficially become the public space for expats and tourists who can pay the entry fees (approximately $10–$30 USD). This was reaffirmed with the arrest of three Indian male migrant workers who were caught taking a break on the beach and arrested for inappropriate behavior (meaning they were accused of harassing the tourists, when in fact they were merely unlucky enough to be at the wrong place at the wrong time). Malls, too, are supposed to be public, but migrant workers from India, Africa, Pakistan, and parts of Southeast Asia are frequently turned away by security guards if they cannot prove they work there. Such instances of discrimination have led some residents to begin organizing to contest these unofficial boundaries.

During the summer of 2008, we saw very few women in public places other than malls or parks and playgrounds. When Chris and I took a trip to the bazaar on one occasion, located in the old part of town, we were the only women present both in the bazaar and on the busy surrounding sidewalks. The space was populated exclusively by males, merchants and customers from a wide variety of backgrounds (though none Emirati). As the only women walking through the narrow alleyways, we attracted a lot of attention and confusion, which filled us with a sense of unease at being hyperscrutinized at every turn. A few days later we would experience this same feeling when looking for a restaurant along the streets of Deira in Old Dubai. Again we were the only women in view, and several cars slowed down to ask us if we were sex workers, a scene that would repeat itself throughout our fieldwork as we would find ourselves walking along half sidewalks or on the shoulders of busy highways or roundabouts looking for a taxi or an obscure address. Taxis often refused to stop for us, assuming that unchaperoned women dressed in Western attire might indeed be sex workers and presumably not worth the fare.

On one particularly hot afternoon a similar occurrence provoked me to tears. We had gone to visit some of the religious groups that did outreach to migrant workers in Bur Dubai and had attended noontime services. At around 1 p.m., the hottest part of the day, we walked out of the church to look for transportation back home. There were four of us: myself and three of my students, all women, all dressed discreetly in jeans and linen tops. We walked to a corner, our eyes tearing from the heat, and began trying to wave down a taxi. Instead, a series of men in SUVs pulled over, asking us "how much." I finally managed to get one taxi to stop, but when I called over the others the

PHOTO 4   Looking out to Deira. Courtesy of Abby DiCarlo.

taxi driver took one look at the scene of four unaccompanied women and shook his head and drove off, leaving me in his dust. A few moments later a young man in a forest green Range Rover drove up and parked next to the corner where we were standing. As he, too, inquired how much, I shook my head and ignored him, hoping he would leave. My heart was now pounding to match the throbbing headache I was developing from the heat. The hot desert sun burned my skin and my ears felt like they were on fire. The man in the Range Rover wasn't leaving. Instead, he leaned back in his tanned leather seats, enjoying the refreshing air-conditioning while sweat dripped down my entire body, causing my jeans to cling. No taxis were stopping, and we were all starting to feel faint in the approximately 120-degree heat. We needed water and air-conditioning, but neither was within sight as Chris signaled yet another cab unsuccessfully. For the first time in a long time, I started to cry, grateful that I was wearing dark sunglasses so my students would not be able to witness my breakdown. After a few minutes, I pulled myself together and told two of the women to wait in a patch of shade I had spotted across the way. After what seemed like an eternity but in fact was only minutes, Chris and I managed to hail a taxi, pile in with the others before the driver had a chance to say anything, and head home.

The following year we discovered that the southern part of town, or New Dubai, was a more female-friendly neighborhood. Walking the boardwalk of the Dubai Marina we saw more women (mostly from the United States, Europe, and Australia), and it seemed that our presence was more unobtrusive. Though we had moved to a part of town where unaccompanied women were a more common sight (passersby probably assumed we were tourists), we would experience gender segregation in other locales. Having decided to rent a car, and perpetually taking wrong turns, we stumbled into other male-dominated spaces on several occasions. A few times we ended up near construction sites, and when slowing down to ask male migrants for directions we were either laughed at or ignored. In the police station, and in our subsequent visits to the traffic department to pay our fines, we were again the only women in large, male-filled waiting rooms. The moment we would enter, all eyes were on us; not only because we were women, but also because they could not immediately peg our ethnic or socioeconomic backgrounds. In these moments we would become acutely aware of how race and class, apart from just gender, also played a large role in Dubai's social and physical layout.

Several conversations and incidents with various friends in the UAE confirmed this phenomenon. One night we had decided to go for a drink at the Atlantis Hotel, located on the Palm Islands in a more affluent part of town. We had invited two new friends of ours, Indonesian sisters who were raised in Australia, had lived in Miami, and had recently moved to Dubai to set up a real estate business. In their spare time they worked as volunteers for an informal group that did outreach to female migrant workers. That night, Chris and I were waiting at the Atlantis Hotel for them to arrive when one of them, Shana, called my cell phone.

"I'm stuck at the gated entrance, they won't let me drive in," she said, her voice an exasperated whisper.

"What's going on?" I asked her.

"The guard won't let us in," she said, this time more audibly. "He thinks we are prostitutes and don't belong in there." In the background I could hear the gruff voice of the security guard telling Shana to turn around.

"Tell him you are meeting friends inside," I told her.

"No use, they think because we are Asian—I think they think we are Filipina—they assume we are trying to pick up customers in there," she said, the frustration in her voice palpable. Shana didn't make it into the Atlantis Hotel that night, she said, because certain types of people didn't belong in certain parts of Dubai. "If you aren't Paris Hilton, or don't look like her, you don't get to enjoy all that Dubai has to offer," she told me the next day.

On another occasion we were meeting with an officer of the highest-ranking police squadron in Dubai, named Ahmed. A large man with broad shoulders and the build of a wrestler, Ahmed was born and raised in the Gulf and now worked on policing illegal immigrants in Dubai. Ahmed told us he "just knew" who belonged in what part of Dubai, reflecting ways in which racial hierarchies were reproduced at the law enforcement level. When we asked him how he knew this, his response was a bit startling. "I know from their faces and where they are. Certain types of people don't belong in certain places, and when I see someone who looks out of place somewhere, I know. I know that they are doing illegal things to get there," he explained. We were confused by his answer and pressed him for further explanation. We were sitting at the Mercato Mall, a relatively upscale shopping center located near the southern and more affluent part of town. Ahmed scanned the section of the mall we were sitting in and then pointed to a group of women who looked like they were from Eastern Europe. "See those women over there? They are probably prostitutes, and have overstayed their visas," he said. Ahmed explained to us that in his opinion the UAE should not allow single women into the country on visit visas so readily. He said that his job was made more difficult because the women were allowed in as tourists and then overstayed their visas. His specific mandate was to find migrants who were working illegally in the informal sector in Dubai and who had out-stayed their visas, in order to arrest and deport them. He told us he spent most of his time arresting women who he thought were sex workers, a fact that continued to unsettle us and reflected gendered and racialized tropes shared by other security guards.

"Why do you say that?" I asked Ahmed.

"Those women are probably Russian and they were probably poor be-fore coming here; they don't belong in a mall like this, how do they have the money?" He told us that it seemed perfectly normal that we would be in the mall, "because I can tell by your face and dress you are coming from America," but women who seemed to be from Eastern Europe, or "worse," Southeast Asia, probably did not belong in a fancy mall near the southern part of town. "Those women should stay in Bur Dubai, or Satwa where they

are living, unless they work at the mall," he had said during another conversation. "Certain people just don't belong in this part of town."

Working with sex workers also led me to understand the intersections of
race, space, and place more clearly. In recent years the sex industry in Dubai
has grown to include women from the Middle East, Eastern Europe, East Asia,
and Africa. With the increase in sex workers from different ethnic and racial
backgrounds has come a form of racism that is embedded in structures and
desires seen within specific locations. In other words, there is a hierarchy of
demand for sex workers in Dubai, and this demand both affects and is affected
by the locations within the city in which sex workers perform their labor.
Women from Iran, Morocco, and some parts of Eastern Europe (perceived
as white) command the highest price and thus invariably work in the higher-
paid and more comfortable environments of expensive bars in Jumeirah and
Dubai Marina, and inside luxury apartments in higher-end parts of town.
Women from South and Southeast Asia (perceived as brown) form a middle
tier and often work in lower-end bars and clubs in Deira or Bur Dubai, or in
brothels and massage parlors throughout the city. Finally, women from Africa
(specifically sub-Saharan and East African and raced as black) are still conspicuously overrepresented in the poorest and most dangerous sectors of the
trade, namely in street work.

Living Dubai

The influx of a huge migrant population allowed the Sheikhs to achieve their
dream and vision of Dubai as a major cosmopolitan center and financial trading hub. However, while Dubai has developed financially, labor reform and the
social infrastructure needed to provide services to the large migrant population are lacking. Dubai is now struggling to keep pace in terms of social development with its rapid emergence on the economic front. The vision of the
sheikhs is to create a place that is admired and loved by all and that is attractive
to merchants, migrants, investors, and tourists from around the world. For this
reason, image is very important to them. They do not want to be known, as
their neighbors are, as "rogue states." They want to be seen as safe, neutral, and
stable. However, as Zahra told us at the Sheikh Mohammed Center for Cultural
Understanding, Emiratis also want to hold on to their culture and don't want
to lose sight of their collective identity in the face of the many changes and the
influx of different cultures and nationalities.

This duality of purpose is apparent in the legal and social framework of Dubai's development. While on one hand, Emiratis are dependent on migrants to fulfill their vision of building this cosmopolitan city, on the other, they do not provide migrant workers with strong labor laws, and nonlocals face harsh discrimination in business and law and in their lack of access to social and health services. In response to recent criticism of its lack of human rights standards, Dubai has hastened to pass a series of laws designed to curb rights violations and regulate migration. These rushed laws—such as tightening borders, increasing the police force, and implementing measures to restrict the migration of women—are paradoxically resulting in a situation where many migrants gravitate toward illegal avenues in the informal economy, in areas such as sex work.

The lived experience of migration and labor in the formal and informal economy of the UAE is affected not only by international policies, but also by the historical, economic, and social context of the Emirates. Migrants are drawn to the UAE because of its long legacy of employment opportunities and its history as a place where migrants of all backgrounds can come to reinvent themselves economically. While the Gulf continues to offer migrant workers many economic and employment opportunities, transnational laborers must confront the scarcity and lax enforcement of labor laws in place to protect their rights. Furthermore, global policies on trafficking and sex work have ignored the reality of lived experiences in the formal and informal economies of places like the UAE. To change this, migrants' voices need to be heard. To understand the disconnect between policy and migrants' own stories, we must be able to trace their migration trajectories even into the informal economy of sex work and street work. Then, perhaps, we can mold domestic and international policies on trafficking and forced labor to migrants' needs and benefit.

3

SEX WORK

I have talked to dozens of trafficking victims here in Dubai. These poor prostitutes were fooled. They were told they were coming here to be maids or cooks but end up in a brothel. There are just so many of them.

Director of a Women's Shelter in Dubai

Migrante International: We do try to help migrants, but they, their papers are legal, it's not as important as the, uh . . . the women trafficked to be sex slaves.

PM: So you are saying that trafficking is when sex work is involved?

MI: Yes.

PM: But what if they weren't exactly forced to go into sex work?

MI: But they *were* forced. Because they are forced. No one chooses this life, they are trafficked into it.

Director of Migrante International, Filipino NGO
working with Overseas Filipino Workers Globally

The Iranian women in Dubai, well those in the sex industry anyway, can be placed in two distinct categories, at least in my view. There are those who are victimized by the system, who are kidnapped and brought here as sex slaves, and then those who are trying to work the system and have come here to find a rich Arab husband. These ones are just the most glamorous women you have ever seen, but also the most dangerous.

Arab-American psychologist in Dubai

I came [to Dubai] to make money. I came to make money for, for my family, for my daughter. I knew I could make a lot of money doing this, and could make that money in a short time, so I did it. I gathered up my courage, left my husband and family in Tehran, and came here, but I will be leaving soon.

Leila, a sex worker from Iran

THE FACT THAT SEX WORKERS predominantly exist in the underground, economy of Dubai contrasts sharply with their visibility within global conversations on trafficking. They are at once invisible in the local landscape of labor and formal migration, while simultaneously hypervisible within the trafficking debate. Unfortunately, much of the discourse about sex work and trafficking is based on rumors and stereotypes; it rarely draws from the actual narratives of those who work in this industry and their experiences.

During my time in the field I heard various stories about motivations for engaging in the sex industry in the UAE. When I began talking to sex workers in Dubai in 2004, I noticed a disconnect between the ways in which sex workers narrated their own experiences and the stereotypes swirling about them. The caricatures drawn by Emiratis and expatriates living in Dubai about sex workers from a range of ethnic backgrounds were based on myths and rumors. Both the global imagery about sex work and trafficking (as seen in films like *Taken* or *Call and Response*) and the national imaginings regarding sex workers and trafficked women in Dubai evoke stereotypes that counter women's own stories and further ingrain negative attitudes toward sex workers. Most damaging is the idea that all trafficking is sex trafficking and all sex work is trafficked, which serves to marginalize laborers outside of sex work who face abuse while hyperscrutinizing all women in the transnational sex industry regardless of the conditions under which they entered or their experiences as commercial sex workers.

Global Mythology

Global policies center around a series of myths that feed on one another and that tend to equate trafficking with sex work.[1] The first myth is that all sex work must be forced, therefore all transnational sex work must result from instances of trafficking whereby women are tricked or kidnapped and taken unwillingly across borders to be coerced into sex work. Certainly, there are women who face abuse within sex work, and some who are tricked or trafficked into the sex industry, however this is not the case for all commercial sex workers. This myth feeds the "rescue rhetoric" that focuses on the need to "save" all women allegedly trafficked into sex work. The idea that sex work isn't always forced, or that force and choice can sometimes coexist or operate within a continuum, works in direct contradiction to the fundamental beliefs underlying current policies that hold saving these women as their central mandate. Contrarily, if the women were not forced, it is assumed they would not need to be rescued and thus would not need the services of social service providers whose existence is predicated on these myths. Mario Pechemy has pointed to a "fetishization of victimization" whereby social actors and policymakers exclude narratives that do not fit their victim paradigms. Objectifying the stories of "victims," he argues, submerges the self-identities of those whose fate is determined by policymakers without their input.[2]

The second myth, predicated on sex work as an identity rather than a source of income generation, fails to recognize sex *work* as labor, and thus prevents access to potential protections that could be provided by strengthening labor laws. The research and findings of Siddharth Kara of the organization Free the Slaves, and John Miller, former Ambassador to Combat Trafficking, rests on the assumption made through interviews only with women at shelters, not with sex workers at their workplaces, that all women in the sex industry are slaves. In order to help these women, argue Miller and Kara, they must be saved from slavery, dismissing outright the perception of sex work as labor. Discussions about trafficking also reveal a xenophobic dimension; namely, that women from the Third World make the "irrational" choice to migrate and are duped or tricked into sex work. In my experience, the migrant women I met in Dubai were neither stupid nor duped. Instead, they had made a difficult but rational choice to leave family and loved ones behind in search of wage-earning possibilities, adventure, or stability. Absent from global portrayals of trafficking is the recognition of the courage some of these women demonstrate, and the central fact that they are sometimes forced to choose.[3]

The final myth implied in the global rhetoric is that ending trafficking depends on ending a demand for sex work, or ending the margin of profit for prostitution.[4] Beyond the fact that this assumption further collapses trafficking and sex work into the same concept, there is simply no proof that demand for sex work is determined by the availability of prostitution. Those who make this claim ignore the historical evidence that across time, place, continent, and culture, commercial sex work has existed and often flourished under a diverse set of conditions. The question also remains: What industries can these women turn to if they cease to work as commercial sex workers?

Local Discourses about Sex Work in the UAE

Conversations and rumors about commercial sex workers in the UAE invariably display the heavy moral overtones outlined above. My fieldwork revealed that expatriates and Emiratis, as well as some activists in the emerging anti-trafficking campaign in Dubai, tend to place sex workers into three distinct categories that reflect racial or, more accurately, ethnic stereotypes. The first paradigm classifies sex workers (especially those coming from other parts of the Arab world and Iran or Russia) as "glamorous" or "high-class girls" who engage in sex work as a strategy for what was referred to as "husband hunting" or "home wrecking."

The first time I heard the topic of sex workers discussed in the UAE was during my first visit to Dubai in 2004. I was spending an evening with a group of young Arab-American, Pakistani-American, and Iranian-American men and women. We had made our way to one of the more popular bars on Sheikh Zayed Road, in a complex that featured seven different nightclubs and bars and was a popular hangout spot for tourists, expatriates, and, as I would come to learn, "working girls." As I looked around the bar I saw many women dressed in fashionable attire and what seemed to be expensive jewelry and accessories (such as Chanel handbags, Gucci scarves, and Prada shoes). I made a comment to one of the young men I was with that I always felt underdressed in the Middle East.

"Don't worry, you aren't supposed to dress like *those* women," he said. I was puzzled.

"Oh, is she worried about the prostitutes?" asked another young man next to him.

"Did she just notice the prostitutes?" asked yet another young man.

"What do you mean, what is going on?" I asked, shouting over the blaring music playing in the club. To me the women looked like many of the highly fashionable Iranian and Arab women I would see at the grocery store in Los Angeles; I told the group that many Middle Eastern women are often overdressed and quite made up. "These are different," said another young man in our group.

"These women are working girls, they are special, they are expensive, and they are looking for a husband," he continued.

"And they are trouble," added his girlfriend who was visiting from Jordan.

Everyone laughed and then continued explaining to me about how these "gorgeous," "made-up," and "expensive" women were actually quite predatory in their quests to "poach" a wealthy Arab, Iranian, or European expatriate husband. "They see Dubai as their ticket to a better life, and we, well, a lot of guys here, we hold that ticket," said another young man as we were leaving the bar.

The topic was often revisited during my fieldwork. One Emirati English teacher with whom I spoke in 2008 said that she was very worried about and wary of Iranian and Arab sex workers in particular. "I guess this isn't the case with all of them, but many of those glamorous Iranian women you see here are out to get our husbands. And sometimes they win, too! They beat us out! Because of how they dress and act, and they really are beautiful, but they somehow just know how to get men." Another man who works at a hospital in Dubai as an administrator noted that he was afraid that sex workers were "ruining the culture" of Arab families. "I am an Arab man, and I am supposed to have strong character, but I see these women, and I think . . . well, I don't know. This is bad because it ruins marriages and families. I wish they weren't here so my family wouldn't be exposed to it," he explained. His colleague who was the head of surgery at the hospital also echoed his sentiments, worried about "the effect on families of having these women here." Another group of American and European expatriate women who hosted periodic lunches for expatriates in Dubai told me in 2008 that "the women [sex workers] here are the most glamorous, and they get the highest price. We aren't sure why that is, but they are so expensive, and so high in demand, they are definitely in charge." This sentiment was corroborated by a team of British journalists who were in Dubai to make a film about Iranian and Arab women in the sex industry (not yet released). They indicated that they had chosen to focus on these women precisely because of the perception that they were "glamorous, expensive, and on the prowl," as one of them explained.

The second response to commercial sex work within the UAE was more severe in its assessment of the women in question and was voiced principally by government officials, policemen, and a few local health care providers. This paradigm focused on the "cold, calculating woman" who was taking advantage of the system. One government official who was now volunteering at a local shelter told me:

> There are some women here who were trafficked. But more important, there is another group of people who play the system. There was a woman at our shelter who knew all our laws and worked them to her advantage, and she isn't

the only one, but I'll tell you about her as an example. She came, I think she came from Uganda or somewhere in Africa, and she never did any work. She wouldn't help out at our shelter, and she didn't want to get a job. She came to us saying she had been raped. But we knew she was a prostitute, the police had told us so. And she came saying she was raped and beaten by her employer. But then whenever any men came around, especially Arab men, she would run up to them and start trying to kiss them. She knew that if she got impregnated by an Arab [Emirati] man that our laws and our men would protect her. So she was trying to work the system.

This interviewee is not reproducing the rhetoric about women being forced, tricked, or duped into migrating, but rather sees their circumstances as a deliberate choice—one, however, that was made in order to take advantage of the UAE's immigration laws. Some of this person's colleagues who work as health care providers to migrant women also felt that some women had not been forced into the sex industry, but had made a conscious decision. "I think everyone who gets here is with their will," began Rania, an Emirati physician in Dubai. "It's because they need the money. They want to come here and work because they can make money here. But not against their will, I don't think so," she reiterated. Rania believed that while some women do face abuse while engaging in the sex industry, they should not "deserve health services" because they have come to Dubai, made a choice to be in an illegal industry, "and that's what happens when you try to take the easy way out." Yet another woman, a professor at a local university in Dubai, explained this viewpoint in the language of trafficking.

Let me put it to you like this. I don't think that they [sex workers] are trafficked. I don't buy it. I think they traffic themselves. Does this disturb you? Because, I mean it's really them who will describe it to you. Because they are better off when they are here. I think that these women really traffic themselves. I don't know if I would call this agency, but that is what they do because things are really bad where they are coming from. So all that they go through here, rape or abuse or whatever, well it's better than over there where they came from.

This woman spoke to an issue that was reiterated by several interviewees; that whatever trouble sex workers faced while in the UAE was comparatively better than in their sending countries. The idea that "here is better than home" as one British man who frequented sex clubs told me, was pervasive and contributed to feelings that perhaps women did not need the benefits of services, nor suffer from the drawbacks that might come with deportation. In this troubling viewpoint, rape or abuse becomes tolerable if it is presumed that the person suffering from the abuse would suffer even more at home. This paradigm was tied to the perceived guilt and complicity of women who found themselves in abusive situations within sex work.

The person who was perhaps most articulate in expressing this paradigm, however, was Ahmed, a police official (introduced in chapter 2) who had been appointed to serve on the special anti-trafficking squad of the Dubai police force. Ahmed was intimidating, but his willingness to speak so candidly about his views on trafficking and sex work were helpful. We had the opportunity to interview him on a few occasions where he made his opinion about sex workers and trafficking in the UAE abundantly clear.

"They agreed to sell their bodies, sometimes they have a contract, they came into this knowing exactly what could happen," began Ahmed the first time we met him in 2008. He constantly reiterated his skepticism that women could really be "trapped" in sex work. He argued that men would not want to sleep with abused women covered in bruises and that it would be bad for business if their traffickers beat them up.

"If they are forced, or something bad is happening to them, why don't they come to us to complain?" he asked angrily. "Could they really not come to us, make a phone call, shout out a window? They must come and complain. But it doesn't work this way, they won't talk. These people, they don't need our help," he insisted, his voice rising and his comportment becoming slightly menacing. "These people are like sheep. If you go to a nightclub, you see them all around, and they are happy. They like being illegal, they like all illegal things, it's in their contract not to talk," he explained before sitting back down to resume eating his pizza.

When we worked up the courage to press him further about why he thought people "liked being illegal" he came up with an analogy. "What if someone walked up to you and offered you a brown bag full of $100,000? What would you do?" he asked us.

We told him we wouldn't take it.

"Why not? You turn down free money?" he said, his voice rising again.

"Well, well, I would assume they would want something from me later. I, I just wouldn't feel comfortable taking it," responded my assistant, Abby.

Ahmed became angry and threw down his pizza. "Well, most people aren't like you. They would take it, they would take the free ride, even though it's illegal, because it's easy," he said, crossing his muscled arms over his expansive chest. "So, if things go wrong for them, I don't have any sympathy. It's their fault, they shouldn't be here in the first place."

The "free ride" Ahmed was referring to was the opportunity to make money. His feeling was that if people were willing to do something illegal to make "fast money," as he would say, then they would have to pay the price of the risks they were taking. Ahmed and many of the others with whom we spoke believed that sex workers were predatory, calculating, and by definition guilty, and thus not deserving of services or protection in the event of abuse. Ahmed frequently spoke of women "deserving" these abuses for "making bad decisions."

The third paradigm I heard about sex workers, mostly from members of the informal civil society in the UAE, was a discourse about "innocent young women and girls" who had been "tricked, duped, kidnapped, or trafficked" to Dubai and were in need of "saving." This viewpoint came into vogue around 2008, arguably because the global moral panic about trafficked migrant women was then in full force. This was also the period during which the George W. Bush Administration was adamant about "rescuing" trafficked women, and when many films and docudramas were being made about sex trafficking.[5] Against this background, some Emiratis and expatriates in Dubai joined in the hyperbole and were using U.S.-based anti-trafficking rhetoric to fortify their paradigm about commercial sex work in the UAE.

One activist in the local campaign against trafficking in the UAE noted, "yes, it's terrible. These poor girls. They are stolen from their families and told they are going to be waitresses or store workers, and then when they get here, their passports are stolen from them, they are slapped around, and forced into sex slavery. It's really horrifying." The script inherent in this woman's version of the events, which was echoed by at least seven other interviewees, is similar to other discourses about "trafficked" women popular in EuroAmerica that are based on hearsay rather than the experiences of the women concerned. When I asked this activist if she had spoken to any sex workers who had had this experience, her response was a simple, "well, I don't speak their language, so, no." She indicated that her account was based on stories she had heard, but admitted that she had never interviewed any women in the sex industry.

Agency and Rescue

The image such stories paint of women, ignorant or duped into terrible situations, disregards the capacity of these women as agentive subjects and serves only to legitimize brothel raids and "rescue" efforts, often to the detriment of the women involved. While some women may be tricked or forced into sex work, others have made the conscious decision to enter the industry based on a range of reasons. Myriad experiences within sex work are overlooked when all sex workers are presumed to be trafficked and assistance hinges on their perceived guilt or complicity in determining their own fates. Perhaps it is seen as necessary to script sex workers as in need of saving in order to justify the need for civil society to combat trafficking. That civil society is necessary to address human rights violations is absolutely not contested, but hearsay in international discourse should be supplanted by women's actual stories and needs when program and policy formation is at stake.

Another government official I interviewed in 2008 also talked about the sex workers who were in Dubai and in need of saving. "Yes, it's really just horrible. They are tricked, brought here, abused, and the whole lot. We need to save them. We need to rescue them and take them home, get them out of this mess," she explained to me. In another interview I conducted with the same policymaker four months later, she was quite puzzled as to why the women she had been trying to "rescue"—through a police-run brothel raid responsible for arresting and deporting thirteen women—were now trying to come back to Dubai, or why many of them had run away from her team of "rescuers" that had raided the brothel. "I just don't understand," she told me later that year. "We are trying to help them, to save them. But they aren't cooperating. We sent them home, but now they are just trying to come back. I don't know what to do anymore."

Wendy Chapkis, Gretchen Soderlund, and others have pointed out that the problem with the "rescue rhetoric" is that many women do not necessarily want to be rescued.[6] While some women understandably find the experience of the "saving effort" frightening (the experience can simulate being arrested, wherein women are often held in prisonlike cells before being deported), others adamantly do not want to return to their home countries. Still others feel that they need to earn more money before leaving, or feel that they cannot return home due to the stigma of having been involved in the sex industry. These sentiments, expressed by many of the women with whom I spoke, have not been addressed or explored by members of the government-approved, civil society–oriented groups seeking to save the women in the transnational sex industry. Most of the officials who interact with the women, from police rescuers to government officials in the campaign to end trafficking, lack the necessary social work or mental health training to work with this population, often holding outmoded notions of the women's actual experiences, needs, and desires.

The discourses about sex workers in Dubai silence women's voices and seek to script their narratives into convenient paradigms without recognizing the nuances of their stories. The question of representation and the erasure of certain narratives go hand in hand. This was made most clear to me when interviewing Susannah, the former director of City of Hope (a private shelter for abused women that has since been closed) about the women in her shelter. While at her shelter, I was in the midst of conducting an interview with a former domestic/sex worker from Ethiopia who was living there. The disconnect between Susannah and the woman I was interviewing became blatantly apparent when I asked my interviewee to talk about how and why she had come to Dubai. She gave a long answer, alluding to coming for work and recounting how she left a bad economic and political situation in her home country in order to find work in Dubai. Susannah, who was also in the room with us, immediately reduced the woman's detailed narrative to a simple phrase: "Ah, she was trafficked." It is notable how the director of the shelter applied her own script to the narrative expressed by the interviewee, despite a marked dissonance between her version and the woman's lived experience.

I do not mean to minimize the abuse that some women face within commercial sex work or other service-sector industries. Some women are indeed tricked and forced into situations they had not bargained for. But prevalent attitudes often tread upon women's own experiences. Many women do in fact choose to migrate into sex work, and the paradigm that paints them as cold, calculating, predatory, or guilty and deserving of abuse denies their human rights. The paradigm that paints them as innocent by assuming they are tricked or kidnapped into transnational sex work denies their agency. Furthermore, there is no recognition that most women fall somewhere in between these two poles. The discourses have been constructed by policymakers or activists with an agenda, and this agenda rarely applies to women's situations. The reality is that each story is different. The only thing that these women have in common is the process they have all undertaken: they have migrated from an elsewhere and are now in the UAE to make money. While acknowledging the existence of trickery and coercion in the trafficking phenomenon, all of the women with whom I spoke were their own agents and had made a difficult choice. Their involvement in paid sex constitutes a form of labor and functions as a strategy for immediate economic survival or long-term gain. These women must be seen as agents of change because they are making deliberate choices and seeking to improve their economic situations, and, as reflective of the larger and longer structural processes of economic change, drastically impacting countries in the developing world and economies in transition. Rather than concentrate on women's degree of compliance with their situations, it is more to the point to look at the living and working conditions of women in the commercial sex industry in order to determine where the human rights violations are occurring, what types of structures enable such violations, and what types of responses could mitigate and ultimately prevent these abuses.

Sex Workers in Dubai

One of the first times I walked into a venue designated unofficially as a sex worker club, I was immediately struck by two things: the heterogeneity of the sex workers and the clients, and the way in which the club was sectioned off according to the ethnic backgrounds of the workers. The club, located as many of them usually are in a hotel lobby in Deira, was small.

As I entered the space, my lungs filled with smoke and several men from a range of ethnic backgrounds turned to look at me. I immediately put on my coat even though I was sweating from the heat. Loud music blared from the speakers and all around me were groups of men and women, leaning in toward one another and speaking in hushed tones. I scanned the room, avoiding the eyes of South Asian, East Asian, Southeast Asian, African, European, and American men. It took a few minutes before I found a few Iranian and Arab men, but the majority of clients this evening were not locals, and neither were the sex workers. In fact, the sex workers gathered at various sections of the bar according to ethnicity. I looked up to my right and my eyes locked with a tall blonde woman who was speaking English with a Russian accent. She was standing with a group of four other tall blonde women who were talking to a group of South Asian men. She looked at me, angry because I was standing in her area, and jerked her head toward the back of the room. I looked at her in confusion and then spun around to come face to face with a group of East and Southeast Asian women, all wearing four-inch stiletto heels. One of them walked up to me and stared down at me, while the other leaned into the African man who was talking to her as he lit her cigarette.

"What are you doing here?" the woman asked me.

"Hi, I'm Pardis, nice to meet you," I said, holding out my hand. The woman did not respond. "Can I buy you a drink?" I asked her, trying to break the awkward silence.

Frustrated, she leaned back onto the purple velvet sofa she was standing in front of and cocked her head to one side, squinting at me. "Where are you from?" she asked.

"Well, America, kind of, but I'm Iranian. Where are you from?" I asked, nervously.

She clearly didn't want me in her space and I was starting to feel uncomfortable as the rest of her group stared at me, now that the African man had moved on.

"Thailand," said one of the women, adjusting her red halter top.

"China," said the woman I had been talking to. "But you should make your way back there," she added pointing to the back of the room.

I could tell that they were frustrated and feeling that I was wasting their time by talking to them. "I'm sorry, I'll be on my way," I said, glancing in the direction of the area she had pointed to. A group of Middle Eastern–looking women were standing in the back of the room being courted by European and American men. Nervous about joining that group, I stood in the middle of the bar, to my left the East and Southeast Asian women, to my right, the tall blondes from Russia and Eastern Europe. In front of me was a group of South Asian women, and in the back, the Middle Eastern women glared at me. Frozen, I stood there unable to decide where to go next.

It took several trips to this particular club and other venues like it before I worked up the courage to talk to the women or the male clients, though I never managed to feel fully comfortable in these spaces. One thing I did note each time I was in such clubs was the multiplicity of ethnicities present, both in terms of clients and sex workers. Each club I visited had the same type of spatial division based on the ethnicity of the sex workers, and each club was also comprised of clients from around the world. A direct challenge to the stereotype of Dubai being a major trafficking venue due to the sexual insatiability of Arab men (as seen in films like *Taken*), these venues featured clients from many different nations, with local men clearly underrepresented. When speaking to the sex workers about their client base, or "johns," they corroborated my observations and noted that their clients displayed a wide range of backgrounds but did not often include local men. "I mean, I have had one or two locals," explained one Iranian sex worker I spoke with at 360, a popular club I visited in 2008. "But the majority of my clients are from Europe, like London or Germany or those places," she explained. At least ten other sex workers with whom I spoke echoed this statement. When I told Ayesha, an Emirati friend from Abu Dhabi about this finding, she smiled and said, "I told you it's not just our men that are so into this, in fact it's mostly the foreigners. That's at least one myth dispelled. You have many more to go."

                                          ▪ ▪ ▪

"I came to Dubai to make money," was the phrase I heard from over a dozen sex workers during my time in the field, one of the only similarities I encountered among the many different narratives about women's motives for migrating to the UAE to engage in sex work. Several women noted that Dubai was particularly attractive given its relative proximity to their home countries (such as Iran, Morocco, Ethiopia, and Russia) and the fact that obtaining a visa to travel to the UAE was relatively easier than for elsewhere. "We come here on tourist visas, it's really easy, and then we just stay," explained Sanaz, an Iranian sex worker I met in 2004. Dubai was also chosen because of its reputation as a global playground. Many women expressed their hopes that they would find clients from the United States or Europe who would presumably pay more than clients in their home countries.

Some women saw Dubai as a stepping-stone or gateway for eventual migration to Europe or elsewhere. Still others described fantasies of falling in love and marrying expatriates and moving to the West, adamant that they would have to be in love in order to migrate.[7] "In Iran I can't meet anyone. Not anyone that I can connect with anyway," said Tannaz, an Iranian sex worker I met in 2004. "Look, I don't want to be doing this forever. I want to work in Dubai, meet a great German or French man like my friend Goli, and fall in love, and move to Europe," she explained.

Another young woman from Morocco, Mouna, described a similar fantasy, but narrated it in terms of job opportunities that came with sex work in Dubai. Mouna spoke to a theme alluded to by four of my other interviewees; namely, the idea that for some women sex work felt "easier" than domestic work or what they referred to as manual labor:

> This kind of work is better for me because it has hope and possibility. I could
> have gone and worked as a maid or cleaned toilets somewhere, but this business

is good, easier . . . it suits me more. And especially in Dubai where I get to meet all kinds of people. One of these days I'm going to meet a great guy, maybe a guy who lives in America, and we'll fall in love and move to America. What other job gives me this opportunity every day?

Another young woman from the Philippines, Ana, echoed this sentiment and indicated that she aspired to work as a full-time sex worker (rather than to merely supplement her income as a beautician in a mall) because "that way I can meet more boyfriends . . . and have more, well, more pen pals. Then one day one of my pen pals will invite me to America . . . Working as a waxer for women won't help me get to America; my pen pals will." Ana's friend Lucy added, "plus, working with men, it's much easier, and feels more fun than other kind of work."

Not all of the women who engaged in sex work in Dubai identified themselves as sex workers or were involved in sexual labor in their home countries. Many of these women were not committed to working full time in the sex industry and indicated that "doing this kind of work on occasion is okay because I have to make money to feed my family," as Ellie, a young woman from Ethiopia, explained. Another interviewee, Ladan, took this a step further. "I think it's okay to do this on occasion because it's fun, and I am treated well by these rich Arab sheikhs (referring to Saudi Arabs) who put me up in a great apartment, and I make a lot of money," she said. Ladan is an Iranian woman who does not see herself as a sex worker, but indicated that she engaged in sexual labor to supplement her income. Ladan reported traveling to Dubai for a month every six months to earn large sums of money that allowed her to maintain her apartment in a middle-class neighborhood in Tehran and send her son to a private school.

> I really like what I have with these Arabs. It's easy work, easy money, and I get to feel like a princess for a month every now and then. And they are great. I get to leave Iran, breathe freely [referring to the fact that in Dubai women are not required to wear Islamic dress or obey Islamic moral laws], and it's like a change for me. I like it.

Another young woman, Sussan, indicated that she had had no intention of engaging in the sex industry, but that she accidentally became involved during her first trip to Dubai, and then was attracted by the monetary gains she achieved from it.

"The first time I went to Dubai, I just went with my friends, to have fun," explained Sussan, a student at Azad University in Tehran who engaged in commercial sex work in Dubai during the summers. In an interview in 2008, Sussan described how she became involved in the sex industry in Dubai.

> So we were just out one night, and then as we were leaving the club we were standing outside in the street looking for a taxi. Suddenly this really nice car, I think it was a latest model [Mercedes] Benz, drove up to us and two guys started talking to us. They said they would pay us 200 Dhs [$50 USD] for our phone numbers. They seemed nice, and that was a lot of money for us, so I gave it to them. They called the next day and said they would pay 1,600 Dhs [$400 USD] for a night with me. Well, I was not in the habit of doing this, but it was just so tempting so I did. And I've been doing it as an on-the-side thing, kind of like a summer job, ever since.

Sussan was not the only one to find herself engaging in sex work in Dubai as a side job or to create supplemental income. Leila, the Iranian woman quoted at the beginning of the chapter, also described a similar experience.

> L: Well, yes, I am here to make a lot of money and then go back home to my husband and children in Tehran.
>
> PM: How did you get involved in the commercial sex industry in Dubai?
>
> L: Well, I came to Dubai one summer looking for a doctor for my daughter. She is very sick, and she needs complicated procedures. We found a doctor who can help her, but it is very expensive. What she needs is very expensive, and we just don't have the money. My husband and I are both educated people. He is an engineer, and I trained as a teacher but there is no work for me in Tehran. So we are suffering. Well I guess everyone in Iran is suffering.
>
> PM: So you came to Dubai to find a doctor. Is that when you became involved in commercial sex work?
>
> LM: Oh, well no, it wasn't then exactly. But on that trip I met several Iranian women who were doing this as a side business. They told me how much they were making and I was shocked and impressed. One of the girls I met that time told me I was pretty, and because I was Iranian, I could make a lot of money. She said that Iranian women make a lot of money here. So when I went back to Iran, I told my husband everything. I told him that I found a way out for our daughter. A surgery that would make her well again. But I told him how expensive it was. He was discouraged. Then I told him what I had heard. I told him that I had heard Iranian women could go to Dubai and make a lot of money doing this, and in a

short time. He didn't like it at first. I didn't like it at first either. But it's for my daughter. So we agreed finally that I would come here, stay for three months, and then go home. Whatever I make will go for her operation. That's it, that's just the way it is.

The phrase "that's just the way it is" was something I heard repeatedly from the women who engaged in the sex industry in Dubai. Virtually all of the women I spoke with from Iran, Russia, Ethiopia, the Philippines, and Morocco described becoming involved in the sex industry for economic reasons. They cited the worsening employment situation in their home countries, as well as the increasing economic pressures placed on women to provide for their families in the face of male unemployment or abandonment. "Look, this wasn't my first choice of things to do," explained Trish, a former sex worker in Dubai who had recently returned to the Philippines. "But I did it. I went to Dubai and did it, because my dad lost his job and my brother left us and we had no money. It was up to me, and now I've remodeled my house," she said, pulling out a picture of a villa from her purse and handing it to me. She smiled and continued:

I did that for my parents. And it was easy. I would not have been able to do prostitution here [Manila] because then people would see me, my parents would be shamed. But this way, I was away and they could just say that I was working as a model or hostess or something, and I sent the money home. Made more sense this way, and I made more money this way.

Four other women said that sex work would not be their first employment choice, but indicated that it was the best option available to them given the deteriorating economies at home. Aber, an Ethiopian woman who had come to Dubai to work as a domestic worker but who had turned to the sex industry instead, explained her decision-making process:

Ethiopia bad. No work, no food. My family, nothing. Me, I come to be housemaid, but is no good. Is no good to be housemaid here. Peoples is mean. They treating you bad. Making you sleep on the floor, no food no water. Me, no like this. Me tell boss is no good. He mad me, throw me on street. Me no go home, no money. Then someone telling me more money more easy to work in clubs. With men. I see more easy, men more nice in club. So I do. I make money. I go back home, to Ethiopia. With money.

Several of my interviewees indicated that they were not happy about engaging in sex work, but that they had decided to put aside personal struggles through their rationalization of economic benefit or necessity. One young woman from Thailand explained, "I didn't want to come [to Dubai]. I wanted to stay home and go to school or work in my village at home or in Bangkok, but the money was good. Everyone told me that this way I could make money, provide for my family, maybe even make my parents proud, so I came. But it is a hard life." Another young woman from Poland echoed this sentiment.

> I didn't want to leave home. I wanted to stay with my family. To study there. To live there. But it wasn't meant to be. Everything changed, and then one day someone told me I could make a lot of money by doing this in Dubai, so I said I'll come. Nothing for me in Poland, I'll try in Dubai.

At least five other women had narratives similar to these two women whereby they indicated ambivalence or dislike toward the work they were engaging in but chose it either out of a need to provide for themselves or their families or to search out opportunities abroad that were unavailable at home.

Some women noted that Europe or the United States was their first migration choice, but that Dubai was a good stepping-stone in the hopes of further migration and economic possibilities. The need to create new economic opportunities was a common theme among women's stories, and Dubai was seen as a place to generate such opportunity. As Tina, a sex worker I met in Tehran in 2004, put it:

> Everyone knows that Dubai is the place to go as a woman to make a lot of money. I mean, you can't even walk down the street or be in a bar in Dubai without getting propositioned, or an offer. And you can make a lot of money. It's attractive.

What Tina alluded to, namely a constant stream of attention from men (mostly foreign) and several propositions a day was something I experienced during my fieldwork in Dubai. On several occasions, waiting for a taxi or a ride, even in the middle of the day, men would stop and offer me a large amount of money. Similarly, there would be times when I was at dinner or lunch with a female friend, when we would mysteriously be sent a dessert, or someone would offer to pay our bill. They would then come over, introduce themselves, and subtly make insinuations or offers. Though my friends and I always politely declined, one could see how many of these instances could be attractive, especially to economically motivated young women.

While some of the women with whom I spoke indicated they worked with pimps or recruiters, others noted that they had come on their own and were working as independent contractors. Some of the women explained that they wanted to come to Dubai to "take a break from repression in Iran" or "to leave the dirty streets of Manila for the clean, wide Dubai streets." Others said they wanted to "see the world," and still others said they were coming to have "new experiences" or "fall in love." Nearly all of my interviewees had different experiences and different reasons for coming to Dubai. However, none of them indicated being forced, kidnapped, or "trafficked." While I do not deny that trafficking occurs, I did not encounter any trafficked sex workers during my time conducting this research.

Though it is possible that victims of sex trafficking are hidden and reaching them is difficult, it is important to note that a number of sex workers have come to Dubai of their own volition (exact numbers are not known, but I met over two dozen). Their experiences with force or abuse in Dubai typically came from the imported police or middlemen recruiters who benefit from the illegality of sex work and women's economic vulnerability. Indeed, at least five of my interviewees noted that they had been severely abused at the hands of the members of imported law enforcement squads. Due to high demand for law enforcement personnel (which became even higher due to recommendations in the TIP report), Dubai customarily imported police officers, often untrained, from neighboring countries such as Iran or Bangladesh. These officers did not receive training of any sort and were often not held accountable for their actions during raids or arrests. Women who worked as street-based sex workers reported more abuse than women who worked in "safer" environments (at indoor clubs or in private brothels) and indicated feeling very vulnerable to police officers who would sometimes harass them while working, or worse, rape and abuse them during arrests.

Segmenting Sex Work in Dubai

The first time I met Ziya she was living with a group of Indonesian and Australian real estate agents in the Jumeirah Beach Residences, a high-end housing complex located in the southern, newer part of Dubai that has emerged as the more affluent part of town. "Here, I love. JBR very good," Ziya said, referring to her current housing situation. "Me, I'm not liking Bur Dubai. Living on street, living in bus station. Bur Dubai dark, bad. Marina, nice," she said, contrasting the two very different parts of town she had inhabited since migrating to Dubai in 2007. She took me to the balcony of her current home to show me the breathtaking view of the Persian Gulf and accompanying Palm Islands as she settled in to tell me her story.

Ziya migrated out of Addis Ababa in 2007 after her husband left her with two children and deeply in debt. Having heard from friends that there was an abundance of work in the Middle East and "a lot of money there," she decided to migrate to Dubai to find employment as a domestic worker. When she arrived, however, she was placed with a family that was highly abusive.

"They burn my clothes, throw cups at me, very difficult," she told me in the summer of 2009. When Ziya made the decision to run away from her abusive employers, she automatically became an illegal alien. "I run away, but no passport, no place to go," she explained, reflecting on a tumultuous time in her life barely six months earlier. Without her passport (which her former employers continue to hold), legal working permits, or any money, Ziya entered the informal economy,[8] working as a sex worker and sleeping in airport terminals, bus stations, or on the streets of Bur Dubai, the older part of town which is now somewhat of a working-class neighborhood populated mostly by migrant workers of South and East Asian origin.

After six months of living and working on the streets of Bur Dubai, where she faced regular abuse from clients, police, and sometimes others in the business, Ziya found an informal organization, supported by locals and expats alike, that provided outreach to street-based sex workers and "trafficked" persons. The members of this informal group mobilized to provide housing assistance for Ziya while they worked to sort out her legal paperwork so that she could procure a new work visa. When I last spoke with her in September of 2009, Ziya had found a job as a nanny for a family in the same building as her temporary home. She laughed as she said, "I am happy to make money now like this to send home to my family. Next time I go home to Ethiopia, I am happy and proud."

ı ı ı

When I met Maryam, a high-end call girl from Tehran, she was also living in a modern high-rise skyscraper overlooking Dubai Marina. By the time I left Dubai in 2009, however, Maryam was sleeping in a half-built metro terminal in Bur Dubai (the metro system in Dubai was under construction during the summer of 2009 and had been slated to open the following fall) and trying her best to avoid the authorities, who had a warrant for her arrest.

"I guess I'm a rags to riches story, but in reverse," Maryam told me when I talked with her on the phone shortly before my departure from the field that summer. "Remember when we first met? I was making thousands of dollars a night, living the good life. Now look at me. I can't stay here [in Dubai], I am in debt because of my legal cases, and I can't even go back to Iran. Worse yet, no one wants to help me here," she lamented.

I had originally heard about Maryam through her friends and colleagues in Iran. Because Iranian and Moroccan women were the two ethnic groups of sex workers in highest demand in Dubai, these women made up to 12,000 Dhs (about $3,000 USD) per night. Many of them lived in luxurious apartments paid for by their regular clientele, while others financed their own accommodations in the nicer part of town with their high salaries. Maryam used the semiprivate space of the Internet to attract her customers, and up until 2009 she had a steady flow of clients that allowed her to make more money than most of the businessmen I met while in Dubai. She and her friends enjoyed the safety provided by the discretionary nature of their work. "No one is going to find us here, and if they do, they can't prove anything, can't prove we are prostitutes, so it's OK," Maryam had told me in 2005. When I asked about physical safety, she pointed to a series of cameras in her apartment and indicated that she and her friends had hired a full-time guard who would provide assistance should any problems arise. "We are living the life," her friend Sayeh told me in 2008 when I visited their five-bedroom apartment, marveling at the view afforded by the prime real estate location near the Palm Islands.

In 2009, however, all of this changed when the jealous wife of one of Maryam's Syrian customers found out about her husband's activities and called the police. Maryam was arrested immediately, and she spent most of one year's income on legal fees and posting bail. She was permitted to leave her holding cell in early 2009 but was told she could not leave the country while her case was pending. She was charged with the crime of adultery. When another client's wife found out about her, she charged her with a series of crimes ranging from espionage to theft. This time, however, the authorities couldn't find Maryam. Her friends had rented her room out to another young woman from Tehran in her absence and told Maryam not to return due to unwanted attention she or her clients' wives might bring. Maryam was relegated to working in hotel lobby bars and clubs, and occasionally turned to street-based sex work to make ends meet. She began sleeping at the homes of clients or in airport or metro terminals. When she sought out assistance from informal outreach groups, she was turned away.

· · ·

Why the discrepancy? Why was Maryam turned away, unable to access services and assistance while Ziya was taken in? The answers to these questions have everything to do with perceptions of female sex workers based on their countries of origin and the conditions and areas in which they work. Women who work in street-based sex work are seen as vulnerable and innocent by those who provide outreach in the form of social support and services, while higher-end sex workers such as Maryam are viewed as predatory, guilty, and a threat to the moral fabric of society. Their perceived complicity in determining their fate is taken as license to mold their stories into predetermined scripts that support programmatic paradigms of "victimhood."[9]

The physical spatialization of sex work in Dubai is tied to a sex worker's perceived race or ethnicity and also determines his or her income-generating potential. Deploying the term *race* in this context is complex, especially because locals equate it with *nationality* and were generally unmindful of its nuanced ramifications. The hierarchical and racial structures in place in Dubai effectively barred dark-skinned Ziya from accessing work in the somewhat safer spaces of high-end brothels, hotel lobby bars, or clubs; whereas light-skinned Maryam had previously enjoyed the luxury of working as a high-end call girl in her own apartment on her own terms.

Demand for sex work in Dubai, as elsewhere, is stratified according to migrants' perceived skin color and national origin. Women from Iran, Morocco, and some parts of Eastern Europe (described as lighter skinned and labeled as white) command the highest price, and thus invariably work in the higher-paid, more comfortable environments of expensive bars in Jumeirah and Dubai Marina, and inside luxury apartments in the wealthier parts of town. Women from East Asia, the Philippines, India, and Pakistan (perceived as brown) form a middle tier (based on earnings) and often work in lower-end bars and clubs in Deira or Bur Dubai, or in brothels and massage parlors throughout the city. Finally, women from Africa (specifically sub-Saharan and East Africa and perceived as black) are still conspicuously over-represented in the poorest and most dangerous sectors of the trade, namely in street work. That specific physical spaces are designated for women from different racial groups is a function of the interplays of race, space, place, and demand, each affecting the other in multidirectional ways.

' ' '

Demand for sex workers along ethnic lines is driven by the association of attributes to a particular race or ethnic group. Iranian, Moroccan, and some Eastern European women are in highest demand, making three thousand dollars or more per night and most often contracting work through the semiprivate space of the Internet, telephone, or informal, word-of-mouth client networks. When I asked clients of sex workers about reasons behind the elevation of these particular ethnic groups to the top of the chain of demand, responses were constructed along the lines of supply and demand, linguistic and cultural compatibility, and in some cases resemblance to pornography actresses. Some johns alluded to the fact that the ability to have discretionary relationships—the women lived in apartments and could be contacted online—was one of the benefits of engaging in relations with high-end sex workers. "I like that they aren't in clubs or on street corners, it makes it seem more classy and less seedy," said one Iranian man who frequented Maryam's apartment. Many of the more socioeconomically privileged men in Dubai are Middle Eastern of Arab or Iranian descent. For these clients, the ability to relate to the sex workers was also described as essential. "Believe it or not, I actually want to like the person I'm with," explained Arash, a wealthy Arab-Iranian merchant who frequented a high-end sex work venue in Dubai. "For me, I like that I can speak in Farsi or Arabic with them, and a lot of my friends feel the same way," he explained. His Egyptian friend nodded in agreement.

Two Moroccan women who work as high-class escorts in Dubai once created their own website called "Sex and the Dubai Hotspot," a blog written in French, Arabic, and English that lends a trilingual testament to their level of education and class status. Saba, author of the many postings on this site who entertained readers by relaying her encounters with clients, said, "Who do you think has the most money to spend in town? Right, the guys that want us to talk dirty in Arabic."

Other johns espoused a supply-demand narrative, reasoning that Moroccan and Iranian women were most in demand because they were most limited in supply. "There are tons and tons of Russians, that's why they aren't the most desired anymore," explained a Romanian client. Two British men who use Web-based escort services added, "If I'm in Dubai, I want to be with a Middle Eastern woman; if I'm in East Asia, I will go with an East Asian." Eastern European women who also worked in high-end brothels or through escort services reported that their clients liked that they looked like the actresses seen in popular pornography films. "I guess a lot of the porn actresses are blonde," said Irina, a woman from Poland who had been working as a call girl in Dubai for four years. "That works for me because a lot of the men—Arabs, Iranian, Indian, and sometimes [East] Asian—will pay me a lot of money. Probably it makes them feel like they are in one of the films," she added. Irina, Saba, and other women at the top of the pyramid of demand for sex work mostly worked inside lavish apartments in the southern (higher-end) part of town, Dubai Marina, or Jebel Ali, or on the Palm Islands. These women rarely had pimps or agents and often shared residences and worked with other sex workers in order to manage their clientele. Compared to their counterparts who work on the street, they enjoyed a degree of privacy and remained relatively undetected by the surveillance powers of state authorities, a fact that made them further attractive to their clients.

⦁ ⦁ ⦁

High-end sex workers and low-wage, street-based sex workers are largely invisible in writings and discussion about sex work in Dubai. Most journalistic and media representations of sex work in the Emirates focus on the middle tier (labeled as such because of income-earning potential) of sex workers, namely those who work in hotel lobby bars, nightclubs, and massage parlors in the older (northern) part of town.[10] Reliable figures about numbers of sex workers in each category are hard to come by, but the middle tier of sex workers is certainly the most visible, which makes it seem as though this type of sex work forms the bulk of transactional sex taking place in town. Hotel lobbies in Bur Dubai and Deira play host to a revolving series of nightclubs. Some clubs are known as homes to certain ethnic groups more than others—for example, the Rattlesnake is considered a gathering point for Southeast Asian women—but the majority of women who work in hotel lobby bars are of Russian or East, Southeast, and South Asian descent. With the exception of Russian women, then, these women are largely from the global south and typically earn roughly $100–$1,000 USD per evening, depending on the season and their location.

In many of these popular clubs, women stand in a small circle in the center of the club, encircled by a larger group of male clients. Both groups rotate, women clockwise, men counterclockwise, looking for evening companions. These clubs presumably have an arrangement with the hotel staff or owners to offer relative protection to the women working inside, but such protections and privacy are not valid against law enforcement personnel, who occasionally raid clubs, revoke bar licenses (as in the case of Cyclone, the club featured in the hit movie, *Body of Lies*), and sometimes arrest all the "working women" inside, which can ultimately result in their deportation. Sex work is often a side job for club workers, who might be legally employed as mall workers, beauticians, domestic workers, or caregivers. Some are working off debts or waiting for legal work permits, and all are vulnerable to abuse from clients who escort them "home" or to other unknown locations. These women frequently work with informal social groups of coethnics (with whom they often share housing to minimize costs and build social capital) in order to manage their risk, with varying degrees of success.

. . .

Most of Dubai's street-based sex workers are women from sub-Saharan Africa, who sometimes reside and work in the winding alleyways and streets of Bur Dubai in the northern, older part of town. On occasion, these women will venture into hotel lobby bars, but they face serious backlash from other sex workers or hotel staff at these venues. Kimberly, a part-time hairdresser from Nigeria who engages in sex work on the side, noted, "people look at me kind of funny when I walk into the hotel lobby bars. It's because of my skin . . . they don't want me there, and I don't think I can make as much money in a place where I get dirty looks." Kimberly and some of her friends explained that working on the streets of Bur Dubai was easier than the tense and racially charged atmosphere of the clubs. Though they articulated feeling physically safer in the clubs (where police raids, arrest, and abuse were less likely), they noted that working on the street was a risk they were willing to take in order to avoid the regular hostility they felt from hotel employees or sex workers from other backgrounds. Clients of street-based sex workers tend to be lower-wage laborers; on occasion these women are taken to labor camps to provide sexual services and are paid a lump sum. Many of the women working in the informal economy of street-based sex work report regular abuse at the hands of policemen or clients. Given the illegal nature of their work and the fact that most have overstayed their visas, their recourse to social support is practically nil.

The raced dimension of demand for certain sex workers over others continues to privilege high-end call girls who operate in more "respectable venues." Their location in luxury apartments in the better parts of town in turn allows them to demand higher wages and gives them an advantage, until this cycle of relative privilege is broken by abuse or entanglement with authorities. In contrast, women who work on the streets of Bur Dubai do so because the racist structures of demand do not allow them to command sufficient wages to work elsewhere. Further perpetuating this cycle is the fact that their location on the street is pointed to as making them more dangerous, thus transactions with them are perceived as not being worth as much money as those with women who work in safer venues.

Assuredly, many female sex workers cross racial categories and spaces, such as white women working as street-based sex workers, brown women working as high-end call girls, and sub-Saharan African women working inside hotel lobbies. Moreover, women can potentially move up or down the ladder, as was the case with Maryam, who went from living and working in a luxury apartment in the Marina to the streets of Bur Dubai. Beyond the physical segmentation of sex work, however, it is interesting to note how race-based structures orchestrating the various ethnic groups participating in sex work in the UAE stand in sharp contrast to the predominant hierarchy within the discourse on "victimhood" and "rights." Historically and globally, sex work has been compartmentalized according to race and degree of economic autonomy, but particularly interesting and salient in the case of Dubai is that while racism relegates certain groups of women to unsafe, street-based sex work, it also, paradoxically, enables them to access informal social services and assistance. In Dubai (as in many other parts of the world), sex workers' access to social services hinges on their perceived guilt or complicity in determining their fate.[11] Women who work in street-based sex work and those found in lower-end hotel bars or clubs are constructed as innocent nonagents, understood as forced, duped, or tricked into sex work by conspiring male pimps or traffickers. This attitude is not limited to Dubai but is instead a pervasive stereotype held by anti-trafficking organizations around the world that seek to save "innocent" or "fallen" women.[12] These sex workers are regularly described as trafficked (an assessment relating to their perceived innocence and lack of agency and not to the particular conditions of their travel and employment process) and in need of saving. This narrative fails to recognize transnational female migrants as active agents working in pursuit of their own objectives and relies on an artificial dichotomization of force and choice.[13]

None of the sex workers with whom I spoke conceptualized themselves as victims.[14] To the contrary, they each narrated a similar set of desires: to earn money, support their families, and provide a better life for themselves and their loved ones. Interestingly, however, the rhetoric that casts these women as victims, while refusing their agentive capacity, works to their immediate advantage in that they are painted as innocent, unknowing, and nonconsenting. Women thus characterized are seen as worthy of the support and resources provided by social services and outreach work. This is the type of logic that undergirds well-intentioned but uncritical, deeply flawed EuroAmerican anti-trafficking feminist campaigns to save, enlighten, or civilize the lost and fallen woman or childlike native.[15] Unfortunately, in recent years these campaigns have spread from EuroAmerica to other parts of the world, influencing local efforts in places like Dubai to attempt to end trafficking by ending prostitution. While this was not always the case in Dubai, in recent years sex workers have come under increased scrutiny due to the elevation and politicization of the trafficking issue, through U.S. policy such as the Trafficking in Persons Report (TIP) and international policy such as the United Nations' Palermo Protocol. The global moral panic that equates sex work with trafficking has created unhelpful stereotypes about sex workers that effectively limit their access to social services.

Across the globe, distinctions have been made between consenting, guilty (read scheming or predatory) sex workers and innocent or unknowing women who were tricked or forced into sex work.[16] Only the latter category is seen as deserving of assistance or protection, which may well amount to detainment or deportation, against the wishes of the women being "helped."[17] In Dubai, the concept of race that filters demand for sex workers also dictates particular locations for conducting business correlating with different levels of risk, and adds yet another layer to the false dichotomies of guilty/innocent and force/choice. Women from certain backgrounds (including Iranian, Moroccan, and Russian) are perceived as guiltier than their darker-skinned counterparts because they are seen as having consented and even strategized for their positions.

⁘

Contrast the cases of Maryam, from Iran, and Ziya, from Ethiopia. Maryam earned a high income and was able to work and live in Dubai Marina. But when she ran into trouble, no one would take her in and she was relegated to living on the streets of Bur Dubai. Ziya had the opposite experience. Earning 120 Dhs ($30 USD) per night on the street and vulnerable to arrest and abuse on a regular basis, the former domestic worker was able to find assistance and support from local groups when she decided she could no longer continue in that line of work. Maryam, however, was further marginalized in her time of need because of the perception of Iranian women as guilty or predatory sex workers scheming to destroy happy families.

Ironically, the very racism that condemns women like Ziya to the streets of Bur Dubai works in their favor when it comes to social service provisions. The creation of formal, government-recognized NGOs is prohibited in the UAE,[18] yet many informal groups of coethnics as well as groupings that coalesce around particular issues, such as domestic violence or migrants' rights, have formed in recent years. The more successful groups, and those that provide outreach to women in Dubai, are typically comprised of local Emiratis and Western expats, usually women, who have been influenced by anti-trafficking rhetoric prevalent in the Bush era in the United States.[19] Within these discourses, sub-Saharan African women are depicted as ignorant, duped, or tricked into the dangerous situations in which they find themselves. In contrast, women such as Maryam and her Iranian and Moroccan counterparts are cast by some as villains who have come to Dubai to corrupt Emirati society. They are constructed as guilty and thus deserving of any misfortune that might befall them. This was evident to me when speaking with various groups of informal activists seeking to provide outreach to sex workers who have faced abuse or are in need of assistance. While they had no trouble conceiving of Ethiopian or other sub-Saharan African women as in need of services, when I asked if they would be willing to assist Maryam, the response quickly turned negative when they heard she was Iranian. When I asked a group of Indian volunteers if they would be willing to help Russian sex workers, their similarly negative responses evoked existing caricatures and stereotypes regarding Russian, Iranian, and Moroccan sex workers.

Accessing Services

Beneath informal humanitarian interventions lurks a racialized morality that merits scrutiny. Women's bodies are racialized and spatialized in the physical geography of Dubai, while simultaneously racialized in the moral sphere of social service outreach. Street-based sex workers have greater access to services than women in relatively safer environments, yet this directive stems from an underlying "saving" sentiment that often works against the women's best interests.[20] Infantilizing and condescending, this racialized and moralized approach limits the types of solutions and responses that social service providers are willing and able to consider.[21]

Compounding this difficulty, many of the informal social service providers seeking to address the issues of migrant laborers and abuse are themselves segregated by ethnicity. Ethiopians organize to help Ethiopians, Indians to help Indians, and so on. Locals are willing to donate money to various causes, but many Emirati women in particular have strong reservations about sex workers from certain backgrounds (such as Middle Eastern and European), and they are adamant about not wanting to support women whom they view as predatory competition. This unevenness in the response by civil society combined with patronizing attitudes about who deserves assistance, serves to entrench the racialized hierarchy of the sex industry in Dubai. While there is a need for social services that are available to all regardless of employment industry or ethnic background, it is also important to encourage various ethnically-based informal groups to begin working together toward a common goal of assisting all migrant workers in Dubai.

, , ,

Shortly after returning from the field I moved to Washington D.C., where I had the opportunity to interact with policymakers and diplomats working on these and other relevant issues. During one conversation I had with an Emirati diplomat, he asked me:

> In your opinion, do you think it's better to let these prostitutes be wherever they are in the hotels or streets where people can see them, or is it better to push them away to the outer edges so no one can see them and be shamed by them? If people can see them, they might get desensitized, but I don't know, do we want that? Where should they be?

This was a direct question about the spatialization of sex work in Dubai, but racialized undertones did persist. He continued to press me on the question of how to physically organize sex work. "We don't want a red-light district," he said, emphatically. "But we do want to make sure we can regulate or at least keep our eye on what is going on, so in that sense I guess we do want to be able to find them if we have to," he added. In the end we talked about the importance of not pushing the sex industry further underground where abuse is often more rampant. While he agreed with me that marginalizing sex workers further was not ideal, he continued to return to the question of the proper use of space. "We don't want those bad women to contaminate our good women, so perhaps we need to hide them from view." His response spoke directly to the physical and racial stratification of sex work and sex workers in Dubai, in the morally led discourses and outreach programs that exclude certain populations of women.

Dubai is clearly a place of opportunity and hardship for many sex workers. Added to the hurdles are the discourses that make assumptions about their lives and needs and that fall woefully short of sex workers' lived reality. Such paradigms merely present challenges to women's agency and ultimately their safety. As Radhika Coomarasway, the UN Special Rapporteur on Violence Against Women, has noted:

> A discussion of prostitution must accept the premise that prostitution as a phenomenon is the aggregate of social and sexual relations which are historically, culturally and personally specific. The only common denominator shared by the international community of prostitutes is an economic one: prostitution is an income generating activity.[22]

Based on my field research it seems that women often migrate of their own accord, but once in the UAE they are vulnerable to force and abuse. Harsh laws on trafficking and prostitution only exacerbate the situation, as do problems inherent in the legal system and the police force. The current trafficking framework in the UAE as implemented by the National Committee to Combat Human Trafficking seeks to tighten borders (which only drives migration further underground, where migrants become more vulnerable to abuse), criminalize sex work (which makes it harder for women in the sex industry to report abuse), and provide protection only if women are willing to testify against their supposed traffickers (who sometimes are nonexistent, sometimes have vanished, and sometimes include family members against whom most women would refuse to testify).

Revisiting our understanding of trafficking and the challenges that transnational sex workers face based on their actual experience is the first step toward truly helping the women presumably targeted by policy directives. Redefining international sex work as labor is key to implementing labor laws that protect women from abuse. It is important to reiterate that the discourses constructed about women in the sex industry (and indeed the popular discourses about trafficking as a whole) do not currently serve the interests of migrant women or sex workers in any country. Rather than focus on the innocent/guilty or the force/choice dichotomies, we would do better to concentrate on the socioeconomic and political structures that are leading women to migrate, as well as ways in which we can improve migrant women's living and working conditions by addressing restrictive immigration policies and decriminalizing sex work.

Though women who work in the informal sphere of commercial sex work have become the focus of trafficking debates, discourses, and policies, it is important to note that only a portion of their experiences would fall under the umbrella of force, fraud, or coercion. Many of the obstacles they face are brought on or exacerbated by the trafficking debate itself and its ensuing policies, which focus often unwanted attention on women in the sex industry. Current policies have also eclipsed and marginalized the stories of the many migrants who work in the formal economy who have experienced force, fraud, or coercion. Though the trafficking debate has essentially silenced their voices, their narratives are important in broadening our understanding of migration in the Gulf and amending our image of trafficking to include forced labor and other elements not necessarily related to sex work.

4

MIGRATION IN CONTEXT

RAVI WAS LIMPING the first time I met him at Dr. Suparna's clinic, an informal center that offered medical services and food to male migrant workers free of charge. His clothes were tattered and caked in dirt, and he rolled up his right pant leg to show me his swollen ankle and bruised foot.

I introduced myself and said it was nice to meet him as I fumbled with my purse and bottle of water. Ravi stared back at me quietly. "Is your foot

PHOTO 5   Male laborers arrive for work from across the creek. Courtesy of Abby DiCarlo.

injured?" I asked him, stating the obvious, but wanting to make conversation. He looked at me again as we stood there in silence for what seemed like an eternity.

Finally he spoke, one word that he repeated many times throughout our conversation: "Abscond," he said quietly nodding at his foot.

"What is your name?" I asked him.

"Abscond," he said again as one of the staff from the clinic walked up to us.

"His name is Ravi," said the clinic volunteer, a tall man with a slight mustache and warm eyes. "My name is Nitin," he said gesturing to his name badge. "I'm a volunteer here at the clinic. I work with Dr. Suparna now, but a few years ago I was like these men you see here," he said. He motioned to a room filled with male laborers who were waiting in line to receive the food prepared by Dr. Suparna and her team of volunteers.

Ravi leaned against the door frame, quietly observing my interaction with Nitin and the other men gathered in the waiting room. "Most of these men you see here came from Hyderabad, in India," Nitin said, pulling out a photo album to show me some pictures of Hyderabad.

"It looks beautiful there," I said.

"It's okay. But a lot of these guys, guys like Ravi and me, we left; we came here [to Dubai] for work, mostly in the construction industry because there is no work in Hyderabad," Nitin explained.

"No work, India no work, no food," chimed in Ravi.

"Then, a lot of people came here and were abused. They had accidents on the job, or they weren't paid, or they were treated badly, so now they want to go home, even though it's shameful to go home without money. So Dr. Suparna, she helps them get food and out-passes so that they can go home," said Nitin. He stepped aside to let in three more men who were waiting to see Dr. Suparna about a variety of injuries.

Ravi smiled at me and repeated what he had said earlier: "Abscond."

"Yes, he absconded," said Nitin, by way of explanation, smiling. I nodded, smiling back. "It's funny, you know, most of these men, they don't speak hardly any English at all, but they all know that one word, *abscond*."

"Abscond!" interjected Ravi, enthusiastically, his face breaking into a smile.

"So what happened with you, Ravi?" I asked Nitin and Ravi at the same time.

Nitin motioned for Ravi and me to take a seat in the room as they began recounting Ravi's story. Nitin translated from Hindi to English for my benefit,

struggling to keep pace with Ravi's rapid narration and pausing periodically
to verify details.

> He sold everything at home, his house, and what few possessions he had. He
> made a decision with his wife that he would come to Dubai to work for a year
> and then they would buy a nice house and a store and work in Hyderabad. In
> the meantime, he sent his wife to live with her parents, a very difficult deci-
> sion, apparently. Then when he got here, that was seven months ago, I think,
> things went downhill from the moment they decided Ravi would come. An
> agent charged him a lot of money, and then he came here and his passport was
> taken away.[1] He was sent to live in a labor camp and it was bad.

Ravi paused, wiping his brow with his red-checkered shirt and rubbing his
injured ankle a bit. Nitin continued to explain the conditions of the labor
camps, drawing from his own experience:

> The camps are difficult, let me tell you. The one I was in, well it was difficult.
> Eight men to a room, and the water is not very good. It's hot and crowded
> there. Kind of like back home, actually. But you think that if you are coming
> to Dubai, it's not going to be like India.

He turned to Ravi to tell him what he had just told us. Ravi nodded and
looked back at me while cradling his foot in his arms. Sweat dripped from his
chin and he shrugged his left shoulder up to his face to wipe a drop that was
moving down his chin.

"What happened to his foot?" I asked Nitin.

"Oh, his foot, his ankle is broken and he had an accident," Nitin began.

"Abscond!" Ravi interjected again, this time with some anger, as he began
speaking rapidly to Nitin who again struggled to keep up his translations.

"Well, he came and started working at a construction site, but he wasn't
being paid for a long time," Nitin said as Ravi held up his right hand, splaying
his fingers in a high five–type motion. As Nitin spoke, Ravi's face showed a
range of emotions, from angry, to frustrated, to sad, to tired.

> Five months, he says; five months he wasn't paid. So, then he went to his boss
> who is also from Hyderabad, and he asked to be paid. His boss ignored him.
> Ravi went back the next day begging his boss to pay him, saying he needed
> money to send home to his wife. I guess he was really sad because he went to
> his boss and said you are my fellow countryman, why do you do this? Then, a
> week later, he said that he was in an accident at the work site. Maybe, I think

it was not an accident. Anyways, he was working on a building and the thing he was working on crashed to the ground, from sort of high up, and Ravi was hurt badly.

Nitin pointed to Ravi's foot, which seemed to have swollen up more just in the time we had been at the clinic. "Well, his foot hurt and so he couldn't work, but his boss didn't understand. He made him work, but Ravi couldn't. No money, no work, so he absconded," Nitin said. Ravi nodded emphatically.

Nitin explained that Ravi, like many of the other male laborers in the clinic, had left India to come to Dubai seeking work opportunities with a variety of construction companies. They had found their jobs through Indian labor recruiters and were working under Indian managers at European-owned construction sites. Though recent labor laws passed in the UAE require companies to regulate work sites and strive to prevent accidents, these laws are apparently difficult to enforce, and many companies do not abide by them. During our time at Dr. Suparna's clinic we met over a dozen men who had been injured while working at construction sites. More than half of them had been forced to continue working despite serious injuries, and this had led to their decisions to abscond. Some, however, indicated that their managers had paid for them to come to the clinic to be treated, and they were hoping to return to work soon.[2]

∎ ∎ ∎

Ravi was not kidnapped or tricked into coming to Dubai, nor is he working in the sex industry. Yet his experiences could easily be described as force, fraud, or coercion as outlined by the UN Protocol on Trafficking. His story underscores the need to reconceptualize trafficking as an issue of forced labor and migrants' rights regardless of the industry concerned. Like many others whose trajectories will be explored in this chapter, Ravi's narrative shows that even though migrant workers may migrate voluntarily, any number of problems may befall them, ranging from abuse and injury to the withholding of wages. Ravi's experiences also show that migrant workers in Dubai face instances of abuse not only by their Emirati sponsors, but also by fellow countrymen in the roles of middlemen managers and recruiters. His story is representative of the tales of many men and women with whom I spoke who ended up returning home empty-handed and sometimes saddled with significant debt, either to their recruiters or to their bosses.

Ravi's story depicts some of the challenges that migrant workers outside the sex trafficking paradigm face when transplanted to Dubai. He came to

Dubai to make money; some come to escape violent or difficult situations at home, while others come for love or adventure. None, however, is imagined as trafficked within the discourse, which effectively excludes them from access to the rights that the trafficking framework has attempted to lay out. While, in practice, the current response to trafficking includes arrest and deportation, the *language* of trafficking espouses a set of rights and protections within broader global policies. Ravi's story as well as the ones that follow illustrate instances of abuse or mistreatment that can be defined as trafficking in the true sense of the word. Harnessing the trafficking framework to provide rights to those in need, regardless of their industry, is the challenge before us. This broader conceptualization of trafficking within the purview of migrant and labor rights would assist Ravi and other migrants in Dubai who face hardships characterized by force, fraud, or coercion.

In order to highlight the disconnect between lived experience and policy, I draw on migrants' stories in the UAE to emphasize that instances of abuse take many forms and often take place outside the commercial sex industry. While not all of the individuals introduced in this chapter fit within a paradigm of trafficking, all are facing rights issues and some form of force, fraud, or coercion with potential trafficking characteristics. Each of the stories presented here represents a set of challenges encountered by several people I met during my fieldwork. Some show instances of physical abuse, others of negligence, and still others of withheld wages and legal working papers, all of which are issues faced by hundreds if not tens of thousands of migrants in the Gulf. The experiences narrated throughout this chapter further the important connection between trafficking and migration. Though the lines are often blurred, these stories help to illustrate the ways in which the "fight against trafficking is a fight for migrants' rights."[3]

A Note on Structural Violence

I have found the concept of structural violence useful in framing my understandings of the experiences of migrant workers in the UAE. The systemic nature of the inequalities embedded within the *kefala* system combined with the structure of home country and international policies render many migrants vulnerable to a type of structural violence. Used by medical anthropologists such as Paul Farmer, Philippe Bourgois, and Nancy Scheper-Hughes, *structural violence* refers to types of violence stemming from systemic social institutions or structures that result in people experiencing hardship, violence, or social injustice.[4] Poverty, hunger, and infrastructural shortcomings are all described as examples of structural violence that can be intertwined with actual violence in many instances. In writing about the AIDS epidemic in Haiti, for instance, Paul Farmer uses the concept of structural violence to point to ways in which the poverty experienced by a large percentage of the population of the Western hemisphere's poorest nation has exacerbated the experience of the disease and increased the mortality rate. Other examples of structural violence include racism, sexism, ageism, ethnocentrism, and other types of institutionalized discrimination that can lead to shortened life spans, poorer quality of life, and oppression or exploitation.

In looking at my own fieldwork, instances of structural violence can be observed in multiple aspects of migrants' lives. First, structural violence such as poverty, gender discrimination in employment opportunities, or other types of gender, race, or age discrimination in home countries can be major motivating factors that push migrants to leave home in search of work in the Gulf. Some of my interviewees reported a desire to migrate to the Gulf in search of work due to the difficulty in attaining a job at home, and this difficulty was linked for many to their gender, age, or class status. One woman astutely noted, "When we move to Dubai, we can be whoever we want. No one knows who we were back home, and we have a good chance to make a better life."

In addition, some migrants experience instances of structural violence during the migratory process. Because some sending countries have sought to increase restrictions especially on female migrants (in an attempt to respond to TIP recommendations seeking to alleviate sex trafficking), women increasingly must rely on middlemen recruiters or irregular migratory methods (outside legal structures of labor ministries and the like). Recruiters are in a position to take advantage of them monetarily, physically, or both, and because these women are often migrating into the informal economy (meaning outside parameters of the *kefala* system or formal, legal employment; see description in chapter 3) they have limited options for recourse. Their gender makes them vulnerable to this type of violence, while the structures in place have led them to irregular means of migration.

While structural violence can be observed in home countries and in the migratory process, migrants moving into the spheres of formal work and subject to the rules of the *kefala* system in the GCC countries can experience instances of structural violence in the host country as well. The *kefala* system sets forth rules and regulations that workers must abide by but that operate in favor of employers, and as such itself represents an example of systematized structural violence. By its very design, the *kefala* system renders domestic and agricultural workers particularly vulnerable by restricting their mobility, offering few avenues of recourse in the event of maltreatment, and subjecting them to heavy punishment if they are found in violation of *kefala*'s parameters.

Overall, much of the migrant experience in Dubai can be viewed through the lens of structural violence. Andrew Gardner has extensively documented ways in which the threat of deportation and the restricted mobility of employees under the *kefala* system in Bahrain are examples of the day-to-day structural violence experienced by migrant workers.[5] The officially illegal but widely practiced custom of withholding employees' passports contributes to a restricted sense of mobility for many and makes it challenging to address exploitation or abuse within employment sectors. Heavy debt burdens undertaken by many migrant workers also contribute to this sense of structural violence, as many migrants report feeling a need to "tough it out" with abusive employers in order to earn wages and pay off debts. Instances of structural violence are very real in the lives of many migrant workers and can be seen in some of their stories.

Migration Stories

Though I spoke with many people during my time in the field, I have chosen to focus on a few stories of interviewees whose experiences are representative of many others with whom I spoke. The stories I present here are narratives from some of the migrant workers with whom I became very close during my fieldwork, and whose trajectories I continue to follow to this day.

Arnel

Like Ravi, Arnel left the Philippines in search of money and an opportunity to support his family. Also, like Ravi, he ended up in debt and was forced to return home empty-handed after undergoing serious abuse. Arnel's story was among the most harrowing tales I heard while conducting my fieldwork, but his optimism and upbeat persona had not been affected by the challenges he had endured. One of five children, Arnel grew up in Quezon City, just outside of Manila. After high school he moved to Manila for university, where he studied accounting. He told me that he came from a "family of migrants," with his father working as a driver in Saudi Arabia, his mother and sister working as nurses in Canada, and one of his brothers working as a driver in Bahrain. "Every one of them has a story of migration or traveling abroad. All except my one brother who stayed always in the Philippines," he explained.

Arnel lived with this brother and his wife for three years in Manila, where he worked as an accountant before losing his job in 2003. After some consultation with members of his family, Arnel decided to seek work abroad, joining his family as an Overseas Filipino Worker (OFW). He was contracted to work for an American-owned factory in Dubai in 2004, and was thrilled when the letter announcing his job offer arrived. "I was so excited! I had gotten a job! Even though I couldn't be an accountant, I was going to make more money as a factory worker, and I was going to see the world, and work hard. Make my family proud," he said.

Two weeks after he left for Dubai his brother became ill and died suddenly. "But because I was a newly contracted worker, I couldn't go home for his funeral. This was very difficult for me," Arnel said. His eyes widened as he tried to fight back tears.

"The first few months in Dubai were hard," Arnel explained. "I was homesick, missing my family, my friends, missing Manila. But it got easier. Then it got really hard suddenly," he said, removing his orange baseball hat and taking a deep breath. Six months after arriving in Dubai, Arnel was told he was being sent, along with four fellow OFWs at the factory and an American supervisor, to work in Iraq.

"I was afraid, really scared. I thought I was a brave man, but I didn't feel like I could manage, I didn't think I could go to this war-torn country," he said.

"Couldn't you say no? Couldn't you say you didn't want to go to Iraq?" I asked him.

Arnel looked at me and shrugged, his eyes looking down at the pavement as we walked the crowded Manila streets. "Probably, yes, I could have said no. But then I would lose my job, which wasn't good for me. I needed this job. So I had no choice but to accept what I would later find out was an illegal deployment to Iraq."

Arnel took a deep breath as he continued his story. He had spent a total of five months in Iraq, during which he had limited contact with his family or the outside world.

We were suddenly working at a U.S. military base. We didn't know how that had happened, but we were given work that was very dehumanizing, like cleaning septic tanks. Can you imagine? I was afraid there in Baghdad, the war was fully there and it was scary. I wanted to go back to Dubai, so I kept calling my company there and begging them to take me back to the factory. No one listened.

Arnel's tone, his whole comportment, which was usually boisterous and up-beat, had suddenly dropped. His shoulders shrugged forward as he continued to tell his story.

You know what the worst part was? I kept meeting other Pinoys [Filipinos] who told me to stick it out. They told me that when the war had first started that the Filipino government had made a half effort to evacuate the OFWs there, but they had all said no. They said that if they go back to the Philippines that they will die for sure, of hunger, so they would rather take their chances here. That was tough. No one seemed to want to get out as bad as me.

Arnel was silent for a long time, as though remembering the experience and trying to decide how to proceed with his story. "So, it seemed like things were going pretty bad, but then, I think that God answered my prayers," he said. His voice picked up a bit more, a smile spread across his face. "I complained to one of the Americans at the base, I think he must have been an angel, because he said he would help me get back to Dubai," he said enthusiastically. This American supervisor arranged for Arnel's transfer off the base and back to the factory in Dubai.

Leaving Iraq, however, was apparently not that simple. Arnel had to make several attempts at leaving. The first time he went to the airport he was told he needed an exit pass to leave, which he could not get at the airport at that time. During his second attempt, he received an exit pass, but all the flights out of Baghdad were full, given the exigencies of full-blown war. The third time, he managed to get onboard a flight to Dubai.

But the worst part was that we had to be moved from the base to the airport, back and forth and that was scary. We couldn't sleep at the airport, which I would have preferred, because it closed in the evenings due to the war, but finally we got to leave and go back to Dubai. I had never been so happy to see Dubai in my life." [laughing]

When Arnel arrived back in Dubai, the company paid him his five months' salary for the time he worked in Baghdad and gave him a three-day rest period. "But I came from a family of OFWs," he told me. "I knew that we should have gotten wartime damage wages, so I went to the supervisor and demanded my wages," Arnel explained. When the supervisor denied this request, Arnel made an appointment with the Labor attaché in the embassy of the Philippines in Dubai.

> The guy said that it would be difficult to get my war damage wages, but he did give me some good news. He looked at my papers and saw that there was written there, "not to go to Iraq" or something like this. He said I could demand payment since I had been illegally deployed to Iraq! So, I went to my managers and told them this. They got angry and told me they weren't giving me anything, and then they locked me in a room. But I had had enough, I wasn't going to take this anymore, so I escaped, with the help of my friends, and came back to Manila. I wanted some answers from my government, I wanted someone to hear me about what I had experienced there in Iraq. I wanted help!"

His voice, which had resumed his upbeat tone, became so loud we started catching the attention of passersby.

When I last spoke with Arnel, he was living in a dormitory provided by a center for migrant advocacy in the Philippines while he looked for another job abroad. I told him I couldn't believe that after all his experiences working abroad that he wanted to become an overseas worker again. He laughed and told me that despite what he had been through, he remained optimistic. Arnel said that his experience in Dubai and Iraq had been very challenging, but that he was also disappointed in his government, which he blamed for the unemployment that made so many Filipinos look to jobs abroad.

> So it seems that no matter where you are, your own government will not help you. You just have to suffer abuse after abuse, and it is up to you to defend yourself. You can't rely on the government to protect you, because they are the ones who had violated your rights in your own country. It's not fair! I had this terrible work experience, but here I am now, looking for another job abroad because there aren't any at home. It is my government who should do something. They made my parents leave, they turned us into a family of migrants; they should protect us, help us, make it so we don't have to leave our home.

Arnel's experience of homesickness and frustration at not being able to find a way out of a situation that was exploitative was reflective of many other migrant workers with whom I spoke. Arnel had, like Ravi and many others, incurred massive debt and was financially dependent on his employment in the Gulf. When he was told he would have to go to Iraq, despite not wanting to go, he conceded out of fear of losing his job. His inability to find the proper person to approach with his complaints also exacerbated his situation, thus demonstrating how migrant workers can often become trapped in cycles of structural violence. It was not until he was able to speak to a Labor attaché at his embassy that his problem was addressed. In this respect, Arnel was among the lucky ones who did get assistance for his case (though he never did receive his wartime wages).

Marie

Many interviewees who lamented the lack of work back home echoed Arnel's disappointment with his country's government, blaming officials for not work-ing harder to ensure the rights of migrant workers who were sent abroad by their employers. Others blamed their governments for the lack of jobs at home. One example of a migrant worker who expressed this sentiment was Marie.

ı ı ı

"I never thought my life in Dubai would be like this," Marie said, opening the door to her apartment the first time I visited her home in the Satwa neighbor-hood of Dubai. "I'm so sorry for my house, I'm so sorry it's like this," Marie said, her cheeks flushing pink to match the hot pink lipstick she was wearing, which complimented her pink blouse.

"Please don't apologize!" I told her, giving her a big hug. She giggled as she ushered me in and closed the door.

The apartment was small, maybe 400 square feet, and the walls were made of cardboard. There were three makeshift rooms, each with a cardboard-type door that was padlocked. Marie led me over to her room, which was narrow and contained nothing other than a bunkbed and a nightstand. She showed me the one shared bathroom with no shower and stepped around me to show the water hose in the corner of the bathroom. Six people shared the apartment.

"See, this is how we shower. Me and the other girls, we shower [in pairs], one holds the hose for the other one. But it's not good," she said, her laugh fading away.

She then led me back to her room where we sat on her bed, which also functioned as a closet (she had chosen the bottom bunk and hung her clothes from the springs of the top bunk). Her shoes and toiletries were neatly stacked under the bed, and she had folded several T-shirts and pants at the far corner of the bed. The bedspread was a cheerful orange, and she had a large over-stuffed pink rabbit sitting on it. When I came in, she moved the rabbit to her lap and squeezed it in toward her.

"This is my best friend in Dubai," she said, cuddling the stuffed animal. "When I miss my daughter, my mother, I hold onto rabbit even tighter, he is so soft."

"I like your room," I told her, sliding back on the bed so that I could lean up against the back wall. I realized this was a bad decision as my head crashed into the top bunk.

"Oh, I'm so sorry, Pardis," Marie said quickly coming over to me.

"Don't apologize, it's not your fault, I'm clumsy." We both started to laugh.

"But, really, I am sorry. I am sorry for myself. Look at this place. I don't even have my own room. I am paying 700 Dhs ($175 USD) a month for a BED. That's it. That's all I have. And this place, it's not so good. We can hear everyone, everything. There are men living in that room over there," she said pointing to the wall in front of us. The walls only go three-quarters of the way up to the ceiling of the apartment, so I can imagine that there is very little privacy. "And the men are *strangers*!" she exclaimed, emphasizing her last word. "I hate this place. I wish to live somewhere else. Look, if I wished to live in a house like this I would stay in Manila, this is like the house I grew up in Cavite [area around Manila]." I nodded and told her I had visited many similar homes in Cavite while I was in the Philippines.

> I guess it's good because we don't get as homesick. But that doesn't help. We are still missing our home. And we think, why did I leave? Just to come and live like this again? Yes, it's similar to Manila, but it's DUBAI! It's supposed to be shiny and new and nice. That's part of the reason we came!

Her voice rose and became higher in pitch. This must have caught the attention of her roommates because we heard a loud "shhhhhhhhh!" coming from the next room. Marie shook her head, throwing herself back on the bed.

Marie was born and raised in the Philippines. She finished high school but dropped out of university when she found out she was pregnant. "It was not a problem though, because I was married," she told me when we first met in the Dubai Mall. After her daughter turned three, her husband left them to work as a seafarer, but he never returned and failed to send them any money.

"I realized that it was up to me to support myself and my daughter," she said tucking a strand of her thick, long black hair behind her ear. Marie then began working in a series of jobs in Manila before deciding to become an OFW. She started out as a security guard, then worked in a beauty salon, then worked as a motorcycle mechanic. "But no matter what I did, it was not enough money." She sighed.

Then her father passed away and her mother fell ill. When her sister lost her job, Marie realized that she would now need to support not only her own daughter, but her sister and mother as well. "So, when I lost my job as a factory worker when the factories were shut down, we were in trouble, see?"

> So, because my mother is really old now and I have only one sister and she doesn't want to go abroad because she's scared and she's afraid, I knew I would have to go. I would have to leave them to support me and my kid and my mother because she is getting old. Maybe sometimes we don't know everything. We don't know what is happening. She has aches, she takes medication, we don't have money to find for her; she has health problems. So that's why I come here. And then I want to build our house for my mother. Yeah, because my mother and father, they don't have a house cause my father was not responsible and he lost money to gambling and lost the house. So I'm not living with my parents since I was young. Me, I'm living with my cousins, and my sister too. But, then cousins say no more, so we leave. So I'm coming here to make money for them, my mom, my sister, my kid.

Marie was very animated as she told her story. She spoke rapidly and gestured with her hands for effect. Usually quite enthusiastic and upbeat, when she spoke of her family, I could hear sad undertones. "I don't want my daughter to have the problems I had," she explained, handing me a photograph of her now seven-year-old daughter.

> I cannot even buy candy. Not even Barbie dolls I couldn't buy, so I took a water bottle and made a Barbie. That's why I'm thinking I have to be strong. Even though it's hard here, I don't want my daughter to feel what I feel. That's why. I have to work hard for her.

Marie pulled out several more pictures of her family and handed them to me. She paused as she came across a picture of herself sitting on a red Harley Davidson motorbike.

"Is that you?" I asked. She nodded. "Yes! It's me, can you believe it?! I was, what you call? I was a biker chick!" she exclaimed, laughing.

When I asked her about her thoughts on Dubai, whether she liked her job here (working as a beautician in a mall) or wanted to go back to the Philippines, she was silent for a long time.

> Okay, so it's like this. Dubai has some good things, some bad. We try to focus on the good. Like I mean work everywhere it's the same, some good, some bad things. So you go where the money is. I have a job that gives me money here, so I stay.

Marie then proceeded to tell me her opinions about the bad aspects of working in Dubai followed by the more positive aspects of her life here. "So I would say the bad things are these: the housing, you can see it's bad here." She gestured around her room. "And then missing your family, that's bad. And then transportation and the bad things that happen to you because of transportation," she finished. I asked her to elaborate on this last theme, which she did eagerly:

> You know, you don't have peace of mind here. You don't understand how sometimes things happen, especially when you are new in town. When I'm new in Dubai, I have so many fears, someone will come and bother me. One time, one night I was coming home and a man came to me pushed, grabbed, and I am falling down.

She got up from her bed and slapped the mattress as she said "falling down." I asked her what happened.

> A man in the street. Because when I close the store it is ten so I am working until eleven because my work is near. So I take the bus, then get close to my front gate, and then a man calling me. And what happened to me? I fall down. He take my purse, me, my everything. And tomorrow, black, black, black. After that then three days I am still crying. Three days. I tried to fight, but nothing happen . . . he's very . . . And I'm shaking. And I keep shouting; how come I don't have a voice?!

She wrapped one hand around her throat. She sank onto the bed and became quiet. It turned out that this man who had initially mugged her returned a week later and raped her. He began following Marie, threatening her. When she tried to go to the police they told her they could send her back to the Philippines but other than that could not help her. One policeman asked her if the man was her boyfriend, a fact that angered her and led her to lock herself in her apartment for one week. She continued in a trembling voice:

> They told me no choice, go home or stay here and deal with this man. But I couldn't go home, not without the money, so I had to stay. I was stuck. But then after that I learned. I learned, I become tough. So next time I fight. Another time I have to take taxi home, and the taxi driver he's drinking something. I don't know what, and he asks "you want? Drink, drink," he keeps insisting. And my heart is beating. "I like you," he says and blah, blah, blah. Me, I just get out of the car and walk home. I'm scared, but I learn then. I get strong.

She curled her left arm into a right angle to show her bicep. When I asked her what the good things are about Dubai she hesitated for a moment before answering, "The good thing is the money! I can send money for the Philippines. And whatever they want at home we can give. Because in the Philippines we are all . . . we cannot find good jobs in our age, in my age."

I stop her to ask how old she is since I am surprised by this last comment. "I am 30! And in the Philippines you cannot work if you have this age. They will not hire you. They will start hiring 22 or 18 to 25, but not me."

I tell her that this is very surprising given that it would seem that a thirty-year-old is still young enough to work hard, but has the advantage of having maturity and some experience. She laughs and shakes her head. "The best jobs are for the young women. Like even the girls who become dancers or prostitutes, I would love to do that, it's good money. But I am too old, and not pretty like that anymore," she says. She is quiet as she thinks about our conversation. After a moment she turns to me and says:

> You know what though? I have been through a lot of bad things, and I am still scared at night, but still, I am proud to be an OFW. I am working hard for my family, and my country. Things are hard here, but I know I am doing good. We are the pride of the Philippines, and that makes me feel good.

Like Ravi and Arnel, Marie made the difficult decision to leave her family behind in search of a way to support them. Similar to Arnel, Marie also expressed disappointment in her home government for not providing her more work opportunities and faulted age discrimination for further limiting her opportunities at home. Marie's problems with housing and episodes with violence also speak to an issue that many migrant workers face; namely, threats or experiences of violence in host countries, with nowhere to turn. Without organizations or outlets where migrants can seek support or rights protections, abuse often continues, creating a vulnerable position if the migrant wishes to avoid deportation, the only solution offered to Marie and many others when turning to the police for assistance.

Marie often reflected that she should have pressed charges against her rapist, but as a noncitizen she felt that the police did not care what happened to her. She also spoke of a need for a center that migrants could turn to for support and help answering their questions. While Marie was fortunate in that she was on good terms with her employer, who ultimately assisted her in moving apartments, other migrant workers were not so lucky. Some had issues with their employers and could only mitigate these problems with the help of the authorities. Alia's story below shows what can happen when a dispute with an employer leads the latter to withhold not only pay, but also working papers and documents, rendering the migrant worker an undocumented or illegal alien. Like Marie, Alia narrated a story of challenges and spoke of a desire for a center that could provide assistance.

Alia

Alia was born in Addis Ababa in 1986. Upon completing high school, she moved out of her parents' home and into a smaller place with her cousin. After a year of living together, her cousin decided to move to Kuwait to work as a domestic worker for a local family. When Alia's cousin returned to Ethiopia for a visit six months later, she was quite eager to find a job in the Gulf for Alia. Following conversations with a few local recruiters, she found an agent who promised Alia a job working as maid for a hotel chain in Dubai, but she would have to pay 2,000 Dhs (roughly $500 USD) for her trip. Alia was saddened at this news because she didn't have the money.

"I thought, I no go. No money, no go, but then my cousin give," she explained. Her cousin decided to loan her the money for her journey on the condition that she pay it back within a year. "No money in Ethiopia," she said, shyly lowering her lids to look at the floor as we talked. "No money at home, but money in Dubai. So good or no good we must come. We must do it, we must work, make money."

A frail woman weighing 90 pounds at most, Alia always had a wide smile on her face when we visited her. Her long, wavy black hair was always pulled back, and she often wore a peach headband to keep the unruly strands of hair away from her face. Though I was usually sweating in the Dubai summer heat, Alia always seemed composed, calm, cool, at ease. I asked her why she had decided to come to Dubai, what had persuaded her to move. "I come for my family. For my mother and my brother. So he can go to school."

When she arrived in Dubai she was introduced to a group of people, one of whom would be her sponsor. Though she had been told she would be working for a hotel company she was instead sent to a local hospital where she was made to work fifteen hours a day assisting patients and cleaning. "I think hotel visa, but now I am working in hospital cleanup. I don't like because when I make contract at home in Addis, working only eight hours." She sighed softly. Her voice was so low, it was almost a whisper, but she never stopped smiling as she told her story.

> Tell me working only eight hours. But when I am coming here, twelve hours, fifteen hours I am working. And, salary is very very very . . . In my country, when we are signed—you don't like that work, you come back your country. But when we are coming here, making argument, two maybe three years.

She explained that there was no clause in her contract that would permit her to return home if she was unhappy. For clarification, I asked her if she wanted to go back to Addis. "You cannot back," she said. "If you want back to home, from my money, not from company. I, no money. And my cousin . . ." Her voice trailed off. A few weeks after arriving in Dubai, Alia realized she was pregnant. Worried about the effect of her pregnancy on her job prospects, she kept this news to herself.

> Eight months I am working there in that hospital; eight months I am working hard work, even when pregnant. Then after that time, still no have money. They are paid to me $450 [about $110 USD] for monthly. I want to go back to my country. I cannot stay. If you birth here in Dubai, very difficult to get your baby you know? Too much difficult.[6]

Alia pulled a picture of her daughter out of a drawer nearby as she finished her tale. Eventually she managed to borrow enough money from her friends to go back to Addis Ababa to have her child. Alia said she was determined to have her child in Ethiopia and leave the baby with her mother, even if it meant angering her supervisors. She decided to risk the wrath of her employers and bought a ticket to return to Ethiopia to have the baby. When she told her supervisors she was pregnant and wanted to go home to have the child, they did not agree. They were indeed quite angry and told her she would lose her job, but she took the chance. She went home, had her baby, and stayed for an extra two weeks with the child. All in all, she said she was away for five weeks before returning to Dubai to try to get her job back. When I asked her why she returned, she said, "For money! I borrow much money from everyone, I must work for money, and for my girl, to give her better future."

Sadly, however, when she returned, her sponsors would not give her the job back. She said her sponsor was an Arab man from Syria who spoke only Arabic and "treated her like dirt." He also withheld her working papers and documents. Without a proper visa and working documents, and without any money, Alia became homeless, living on the streets, and looking for work in the informal economy. After several months of informal work as a waitress and then messenger carrier, she met a South African family who needed a nanny for their children. Alia started out by babysitting two to three times a week at first. During a subsequent interview she described her new situation, smiling once again:

> This family, very good. They are from South African family, and very good. Even I can go to church. But now, if God will, God has a plan for me. I am asking that company [her previous sponsors] give back visa. Maybe tomorrow I will go. I will go get back, and stay with new family.

With the help of a few local expatriates who had once volunteered for City of Hope, a local group seeking to provide outreach to abused women, Alia was able to retrieve her working papers from her previous employer. "When we got her papers back, you could see the relief in her face. She just did not know how to get done what she needed to do," explained Karim, an Egyptian architect who was living in Dubai and volunteering his time to help the women who had once been sheltered at City of Hope before it was shut down by the government. He said that it was just a matter of knowing who to put pressure on and how to work the legal system in Dubai. This was not an easy task, as I learned in trying to navigate this system while I was there. But, to someone familiar with the system and a native Arabic speaker, it was doable. Today, Alia has moved into the home of the South African family she talked about, and hopes to one day return to Ethiopia to see her daughter.

Alia's case is a clear example of a situation of force, fraud, or coercion resulting in a migrant having no choice but to work "off the books" outside the kefala system and in the informal economy as she or he attempts to retrieve legal working papers. Alia was indeed "frauded" in that she was told she would be working in a hotel, eight hours a day and yet ended up working in a hospital for longer hours. Without benefits such as maternity leave, she was forced into a situation in which she had to decide between her health and her job. Her choice to return to Ethiopia to give birth led her to lose her job and thus become an illegal migrant in the UAE. Alia was not alone in having a dispute with an employer that led to dismissal while the employer retained the migrant's working papers. Many others I spoke with ended up in the informal economy (outside *kefala*) because they could not find avenues of recourse for such problems with their sponsor-employers. Though hers has a happy ending thus far, her experience shows how migrant women outside the sex industry can also be vulnerable to situations of trafficking and are in need of assistance.

Khaled

Khaled's story may or may not have a happy ending. Like Alia, he left his home country of Afghanistan because he had no work opportunities after the economy of Afghanistan fell apart nearly ten years ago. Also like Alia, he described feelings of homesickness but noted that returning home was not an option. When faced with an abusive employer, Khaled was also fortunate enough to find alternative work, first informally, then formally as a taxi driver in Dubai.

Khaled is a tall, lanky man in his mid-forties with tanned olive skin and wrinkles around his eyes that increase when he smiles. He has been living in Dubai since 2002 when he left Afghanistan after the U.S.-backed overthrow of the Taliban. "After Americans coming in, Taliban going out. Taliban going out, no more jobs for me. So I come to Dubai to make money to get my family out of Kabul," he explained in Dari, a language spoken in Afghanistan that is similar to Persian.

I had met him one afternoon while he stood outside the Emirates Hotel towers waiting for a customer. I was waiting for a friend to pick me up and moved over to a patch of shade to continue waiting. Khaled had abandoned his taxi and was also sitting in the shade. I introduced myself and he asked me where I was from.

"Iran originally, but I live in the U.S. now," I told him.

Khaled smiled and began speaking in Dari with me, "I thought so. We are neighbors. How are you?" he asked, moving over to allow me more room in the shade. I told him I was fine and asked him where in Afghanistan he was from.

"Kabul, but I moved here eight years ago. Said good-bye to my wife, my four children; I have two girls and two boys." He fished a pack of cigarettes out of his pocket. "They all go to school. If God wills it, I will make enough money and send them somewhere for university. Education gives them opportunity, a chance, you know?"

I nodded and politely declined his offer of a cigarette. "Do you like Dubai?" I asked.

He smiled, picking at the grass below us. "Well, it's not about liking. I need work, and work is here. I need to feed my family, so I do that here. But I haven't seen them since I came." His face suddenly became melancholy.

"Do you miss them?" I asked before realizing what a stupid question it was. He nodded and looked over at his taxi.

"Is that your cab?" I asked, another stupid question.

"Yes, and I love my taxi. In my taxi, it is my world and it is peaceful. It was not always peaceful, my life has not always been peaceful." He put out his cigarette in the dirt a few feet away from us. I asked him if he had time to tell me a little bit more about what he had just said. He looked around, not seeing his customer, and nodded before continuing.

> Things have been hard sometimes, but thanks be to God, they are better now that I have my taxi. Things in Afghanistan were violent, like I said, so I left. Then I came to Dubai to work for . . . to work in building these tall buildings you see everywhere. But that was not good work. It was hard, and for me, I was not so young, I couldn't do it. My boss was very bad to me, he yelled at me all the time, he was telling me I was not working hard enough.

He wiped sweat from his face but several beads of sweat clung to his chin stubble. "I didn't like my job. And then, something happened." He paused, let out a long sigh and put his forehead in his hands. "After my second year in Dubai, one of my daughters got sick. I used to have five children, but now I just have four."

"I'm so sorry to hear that," I said. I offered him a tissue. He took it, wiped his face, and took a deep breath before continuing, lighting another cigarette while he talked.

> I wanted to go home, I wanted to go back then and be with my family. I didn't want to stay here anymore, I hated my job, and my family needed me; I wanted to go back. But the violence there was more. My wife said that there was no work back there, that the family was struggling to make ends meet. So,

I decided to stay. It wasn't easy to, but I made the decision. But I did quit my job. Long hours, heat, carrying things all day long. That wasn't for me. And my boss was just terrible, yelling at me all day, and not even paying me what I was owed! I couldn't take it. Luckily though, God helped me, because I prayed. I went to mosque one night and met a man from Pakistan. His cousin owned a taxi company so he found me a job driving that taxi.

After that day, I saw Khaled several more times. He had asked me to call him every so often and invited me to eat Afghan food with him at a local restaurant near the place he lived in Satwa (a neighborhood near the northern part of town). He also told me to call him whenever I needed transportation, and that I could count on him. I did call Khaled and met with him many times while I was in Dubai in 2008. He showed me photographs of his family and told me how much he missed them. The last time I saw him in the summer of 2008, Khaled had decided to move back to Afghanistan to be with his family because his wife had fallen ill. "I don't want to make the same mistake I made with my daughter," he said during our last visit. "I will go home and be with my wife. *Insha'allah,* God will provide for my family and we will be okay."

When I returned to Dubai in the summer of 2009 I was happy that I could not find Khaled. I called his mobile phone only to learn it had been disconnected. I spoke to a friend of his at the local Afghan restaurant who told me he had returned to Afghanistan. When I asked if he had any news from Khaled, his friend smiled at me and said, "I have no news, but I think that is good. And even though I miss my dear friend very much, I hope he does not come back to Dubai and stays in Afghanistan where his heart is."

Khaled's challenges with earning enough money to return home were symptomatic of many migrant workers with whom I spoke. He described his expectations of coming to Dubai and earning high wages so that he could support his family and return home in just a few years. However, upon arrival, Khaled, like many others, realized that the pay was not as high as he had hoped, especially when coupled with living costs and the debt he had to pay back to his recruiters. It took him four years to pay back his debt, and during his time in Dubai he earned barely enough to scrape by, let alone extra money to send home to his family. Furthermore, Khaled, like many others, had his wages withheld from him for months at a time, making it impossible to make ends meet. In this experience, Khaled was not alone. Numerous migrant workers described expectations of earning higher wages, only to be disappointed by the small amount they could save and remit.

Fortunately, Khaled's story may have had a happy ending in that he may have been able to return home with enough money to support his family for at least a few years. Unfortunately, "home" is not an option for many migrants with whom I spoke, who described fleeing violence or legal problems in home countries as their primary motivation for migrating. Marjaan was one such woman who left Iran because her husband had put out a warrant for her arrest. Her fleeing to Dubai meant that she arrived on a tourist visa and has had to work illegally in the UAE for almost a decade.

Marjaan

The second time I met Marjaan she was running to catch a bus, carrying four bags in her left hand while trying to hold up her green *abaya* so that she wouldn't trip as she ran. When she missed the bus she was chasing, she resignedly found a place in the shade to sit, struggling to catch her breath. She took off her light green head scarf and used it to wipe down her face. After gathering her hair into a bun, she replaced the head scarf and pulled out a tube of light pink lipstick to reapply to her lips. I had been watching her from a café across the street, squinting to make out her face as I was almost sure she was the woman I had met briefly at a local shelter earlier that week. I had only met her for a brief few minutes as she was finishing up her English lessons and leaving the house in a hurry to get to work, but even then I was struck by her beautiful smile, wide brown eyes, and long eyelashes that she had creatively coated in dark purple mascara.

I waved at her as I crossed the street toward her. She looked up at me, tired and frustrated, but managed to force a smile and a wave. "Hello Marjaan *jaan*[7]!" I said, walking up to her. "Remember me? We met at the shelter," I said in Persian.

Marjaan, still struggling to catch her breath, nodded and let out a long sigh. "Yes, I remember. I'm sorry you have to see me like this," she said, removing the bags she had looped over her left wrist and motioning for me to sit next to her on the bench near the bus stop. I looked at her to see that today she was wearing green eye shadow that matched her head scarf and *abaya*, and her highlighted hair was wavy instead of straight as it had been the previous week. It was hot, as usual, and I moved closer to her so that I could enjoy a bit of the shade in which she was sitting.

"Please, don't apologize," I told her, pulling a water bottle out of my purse and offering it to her. She accepted and took a big gulp.

She wiped her mouth carefully with a handkerchief she had produced from a pocket in her abaya. We sat for a moment in silence, me fanning myself with a newspaper and Marjaan adjusting her bags, which seemed to be filled with lotions, wax, and other beauty supplies. "I missed the bus. Now I'll be late for work," she lamented. "This is my life here, always running, working, running, working, all day long. And still not enough money." I told her I hoped she would get to rest soon.

Marjaan smiled and put her arm around me. "No rest for me, but it's OK. I am here, I have hope, things will change, you will see."

That day Marjaan and I talked for a long time. I took a taxi with her from Jumeirah beach (where I had run into her) to Deira, and she began telling me about her journey. After that day we exchanged phone numbers and kept in touch. When I asked her if I could include her story in my book she was enthusiastic and asked if she could write her section herself. I told her that would be great and two months later she e-mailed me the following account. I have not edited it in order to preserve Marjaan's voice. Here is her story:

> I was born in Iran, in Tehran on May 22, 1962. We were a big family with 10 children. My father was working in a factory and my family were strong in religion (very religious). After I finished elementary my family chose I got married. At that time in my country revolution to change the government. So I have got married with a man he was working in committee for government police. I delivered 3 girls and after that he left my children and I because he wanted to got married again to have a son, in Iranian cultures when the men get married they like to have a son. So I was alone with my children, I didn't have anybody to help cause my family didn't have money or facility to support me and my children.
>
> My husband didn't support my children and I and it was so difficult. I started to continue my studies in high school. I was practice without teacher after 4 years I finished high school and pre university so I could find a good job with a good salary. After 18 years I found a chance to divorce. My husband lawyer, he came to the court and signed the divorce papers. They didn't give me any rights in Muslim religion when woman she wants to get divorce husband has to give all her rights it's written in Koran, but they didn't give me any things.
>
> With one of my friends help we found a car parking to live, 2 years we were living in car parking. After 2 years one of my friends she moved with her fam-

ily to other country she let us to live in her house for 1 year, after that with my friends' help I got some loan from bank to rent a flat.

I worked very hard, my eldest daughter entered to university.

I was working all the time but we didn't have good life, my husband started to have relationship with me, he wanted my eldest daughter to get married with one of his friends son, that time he had high position in president office, I didn't like to accept his offer but he was calling me and every time he told me I don't want to accept he will put me in a trouble. I decided to send my children to other country to save their life and their future; I exited my children from Iran without permission from my husband, I sent them to France and India, they started in university.

My eldest she was studying Electronic Engineer, the middle one she studying law, and the youngest she was studying technology.

After some time my friend let me to know that my husband started to open for me a case in police office and he complained that I sent my children to other country without permission from him and I let to them to get married with non Muslim, so they told me you have to go out from Iran because my husband he was looking for me to put in trouble. I collected 75,000 Dhs [roughly $18,000 USD] and I got resident visa from Dubai. I exited from Iran and I entered to Dubai, but I found with partner visa I cannot work to earn money to support my youngest daughter and so every were I looked for a job, at last I found in a beauty salon with 500 Dhs [$120 USD] monthly without accommodation. It was difficult, 3 months I was working there and I was living in a roof of a building but they understood I couldn't go there so I used to live in outside. Every night I was sleeping in airport or bus station or parks.

During 9 months I had a contact with one of my friends in USA. She introduced me to her lawyer, he started to call me, he got all my papers and he told me he will help me to migrate to USA. He told me my divorce paper is good for emigrate, he got all documents from my children about their marriage and he had all story about my life, every night he used to call me, he was worried cause I didn't have place to stay, he was practice to found a safe place for me. At last he found one of his friend, he was common friend with madam Susannah [head of the private shelter City of Hope] so he introduced me to madam Susannah. I visited her and she promised me and my lawyer to help me. I started to live in shelter, but I didn't used food or any clothes only one bed space because I was thinking it wasn't my rights to use, I could work. Every time I was looking for a job to earn small money.

My youngest daughter she was sick she was in hospital for 2 months I didn't have money to sent to hospital, my lawyer he was preparing to make appointment in USA ministry for me, he told me I have to cancel my resident visa before going to USA ministry, so I canceled my visa. I got my deposit for resident visa I sent to hospital for my daughter. He [the lawyer] asked money from my children to follow my case. They sent for him $3000, he had contact with me and madam Susannah but after 15/1/2007 he didn't answer phones and e-mails, my friend in USA she couldn't find him, I sent many e-mails to him and many times I called he didn't answer.

Now nobody didn't give me resident visa so I had to exit from Dubai to get new visa. I couldn't earn good money to support myself. With madam Susannah permission I brought my youngest daughter to shelter. She told me we can find a job for her, after that I collected money for her ticket to Dubai. She came to Dubai but madam Susannah she left Dubai to USA. I couldn't keep my daughter in shelter her visa was going to finish. I didn't have money to give her to have new visa, so I sent her back to Iran.

Every time when my visa is going to finish I exited from Dubai to Oman and wait to get new visa, but it's difficult; I couldn't find a job with employee visa, I don't have that much money to buy employee visa, every time I have to work for a small money. I don't have a choice, thanks God still I can work and still I have hope to change my life.

My children in France still don't have citizenships. When I sent my youngest daughter to Iran, she became sick. My family took her to a doctor, he told them she is sick, she is not relaxed and she got stress she has to be a safe place. She is afraid that her father can find her, he didn't know where am I or where are my children.

Every time I had to exit from Dubai to get new visa to back to Dubai, I used to go to Oman to stay there wait for visa but every time I have same problem I don't have anybody to open visa for me so I have to pay for my visa, hotel payment, food and phone credit, it's difficult to arrange all so I have to borrow money every time to support myself again. I have to work to money back. I'm tired from waiting, I'm tired from exit, I couldn't find any way to go out from Dubai or find a job with employee visa and I don't like live in this country without visa.

Shelter closed now when I want to back to Dubai I don't have any place to stay I don't have job I don't have money, same problem like before . . . Still I'm alive, I'm looking to find a good future I hope I will find one. Now I'm waiting to get visa but I don't know I will or no. I don't have money at all to hotel payment, now no place to sleep. I'm sure God Is great and he will help me like before.

I have to thanks for all who help, God bless.

Marjaan's story shows the cycles of structural violence in which migrant workers, especially undocumented migrants, can get caught up. Without a visa, illegal workers can be exploited by their employers more easily, as the employers know they are dependent on their income and have very few avenues of recourse in instances of abuse or withheld wages. Because they are undocumented, migrants such as Marjaan must live and operate by working odd jobs and being paid "under the table," and incur substantial debt just to survive. In her story, Marjaan emphasizes that without a visa, she has to spend exorbitant amounts of money to remain in the country, and is constantly afraid of being caught and deported. In her case, as for many others, deportation is particularly fearful, as "home" is not a welcome place due to problems she has with her ex-husband. Marjaan's story also highlights ways in which migrants who have become disconnected from family or loved ones are even more vulnerable and lacking in social support and safety nets.

Natalia

Marjaan was not the only woman I met in Dubai who was fleeing an abusive husband. Contrary to many of the other stories presented here, Natalia did not migrate for work or because she needed to leave her home country; rather, she moved for love. Natalia initially migrated to Dubai to be with her husband, a move that turned out to be the worst decision of her life when he started to abuse her and then left her in Dubai with his debts. She became an undocumented migrant with a debt to the UAE government, which kept her from leaving the country.[8] Similar to Marjaan, her undocumented status has limited her work options, making it almost impossible to pay off her debt. Both women's stories show the cyclical nature of the violence endured by migrants who are in need of support and legal assistance.

. . .

"I was born right near Count Dracula's castle, I know all about him, I could even be related to him," Natalia said one evening as we lay on a couch reading trashy magazines and talking about celebrities. I looked at her as she said this, arching one eyebrow. "I'm serious!" she laughed, tossing her head back, which caused a wave in her shoulder-length caramel-colored ringlets.

"Count Dracula?" I asked her, playfully.

"I know you LOVE vampires," she responded, smiling wickedly as she pointed to the *People Magazine* I was holding. I looked down at my magazine, realizing that I had spent the last few minutes reading about the stars of the movie *Twilight*. Even though the books in the series are supposedly intended for "tweens," I had found myself inexplicably drawn to them like so many other adults.

"How did you know?" I asked Natalia.

"Chris and Abby told me you loved the vampire books," she said, referring to my research assistants. "I can tell you all about them, vampires and Count Dracula I mean. After all, I am from the land of Dracula, and we Romanians know *all* about vampires. But if you want to know, you're going to have to put down that magazine you're reading and give me your full attention," she lectured in her bossy voice to which I had grown accustomed.

The first time I met Natalia, I was taken aback. She was blunt, loud, and at times very bossy. She was living in the home of one of the former City of Hope volunteers, Shana, along with three of the other women from the shelter and Shana's three roommates. All in all, eight people lived in a modest-sized three-bedroom apartment in the upscale project-style housing units known as the Jumeirah Beach Residences. Each time we visited Shana's apartment, Natalia was there, usually giving orders to the other women from the shelter and sometimes to Shana and her sister. Though at first I felt intimidated by Natalia, I quickly grew to love her straightforwardness and matter-of-fact way of speaking. She had a sarcastic sense of humor and loved to perform for her friends, often standing up from the dinner table to give a long soliloquy about her opinions on certain issues, ranging from Michael Jackson's death, to marriage, to love.

"I came to Dubai for love," Natalia had told me one evening over a glass of wine as we relaxed at Shana's apartment. She took a deep breath and let out an audible sigh. "Yes, love," she said playfully, placing her hand over her heart and then giggling. "No, really, this is how it happened," she said, switching once again to her lecturing voice. I remember thinking that she must have made a wonderful teacher back in Romania. She took a big gulp of wine and then shifted on the couch to a kneeling position from which to continue her story.

"Well, it's like this. I met my husband, the bastard, when I was visiting family in Poland and he was, I think, on a business trip from India. He is

Indian, you know that, right?" she asked, pausing to look at me. I nodded and she continued. "Anyway, we fell in loooove, or whatever that was." She made a face as she drew out the word *love*. "So, he was moving to Dubai for work, so I moved to be with him and we got married." She explained that she had made the decision quickly and had quit her teaching job two days after returning from Poland. "That was nine years ago. So, anyways, we got married and . . . and . . . and then we had a beautiful little girl. The light of my life," she said, sitting back down on the couch. "I'll show you her picture later. It's on my Facebook page. You're on Facebook, right?" I nodded. "We should be friends," she said. She quickly walked over to the communal laptop in the corner of the apartment and brought it over to the couch.

As she did so, Shana walked over and asked if she could use the computer to send an important e-mail. Natalia nodded and handed her the computer, promising me that we would attend to our Facebook pages later. She sat back down on the couch and took a sip of wine before continuing. "So let's see, where was I? Oh yes, my husband—the bastard. Well, anyways, when my daughter was four or five my husband started having affairs, sleeping around with lots of people. Well I'm not one to stand for that kind of crap," she said. She rolled her *r*'s and slapped her thigh as she spoke. "I said to him, 'No more! I know you are having an affair and you have to stop!' But me and my big mouth, maybe I shouldn't have said that because that's when the nightmare started." She became very serious and poured herself another glass of wine.

> He started beating me, and then he locked me in the house for three weeks with no way out. He would only come home twice a week, force me to have sex with him, and then leave. It was a nightmare. Somehow though, I managed, in that three weeks' time, to talk to my mother in Romania and send my daughter home to my mother. I just had to get her out. Just had to get her out of the nightmare, you know?

She finished her glass of wine and poured herself another. Natalia told me that over the next three months her husband continued to abuse her. She tried to send him to counseling, but he refused and told her that if she called the police that he would have her arrested. "I didn't believe him of course, but at the same time I was scared, I didn't know what to do." At one point Natalia considered going to the police, she said, but was told by friends that because she was not a citizen and because her residence in Dubai was dependent on

her husband that they would in all likelihood tell her to return home and try
to "work it out."

In October of 2008 Natalia's husband resigned from his job and left the
country, leaving her behind. In November of 2008 his company evicted Natalia from their house.

> It was then that I realized the depth of the shit I was in, pardon my language.
> I wanted to return to Romania, I had given up on Dubai, but then I found out
> that the bastard had given out a check of 35,000 Dhs [over $8,000 USD] against
> a loan in my name. My name! So now I owed money to the government that
> I didn't know about! To add to that, the police want my help in finding the
> bastard! They want me to help them find him so that I can clear my name, can
> you believe it? What I've been through?!"

The bank filed a case against Natalia with the police, and she was forbid-
den to leave the country. The police also tried to arrest her to take her to
debtor's prison, but she protested. "I explained that my husband had forged
the check and that I didn't even know about it," She offered as her voice became very high pitched. Luckily, the police did not arrest her, but told her that
she would not be able to leave the country as long as there was an ongoing
court case against her.

Natalia explained that after she was evicted from her home she began
sleeping at the airport. She looked fervently for a job to make enough income to live and to begin to collect the money that her husband owed so she
could go back to Romania to join her mother and daughter. "I knew I had
to find a job. I didn't have work, I didn't have the proper visa, and I didn't
have a place to live," she said, laughing nervously as her eyes grew wider.
Natalia's visa had been a marital visa, and she explained that she needed
a work visa to gain formal employment. After several months of trying to
find a teaching job, she began to look for any kind of work in the informal
economy. "I started babysitting, cleaning homes, going and giving mas-
sages, whatever I could, but it still didn't help. I couldn't make ends meet."
She shook her head.

> Then one day, one night actually, when I went to sleep at the airport I met a
> friend of mine from church. She told me about this private shelter, and that's
> how I ended up in City of Hope. But then that closed, and my case is still not
> settled. So, I'm living here, working to cook for Shana and trying to do some

work with kids in the afternoons, off the books of course. So I guess you could say that I moved here for love, but now I am loving to move.

Natalia smiled as she raised her wineglass and then brought it close to mine. The glasses clinked as she sighed.

Different Experiences, Common Perspectives

The stories presented here are just a small sample of those I heard from migrants about their lives in Dubai. After speaking to numerous people working in various industries, what we learned was that people had different reasons for migrating to Dubai and had a range of experiences after they arrived. Factors incorporated into the decision to migrate were varied and included "looking for love," as one Nigerian woman working in the Dubai Mall explained; "wanting to get away from my husband," noted a Filipina nurse at Rashed Hospital; "I wanted to set up a business and avoid the complicated tax structure in India," said an Indian shopkeeper in the bazaar; "I came to know Jesus and wanted to practice my faith freely, away from my community and family who criticized me for it," answered a Nepalese construction worker. Many people remarked that they came to Dubai in search of work opportunities, and in the words of a Filipino factory worker, "opting for overseas employment is not merely because of dollars earning. It is about love. It is about a shelter to live in, food on the table, better education for the children, and health for every family member. As migrant families our road to travel is long, winding, and most of the time rough. Let us face these challenges with steadfast hearts."

While each story is different, a few repeating themes emerged when analyzing the narratives of the migrant workers with whom we spoke. More than a fourth of our interviewees spoke of the Middle East as a stepping-stone to immigration or migration elsewhere, such as Europe or the United States. As one Filipina nanny noted:

> For us, it's easier to go here [Dubai] than other places, meaning that here is a stepping-stone. We are told we can come here and work here and make a lot of money. Plus, if you can survive the Middle East, you can survive anywhere, so it's a good practice.

Versions of this sentiment were echoed by eighteen other interviewees, who all spoke of their decision to migrate to the Middle East as strategic in a process to emigrate elsewhere. One Iranian woman who worked as a secretary in an advertising firm added that "gaining experience in an international city like Dubai improves your profile globally and makes it so that you can get a job in Europe or America."

. . .

Another common theme that ran throughout our interviews was the process by which many migrants came to Dubai. Most people we spoke to had heard about work in Dubai through friends, family, or personal networks of other migrants.[9] When talking with migrant workers it seems that most made the decision to migrate on their own or in conjunction with their families, evidence that dislodges the common stereotype of trafficking as primarily linked to kidnapping or the trickery of middlemen.

Several interviewees noted that the tales of returning migrants tend to focus on the positive aspects of migration, either because they wish to forget or have blocked out any negative experiences, or because a rose-tinted narrative conveys a greater sense of pride and perhaps social capital. In this way, myths and rumors circulate about the wonderful opportunities presented by migration. In some countries, such as the Philippines, the number of people leaving the country is so high that migration is a regular part of life. As one Filipino factory worker told me, "there's a running joke that everybody knows somebody who is . . . working abroad, and it really is from all walks of life . . . whether it's somebody who migrated, who became an immigrant, or someone who's an OFW." Another woman, a Sri Lankan domestic worker, echoed this sentiment:

> When there is one migrant worker in a community and he or she goes home, she will . . . tell people about how her work is there and people will want that and be like, oh, okay. I wanna work there too. So they'll end up there, like a whole group of migrant workers from a certain place and all doing the same thing.

Yet another interviewee, a Filipina caregiver, took this one step further, explaining:

> It's always the same industry. If the person who comes home works in construction work, you'll have a village full of migrant construction workers. Like all the people from my village came to Dubai to be caregivers. It's not like, you know, you have a nurse and a construction worker and a caregiver. It's really just the same profession that people go into from one village.

This sentiment was built on by a former migrant worker I met in Manila who spoke of her time working as a domestic worker in the emirate of Abu Dhabi.

> The others see how much money the OFWs are making because the first thing we do with our remittances is build a new house, then everyone in that village sees the new house and they want it too . . . that's how you have entire villages that look like one place, like Villa Milan or Villa Dubai or something like that.

Virtually everyone we spoke with indicated that once they decided to migrate they then worked through an agent or labor recruiter in their home country, usually someone of the same nationality. At least one-third of the migrants we spoke with were cheated by the recruiter in their home country. Some were charged exorbitant fees for services that were never rendered. "I was charged 4,000 Dhs ($1,000 USD) for my health coverage and my paperwork by a guy at home, but when I arrived, I couldn't get medical help and my visa was expiring; I didn't know what to do," said one Nepalese construction worker. Some migrants find themselves in a vicious cycle, trying to keep pace with the cost of living and the obligation of servicing a debt, or of sorting out legal problems caused by agents in the home countries or bosses in the host countries.

"I was cheated by a guy back home, then I got to Dubai and I had a fake visa, but I had to stay to make the money I had paid that agent at home to pay back my friends. That was three years ago, I'm still trying," said a Cameroonian man who worked in the informal economy selling clothing, scarves, and purses without a permit on the sidewalk. A Nigerian man without official paperwork who had found a job working as a chef in an Ethiopian restaurant commented, "we are all in difficult situations when we are not able to stay and not able to go home because we do not have the money to get home or we will face harassment when we get there."

The predicament he alluded to was a theme we heard repeatedly. Many people talked about feeling "stuck," unable to stay whether due to visa complications, health problems, or difficulties/unhappiness at their jobs, but also unable to leave due to the conviction that returning home was simply not a viable option. In choosing to stay in Dubai however (and risking the high cost of fines for overstayed visas), they then automatically became part of the stigmatized category of illegal or undocumented workers.

All migrant workers with whom I spoke faced many similar challenges. Besides the expected feelings of homesickness and missing friends and family back home, many also talked about the barrier of visa regulations and their struggle to navigate the legalities of Dubai's labor system. At least twelve of our interviewees spoke about severe abuse either at work or in their daily lives, while many talked about the hardships and fears precipitated by working in the informal economy. The underlying tensions caused by political/economic structures, such as structural adjustment programs and the conditionality of such lending institutions as the IMF and World Bank, form the often over-looked backdrop to the difficult migratory choices taken up by individuals such as those introduced in this chapter.

It is important to underscore the deeply embedded structural channels of capital and labor flows affecting global migration. Postcolonial and neo-colonial economic arrangements (such as that with the Philippines, or more recently, Indonesia) have led many countries to depend on migrant labor as a major export. Many migrants who would rather stay and work in their home countries cannot afford to do so. Those who do not migrate often work in ex-ploitative conditions in their home countries with meager salaries. Overseas workers who take a chance and migrate in search of better work opportunities (often backed by the explicit encouragement of their governments) sometimes do so in response to struggling or collapsing economies at home. While some migrants manage to send regular remittances back to their home countries, for many migration affords a negligible economic benefit, if any, for at least several years, due to debts incurred by the upfront costs of procuring visas and travel.[10] These larger, macroeconomic structures and the consequences of global economic structuring must be factored in when trying to address the experiences and needs of migrants globally, as it is these broader structures that inform migrants' decisions to move.

The people introduced in this chapter may not have been kidnapped into the sex industry or tricked by a trafficker or locked inside a brothel, nor do they fit the popularly imagined definitions of trafficking in discourse or policy, but they have undoubtedly met with force, fraud, and coercion. The contrast between policy and lived experience is highlighted through the narratives of the many migrant workers who undergo some form of rights infractions while working outside the sex industry and, therefore, outside the trafficking para-digm, and the current hyperscrutiny on sex trafficking only serves to eclipse the challenges that many migrants in the Gulf face on a daily basis.

The stories presented here illustrate the discrepancy between imagined ideas about trafficking and actual realities of forced labor and migration. Beyond a disconnect between policy and lived experience, however, are the instances where policy has had a directly negative impact on migrants' lives by provoking people to leave the formal economy, where they feel they are not protected and are *more* vulnerable, in search of unsanctioned work in the informal economy. The people profiled here still strive to return to the formal economy, yet many whom I met during my time in the field, women in particular, have opted to work outside of it, precisely due to its restrictive and punitive policies. The result is a growing population of laborers who operate outside the law in the potentially abusive space of the underground labor market.

5

LABOR OUTSIDE LAW

So I came as what you would call a "legal migrant," I came to work as a maid for a family. But my debt was too high, and the family didn't pay me what I was promised. My family back home needed more money, but I was still in debt, and no hope for making more money. The family was horrible to me. So, I quit. But I couldn't go back home, not without money. So I decided to work in this business [sex industry], the night business. Now I'm making money, out of debt, and will be able to return home. But it's not what I came here for, and it's not easy.

> Talia, former domestic worker, current sex worker from Ethiopia

If we don't have rights as maids or prostitutes, then we might as well be prostitutes so we can make more money.

> Alice, former domestic worker, current sex worker from the Philippines

IN THE LAST TWO DECADES we have seen a global increase in what scholars term the "feminization of migration." Migration to the Gulf in particular has also become increasingly feminized,[1] with the vast majority of women migrating in search of employment in the semiformal sphere of domestic and care work and some moving into the informal sphere of commercial sex work (not that these forms of labor are mutually exclusive). Domestic and care workers, including maids, nannies, and caregivers of the elderly, are a particularly interesting and important group of migrants to the Gulf because they often migrate through legal channels into the formal labor economy, and while they are subject to the same labor regulations embodied in the *kefala* system, they fall outside the protections offered by the UAE's existing labor laws. Moreover, because domestic workers do not fall under the regularly imagined definition of trafficking they also cannot access the set of international protections or rights that accompany trafficked persons should they face instances of abuse or force or fraud. The lack of legal protection afforded to domestic workers in either their home or host countries under domestic or international law renders them particularly vulnerable to exploitative practices, compounded by the isolating nature of their work. The trajectories of many of the female migrants with whom I spoke highlight ways in which policies can have a detrimental effect on people's lives.

Domestic workers in many parts of the world face common problems such as abusive employers, limited rights, and unregulated hours with very little recourse in cases of abuse or withheld pay, for example. The experience of domestic workers in the UAE, however, is somewhat unique owing to the conditions outlined by the *kefala* system in the GCC countries. Through my fieldwork, I noticed a trend that merited further scrutiny, that of domestic workers who turn to the informal sphere of sex work in search of increased autonomy and higher wages. Worn down by abusive situations with employers and with the restrictions placed on both their mobility and income-earning potential, these women are fed up with being held to the standards of labor regulations without enjoying its attendant benefits of rights.

This chapter focuses on a set of women I met through my work with sex workers and my time volunteering with informal organizations providing outreach to migrants in need. Through these avenues, I started meeting a number of women who had legally migrated primarily into the formal domestic and care work employment sphere in Dubai and Abu Dhabi, but were now supplementing their incomes or working exclusively in the sex industry. Through their stories, I chronicle the individual and larger macro-social factors structuring their transition. While certainly it is not the case that all domestic workers in the Gulf transfer over to the sex industry, the fact that I met over a dozen that did points to an important area of inquiry. These women's experiences highlight the shortcomings of trafficking policies that neglect sectors beyond the sex industry. Their stories demonstrate ways in which global policies on trafficking (such as those advanced in the TIP) and home country protectionist migratory laws (largely seeking to respond to international pressures) that strive to regulate female migration[2] do not, in practice, lessen the probability of women falling into abusive situations under the rubric of trafficking but, in fact, increase their vulnerability to abuse.

▪ ▪ ▪

A common assumption is that most women would do just about anything to get out of the oppression inherent in working in the sex industry. What my fieldwork revealed, however, was a group of women looking for a way *out* of the oppression they experienced in domestic work and *in* to the relative autonomy of sex work. This preference was nurtured by the inadequate global policies, and local, often punitive interpretations of these policies, and ineffectual labor laws that offer women in the domestic sphere little or no protection. People concerned about women being locked up or chained into brothels seem to easily forget that domestic workers, by the very nature of their jobs, must be available and on call 24 hours a day and typically are restricted to small rooms within the homes of their hosts during their nonwork hours. They are often barred from accessing telephones or the Internet, and their freedom to come and go can be severely limited. While not all women employed in domestic work experience these restrictions, several of the women I met during my time in the field reported challenging and potentially abusive situations within the homes of their employers. Some women indicated that they are not given days off, and those that are given a break are often not allowed to leave the home unaccompanied (if at all).

Through the narratives of the domestic workers I present here another story is heard; namely, that of women who are trapped in bad situations or who are in need of higher wages and thus seek out sex work. While sex work may constitute merely another less than ideal situation, the circumstances are generally seen as comparatively tolerable by the women involved. In order to address the vulnerability of women entering the informal economy, it might be beneficial to understand the hardships they face in the formal economy that might drive them to seek out sex work in the informal economy. When policies and conversations aimed at reducing human trafficking focus on ending sex work, people tend to forget the many global, local, and individual factors structuring women's decisions to work in this sector of the informal economy. We also often forget to be critical of those global and state-level policies that, when combined with the *kefala* system, produce a type of structural violence that diminishes women's access to rights and protections within the legal channels of migration.[3]

The challenges migrants face are a product of the difficult choices they have had to make for immediate economic survival, combined with political economic structures of a rapidly changing and globalized world. Though I have argued for recognition of migrant workers' agency in the process of migration, this is not to elide the fact that larger forces also foreshadow the choices they make. Two factors in the larger political economy are important to highlight: (1) the increased feminization of migration, and (2) the role of the state in both sending and receiving countries in shaping supply, demand, and types of migration.

A number of scholars have recently taken up research projects focusing on the issue of migration to the Middle East, writing about the effect of the demand for low-wage labor stemming from "courtesan" states (countries with high demand for labor such as the GCC countries).[4] Their work provides important comparative and background information for understanding the effects of both individual decision making as well as political economic forces behind migration to the Gulf. More specifically, two prominent female anthropologists who have been pioneers in the study of female migrant labor in the Gulf, Anh Longva and Rachel Silvey, have pointed to the challenges inherent in researching and raising awareness of female domestic workers who operate in the private sphere of the home. They note the complicity of both sending and host countries in structuring the challenges faced by migrants (especially female) to the Gulf. Their research supplies further evidence that these particular host countries continue to demand migrant labor without making attempts to reformulate labor laws or recognize domestic work, sex work, or other types of female caregiving labor as work. Home or sending countries, meanwhile, encourage citizens to go abroad to seek employment and send remittances back home. Development strategies that depend on remittances are therefore a contributor to the push factors of migration.

Too often, accounts of migration and state-level measures focus blame for misdeeds on migrants themselves or on specific host-state actors. Moreover, caricatures of the UAE as a hotbed of human trafficking, sex work, and rampant violation of migrants' rights are often predicated on Islamophobia or xenophobic attitudes toward Gulf countries in particular. Both views neglect to factor in complicated remittance-based development strategies in home countries that counteract with international policies seeking to limit or regulate the migration of women. People are on the move everywhere, all the time. The construction of the trafficking discourse today, however, portrays the Muslim Middle East as a particularly heightened spot for sex trafficking and rights violations (as can be evidenced by the number of Muslim countries on the watch list in the TIP report).

A Note on Perverse Integration and the Informal Economy

It is useful to emphasize that the migrant women I discuss experience types of structural violence in their home countries, during migration, and later in the host country. Furthermore, they do not have access to legal protection or benefits in the eyes of law enforcement, which, through the implementation of the *kefala* system, often sides with the employer.

It is no wonder then that many women who migrate into the formal sphere of domestic or care work in the UAE experience frustration and turn to the informal economy for higher wages and increased mobility. It bears mentioning here that the distinctions made between the formal and informal economy refer to work that is undertaken within (in the case of the former) or outside the *kefala* system that structures legal labor in the UAE.[5] In assessing the trajectory of some female migrants from the formal to informal labor sphere, the concept of *perverse integration* can be particularly helpful. Perhaps first used by Manuel Castells in "The Rise of the Fourth World" (1998), the term refers to people's preferences for work in the informal economy. In his book, Castells describes the "fourth world" as a group of people, located in multiple geographies, who are economically and socially marginalized and are motivated to seek out work in the informal economy. Castells notes that "the process of social exclusion and the insufficiency of remedial policies of social integration lead to a key process of perverse integration referred to as the labor force in the criminal economy."[6] He goes on to add that in the absence of new forms of integration for those marginalized workers who are members of the fourth world, the integration will necessarily come in the form of the informal economy.

In writing about homeless street vendors in New York City, Mitch Duneier uses the concept of perverse integration to show how homeless men who find themselves on the outskirts of society use panhandling and illegal street and drug vending in the informal economy as a viable source of income.[7] Through ethnographic research with street vendors in New York, Duneier delineates the deliberate decision-making processes of many men to seek out employment in the informal economy. He notes that the *perversion* of this type of integration is its functionality for many of these men as a regular source of income, but also because aspects of the formal economy become dependent on this type of informal labor, therefore making it integrated. This is supported by the fact that many types of formal work depend on the informal economy or "off the books" labor. A further example of perverse integration can be observed in organized crime, which is illegal albeit lucrative. Similar to illegal vending, organized crime also operates and benefits members of the formal economy, making it an integrated part of systems in many countries.[8]

For the purposes of my fieldwork, the concept of perverse integration is particularly useful in assessing women's decisions to seek out employment in the informal economy of sex work. When confronted with structural constraints in the formal economy, in the form of the *kefala* system or limited earning potential, for example, some women who integrate into the informal economy find that this labor provides them with higher wages and increased autonomy. These women are perversely integrated in that their work in the informal sphere, though illegal, allows them more opportunities. Furthermore, many members of the formal economy seek out their services, which integrates this type of labor even more.

Kefala and Its Discontents

During my time in the field I met several women who had initially migrated to work in the formal economy of domestic work, but who transitioned to the informal economy of sex work for various reasons. Here I delineate the stories of three women whose trajectories were somewhat representative of many of the narratives I heard from women who had made this choice.

Minia

"I used to see my cousins and girlfriends come back to Ethiopia with lots of money, and nice magazines and nicer clothes," Minia told me through her friend and interpreter when I asked her about her decision to migrate to Dubai to work as a domestic worker. When I met her, she was working illegally as a nanny for three different families and occasionally engaged in sex work on the side. She had been in Dubai for almost five years, and in that time had borne a son from an Emirati man with whom she lived for two years. She was very eager to return to Ethiopia to reunite with her family, but was wary of the heavy fines she would incur upon her departure. Migrants who overstay their visas or work illegally are fined $30 USD for each day they remain beyond their assigned departure date. Exacerbating her problem, Minia found herself without her passport or visa, which had been retained by her previous employers.

Minia's trajectory from migrating into the formal sphere of domestic work to working in the informal economy of the sex industry and living as an illegal alien in Dubai was similar to at least seven other women with whom I spoke. Minia told me that after her father died, her mother and siblings were left with a lot of debt. Worried about her family's future, she decided to ask her friends about migrating to the Gulf. "I think, I must make money, I must bring back money for my family," she said pushing back a strand of her braided hair. After announcing her decision to her mother and siblings and receiving their blessing, Minia approached a friend of hers who had told her he knew a shortcut to get her to Dubai more easily. In recent years, the Ethiopian government has passed a series of measures designed to curb the flow of Ethiopians migrating for work, particularly to the Middle East.[9] The state has imposed rules on licensing for recruiters and has been working toward a system of employee training (similar to that in the Philippines) and contract monitoring. Though well intentioned, this increased bureaucracy has caused many women, Minia included, to look for other ways to leave Ethiopia, ways seen as simpler and faster routes for securing transnational employment.

Minia's friend put her in touch with an illegal recruiter who asked for a high fee, equivalent to $2,000 USD, for securing Minia's passage to Dubai (via boat through Yemen) and for drawing up a contract for her to work as a domestic worker. Minia never saw the contract, but was told she would be met by another recruiter upon her arrival in Dubai.

> I was afraid because I knew maybe bad things happen. Before I go, my sister showed me picture of a girl who came back to Ethiopia dead after working in the Middle East. I told her, don't show me that picture, don't talk to me about that. I will be okay, I will be different, I will go and make money and make our family proud.

Minia's eyes filled with tears. She and many other women with whom I spoke indicated that they knew the risks involved with migrating, especially with migrating illegally, but they noted that these were risks and challenges they were willing to face in order to make a better life for their families. As Minia herself told me:

> When you go, you have to tell yourself that it will be okay. That you will be one of those who makes it. You know maybe it won't be okay when you go, but you also know it won't be okay to stay. I know if I don't go, no chance. No chance for me, for my family. In Ethiopia, no money. No work. What I'm supposed to do?

When Minia arrived in Dubai after a long journey she was met by a recruiter and then taken to the home of her new employers, a Lebanese family who had moved to Dubai a few years earlier. The family took her passport and working documents and Minia never saw them again. To this day she is striving to retrieve her working papers so that she can find legal employment and return to Ethiopia someday soon. During the six months that Minia worked for this family, she suffered beatings from her madam (female employer and head of the household) and sexual advances from the male head of the household and his son.

Made to work up to eighteen-hour days, the family often locked Minia in the house when they left and did not provide her dinner on most weeknights. When she complained, she was beaten, and the male head of household would make further advances toward her, making sexual threats that he would rape her one night while she was asleep. She was very afraid of these threats, so one afternoon she ran away from the apartment where she had been sequestered for the previous six months without pay. She managed to find a policeman who took her to the police station and placed her in a holding cell. After several hours, a Bangladeshi policeman[10] came to ask Minia about her situation. "He asked me why I had left the home of my employers, why I didn't appreciate them and all they did for me," Minia recalled. She indicated that there were communication barriers between the police and her, just as there had been with her employers, and expressed her frustration at not speaking Arabic or English.

"After he asked me who my boss was, he called up the family. I thought it was going to be okay, that he was going to get my passport for me, but no, that isn't what happened," Minia said sadly. After talking with her for ten minutes the policeman had called her employers asking them to come to the station to retrieve their housemaid (or *khaddamah*, as they are referred to in Arabic). When the family patriarch arrived, Minia hoped that the police would chastise him for abusing her and withholding her pay. Instead, however, her employer was lectured about the importance of not letting his housemaid out of his sight. He was told to take her home, be more careful, and not to let women like her roam the streets without supervision. When Minia was taken back to her employers' home, she was badly beaten and locked in her room without food for three days. "All day I am crying. What to do? How to leave? And what to do when I leave? No money, no passport, more debt. Only crying." Then on the fourth day Minia decided to run away and this time to abscond from her work as a domestic worker. "I think, I can't do this job. I can't work like this. I can't live in their house, and no one listens to me when I complain," she said. Minia decided that the unregulated space of the informal economy was likely to offer more than her formal work as a domestic worker, where she was bound by the constraints of the *kefala* system.

That day, Minia jumped from the window of her room on the third story of an apartment building. When she jumped, she injured her right leg badly, but instead of going to the hospital or police, Minia decided to go to the church that she had been permitted to attend once a month. "I know other Ethiopians at the church, I know if I can get there, I can get help," she said. However, she did not know her way around town, and her injured leg severely restricted her mobility.

After a few days of living on the street she met a young Emirati man who wanted to help her. "He was so kind to me, he took me to his apartment where he lived alone and said I could stay as long as I wanted. He found a doctor for me, my leg got better, and he even said he would help me get my passport back, he was so wonderful." After a few weeks Minia became romantically involved with this man and eventually became pregnant. The man was very happy to hear that she was pregnant and showered her with gifts and attention. He also promised to get her a legal visa and be her sponsor and potentially her husband. Minia was overjoyed, and during this period converted to Islam and became very involved at the local mosque that her Emirati boyfriend attended.

After their son was born, however, things changed. The young man, who had not yet succeeded in retrieving her working papers or passport, suddenly became agitated with Minia and told her she had to leave the house with the baby. He told her his family had heard about their situation and did not approve of his decision to live with Minia for those two years. He gave her some money for the child and sent her away.

Minia and her son moved in with some friends from the mosque while she tried to look for any possible type of work to earn enough money to pay off the fines she incurred having overstayed her visa, and to procure an out-pass to return to Ethiopia with her son. Limited by not having legal working papers, Minia began by working in a restaurant in the Ethiopian neighborhood in town. After a few months working at this job, however, she was not getting paid. One evening she met a group of women at the restaurant who worked as sex workers in a bar called the Rattlesnake. They told her what her earning potential could be and she decided to join them that evening. This marked the beginning of Minia's work in the informal economy of sex work. After a few months working at the Rattlesnake, Minia was arrested one night in a raid. She was put in jail for three weeks and not permitted to see her son, who was still at the home of her friends with whom she had been living.

While in jail, Minia heard about another Ethiopian woman, Sama, who was rumored to provide complimentary legal assistance and outreach to Ethiopian and Eritrean women in need of services. She was given Sama's number and called her for assistance. In a matter of days, Sama managed to negotiate her release from jail and helped her to find a small room for rent where she and her son could live. Minia told Sama that she wanted to earn enough money to return to Ethiopia with her son, and Sama assisted Minia in finding employment as a nanny in the home of a Jordanian family that Sama knew well. Though she still did not have legal working papers, she was able to negotiate this job with her employers, who agreed to pay her and assist in retrieving her passport.

Minia was adamant this time, however, that she would not live with the family and would return home every evening to be with her son. After seven months, Sama and Minia succeeded in clearing Minia of the heavy fines she had accrued during the course of her arrest and in the many months she had overstayed her visa. When I last spoke with them, Minia was optimistic that she would retrieve her passport, or at least be able to purchase an out-pass to return home to Ethiopia. She was also relieved that she had paid off her debt to the recruiter and had managed to save some money to return home with. "Next time I know housemaid no good. Next time I find job where I have my own home, and my own time," she said. "But I do like Dubai, the city and the people here have been good to me, so even if I go home, I will come back here, to my new home."

Gloria

Not all domestic workers who enter the sex industry do so because they have become illegal or undocumented workers. Some, like Gloria, decide to engage in sex work to supplement their incomes. Gloria was living in a shantytown on the outskirts of Manila with her two daughters, sisters, and mother when she met Ram, a British-Australian man who made regular trips to the Philippines each year in search of women to work as domestic workers for his European clients in Dubai. "Filipina maids are the cream of the crop," Ram had told me during a phone interview.

> I go to the Philippines and handpick them myself. Then I bring them over be-
> cause in Dubai, a family that wants to show their status in town has a Filipina
> maid. I bring my girls over mostly for men who live alone here [in Dubai], and
> I make sure I find the best girls possible for my clients.

I had found Ram through an online listing of recruiters for maid services in Dubai. I was confused at his repeated emphasis that he "brought Filipina girls for single European men." When I pressed him on this, asking whether he brought women to be partners or domestic workers he said, "I bring over maids who are good and well put together. What happens after that isn't my business, but yes, a lot of my girls have gotten involved with their employers."

Confused about the logistics of Ram's employment operation, and the de-gree of agency his employees were able to exercise, I told him I wanted to interview one of the women he had recently recruited. It took many conversations over the course of a year, but I finally managed to convince him to allow me to interview Gloria, who reflected on her decision to accept Ram's offer of employment as a domestic worker in Dubai.

> I couldn't make ends meet. I was working as many jobs as I could to provide
> for my children and my mother who is too old to work. But I couldn't manage.
> I didn't want to go, I didn't want to say good-bye to my little girls, but I didn't
> really have a choice. There was no work for me in the Philippines, and I could
> go to Dubai and make so much money. I could go, become an OFW [overseas
> Filipino worker] and send money back like my friends. I could renovate the
> house. I could send my girls to a good school so they would have the opportu-
> nities I never had, so I said, OK, I'll go.

Gloria responded to an ad Ram had placed in a local paper and decided to meet with him in Manila. Her friends had told her that working as a domestic worker in the Gulf was not easy. "The Middle East is not the first choice for OFWs, but I thought, I will start there and hope to get another, better job somewhere else. Like maybe Europe, but Dubai was good for first." After meeting with Ram, she signed a contract and was on her way in a matter of weeks.

"When I had to say good-bye to my family, that was the hardest thing I have ever had to do. But I kept telling myself, I am doing it for them, I told myself that every day." Gloria had hoped she would be making a lot of money and would be able to send it home immediately, but she soon realized that she owed Ram a large sum of money for her traveling costs and visa procurement. After a few months her family would call repeatedly, saying that they needed money and were facing dire straits in Manila. Gloria still hadn't paid off her debt to Ram because his recruitment fee was higher than others, owing to the fact that he guaranteed employment in under a month. Other registered recruiters in the Philippines facilitated migration at much lower fees, but they required a lot of paperwork and a three- to six-month training program.

"I didn't have that kind of time, so I agreed to go with Ram and just prayed that everything would be okay," Gloria said. Desperate to fix her finances, she had agreed to the terms of the contract in the hopes of paying off her debt quickly. When, after three months, she was still paying back the debt and could not send money home, she decided to speak to her employer, a British executive who had been living in Dubai for two years, about getting a loan from him. Her employer indicated that he would be willing to give her money in exchange for sexual favors.

> I wasn't sure what to do. I didn't leave Manila, come all the way to Dubai to be a prostitute, but I said to myself, this was different. He was my employer, I wasn't working on the streets or in some bar or something. So I said okay.

Gloria felt uncertain about accepting her employer's offer, but she felt limited by not knowing if there were any other options for higher wages. When she talked to Ram, asking for a raise, he had declined her request. Ram told her that she would have to take up any issues she had with her employer, who was also her sponsor, and who was the only reason she was able to stay in Dubai. He also reminded her that she owed him a significant debt because he brought her to Dubai and secured a good work opportunity. Unsure of where to turn next, Gloria began having a sexual relationship with her employer and was able to make more money to send home to her family. Within eighteen months she had paid for a renovated home and both of her daughters were going to private school. "But I missed them too much, and my girls kept calling me, begging me to come home. I knew I had to make as much money as possible, to do whatever I had to do to get home quickly."

Over the course of the next year, Gloria continued her sexual relationship with her employer, and also began a sexual relationship with a friend of her employer's whom she had met at a dinner party hosted in her employer's apartment. The additional income provided by her side job of commercial sex work allowed her to save enough money to return to Manila sooner than she had anticipated. At the end of her two years in Dubai, she had finished renovating a house for her family and had saved enough so that she could remain in Manila for several more years before having to depart again in search of employment abroad. When I last spoke with her, she was in the Philippines and told me that while she was happy to be back with her family, she also missed Dubai and her previous employer. "I had grown to like him and even I had started liking Dubai by the end," she wrote to me when she had returned. "Perhaps I will go back someday soon with my girls for a visit," she said, signing off.

Juju

Financial debts and the desire to support one's family back home were cited as primary factors structuring the desire to engage in sex work. Juju was another example of a domestic worker who turned to sex work in search of increased wages and autonomy. Juju left Sri Lanka after her father died, leaving her mother and siblings with substantial debt and no possibility for income generation. "I was only nineteen, and I was still grieving the loss of my father, but I knew something had to be done," she explained, reflecting on her decision to migrate to Dubai in search of work as a nanny.

Juju was born and raised in a village seventy miles outside the capital of Sri Lanka. The first of three children, she said she always felt a certain responsibility for her family that came along with being the eldest child. After her father died, she said, this sense of responsibility and urgency magnified to the point where she made the decision to seek work overseas. "I knew that there were lots of jobs in the Middle East, many of my friends and cousins had moved there, so I thought, why not me?" Juju had finished high school, where she had learned almost perfect English. She hoped one day to go to college but said that it would have to wait until she had sorted out her family's financial affairs. Juju, like many other women who migrate to the Gulf, are not necessarily members of the lowest socioeconomic strata, as the stereotypes about trafficking would have one believe. Popular discourse suggests that the most desperate (and some stereotypes suggest the most uneducated) women are the most susceptible to trafficking; however, the reality is that many of the women I met were educated and not necessarily desperate, but rather were making a decision to move for a wide range of reasons.

When she went to the government office in Colombo to make a request for an overseas job, Juju was told she was too young and would have to wait a few years. This was not acceptable for her or her family, so Juju went back to the office the next day and asked to see another official. "The next guy told me I had to go to school, and to do some trainings," she said. But this was not a satisfying answer either. "I thought, I have to go now, I can't wait. And I don't have money to go to school, I don't have money for a visa, so I knew I would have to find another way."

Juju's mother knew of a man who made regular trips to their village in Sri Lanka and "knew all about going to the Middle East." When this man visited their village the next month, Juju went to him asking for advice. She told him she needed to move to find a job, but that she had no money. She explained the response she had received from the official government recruitment office and asked for his help. "He told me, 'yes, Juju, I can help you.' I was so happy! I was ready to do anything to go," she said. This man was an illegal recruiter who received large sums of money from migrants and potential employers in the Gulf for brokering transactions with "less paperwork," as Juju later told me. He arranged for her to go to Dubai on a tourist visa (a fact she was unaware of at the time), and placed her in the home of a Lebanese family.

"When I found out I got a job in Dubai, I was so happy! I was thinking, finally, I'm getting out of this village, I'm going to travel the world, make my family proud, and make a better life for my family. That was all I thought about," Juju said, sweeping her waist-length black hair into a bun. The recruiter told her she would have to pay him $2,000 USD for her ticket and the visa processing costs. When she told him she had no money, he told her that she would work off her debt with him in the coming months. "Perhaps I should not have agreed, I knew that this was a lot of money, but I was certain I would make much more money and I was eager to go."

Juju said good-bye to her family and set off for the Colombo airport for her flight to Dubai. When she spoke of her family, her eyes filled with tears; she has not seen them in the two years that have passed since she left Sri

Lanka, and she is desperate to return home. "But I knew then, and I know now, that I would never go back without a lot of money. I would only return when I could hold my head high. When I had worked off my debt and had made enough money to pay off my father's debts."

The recruiter Juju had met was also arranging the migration of four other women that day. He met them at the airport and accompanied each of them to the homes of their new employers. "He dropped me off at a house and said good-bye. That was the last time I saw him, too," said Juju. After a few months, Juju settled into the routine of her new family. She had been told she would be a nanny to their three children, but it turned out that she was also responsible for housekeeping and tending to the elderly mother of her employer. She started working around the clock and was on call twenty-four hours a day. Some weeks she was given only three hours a day to sleep and no days off. Her day began at five o'clock in the morning, when she would wake to begin cooking breakfast and feed the youngest child of her employers who was just six months old. Then she would have to clean the house, cook for the family, and tend to the elderly mother of her employer who required almost constant attention. The baby on her hip, Juju would have to change the bedsheets of the elderly woman routinely when she would wet the bed. In addition to the caregiving and cleaning, Juju often had to assist in household chores such as handy work and yard work. Most days she was working until two o'clock in the morning.

Juju became tired and weak. When she told her employers she needed time off to rest, her boss told her that she had overstayed her tourist visa, and if she left their house she would be arrested. This was the first time Juju heard that her visa was not a work permit. Her recruiter had led her to believe that he had secured a sponsorship visa for her through the employers. "He told me so many lies. He told me that I would only work eight hours a day, make $800 USD a month, and that I was coming on a work visa. Everything he told me was a lie," said Juju angrily. She noted that she had no way of contacting him or anyone else. She thought about contacting her embassy, but worried she would be punished for having violated their rules about migration.

"I felt stuck, I had nowhere to go. They just worked me more and more hours, and there was nothing I could do." Her employers would not permit her to leave the house, and when she complained about the heavy workload, they only punished her by making her work even longer hours, coming up with more chores for her to do. After five months she still had not been paid, and so she asked her employer about her withheld wages. As Juju recounted her story, her dark brown eyes filled with tears:

> He told me that all my money went to the guy who brought me over here, and that I would have to get my money from him, but I couldn't find him. My boss told me I should be grateful for the food and clothes they gave me. I told them I was, but I needed money. He told me to find that guy, but I couldn't. He changed his number and he was gone. That day I cried. I cried so much. I cried for my family, I cried for myself. I cried thinking how many of my other sisters [fellow Sri Lankan women] had been through what I was going through. It seemed there was no way out. I was an illegal. I was stuck in this house. I wasn't making any money, and I was crying every day.

For three more months Juju continued her work, each day hoping that her recruiter would turn up, or that things would change and her employer would seek out legal sponsorship papers for her so she would not be living there illegally. Then one day the family invited another family for dinner, and the visitors brought along their Sri Lankan nanny, a woman named Mediha. When Juju met Mediha she was overjoyed and began telling her new friend of what she had been enduring for the past nine months. Mediha was very concerned for her friend, and told her that she needed to leave the house immediately in search of other work. Juju told her new friend that she did not want to work for another family. Mediha then told Juju about some friends she had met at church who had left their jobs as nannies to work as sex workers in the local clubs. She said that the women made a lot of money, and that the money went directly to them rather than any employer or middleman. "But prostitution is illegal, I told Mediha," Juju recalled. But then it dawned on her that she was already an illegal resident in Dubai. "I thought, I'm here illegally anyway. Why not do work where I can make money and be my own boss? So that night I made my decision," she added.

A few weeks later Juju collected her few belongings and left out the back-yard sliding door. "I guess the only thing keeping me in that house had been fear. I could have run away a long time ago, but I was too scared. Once I made up my mind, it was easy." That night she hitched a ride to a part of town in Bur Dubai where Mediha had told her to go. "The first night was hard. I was scared, but at least I was free of that house." Juju met three other Sri Lankan women who were walking into a hotel bar and asked them for assistance. At first they were hesitant, noting that Juju was not dressed in a manner that would attract male attention, but rather was still in her gray and white maid's uniform. After a few hours of talking, with Juju telling them her story, the women took Juju back to their shared room a few blocks away, lent her some clothes, and brought her back with them to the club they had been heading to.

"I was lucky I met them. After that, I moved in with them, paying them rent and helping with stuff around the house." Juju had been living there just over a year when I met her through an Indian caseworker whom she had hired to procure legal travel documents so she could return to Sri Lanka to see her family. When I asked if she was happy in her new profession she was silent before answering.

> Happy, I don't know. It's not easy. But at least I don't cry all the time any more like I did before. And now I'm making money, and that money goes directly to my pocket. I don't think I'm happy. But I am more happy than before. And I think I am going home soon, so then I will be happy. When I can go home with money and make my family proud.

▪ ▪ ▪

These women's stories break many stereotypes around female migration. Most important, they show the challenges inherent within domestic work and some of the ramifications of the glaring scarcity of laws available to protect women in this corner of the formal labor sphere. They also show that, contrary to popular assumptions that all women must be looking for exit strategies out of sex work, some women find that the space of the informal economy affords more rights, autonomy, and economic mobility than the restricted space of domestic work. The narratives presented here also show that migrant women are not wholly victims of circumstance and can exercise agency in various ways. These women demonstrate their agentive capacities through the decisions they make and the ways in which they navigate their experiences as migrant workers in the UAE.

Minia's decision to abscond, to run away in search of other employment or a way to better her situation, should be read as a resourceful, agentive act, albeit one prompted by an unfortunate, dehumanizing situation. Gloria's strategy of increasing her income by providing sexual favors to her employer should be read as just that, a strategy and a deliberate and well-reasoned act of income generation. Finally, Juju's decision to leave the home of her employers in search of increased autonomy in the sex industry should be read as a deliberate and active exercise of the choices available to her. When she realized she was an illegal employee regardless of her profession, she chose to enter into the informal economy where she would have more ability to maneuver the terms and reap the benefits of her labor.

Many of the women I met during my fieldwork who experienced this particular trajectory had initially migrated with the intention to work as domestic workers or caregivers but had ended up in sex work or other activities in the informal economy due to complications with work permits or disputes with employers that in some cases had led to their arrest. Several women had migrated to work in the sex industry specifically due to failing economies or violence in their home countries. Others had come to Dubai to work as sex workers as part of an entrepreneurial strategy for income generation. The experiences of female migrants who work as commercial sex workers are not monolithic and cannot be captured under such umbrella terms as *trafficked*, *exploited*, or even *guilty* or *innocent*. Each narrative was different, and the only common ground shared by all was their status as migrant laborers in Dubai.

The conditions of domestic work in Dubai and Abu Dhabi ranged from strong ties with families who provided good accommodations and regular time off, to abusive situations such as those described above. Some women with whom I spoke talked about long work days of eighteen to twenty hours with virtually no breaks. Others talked about having to attend to infants, elderly, and animals (such as horses; cleaning stables was even required for some women), while cooking, cleaning, and helping out with gardening and heavy yard work at the same time. While some reported comfortable accommodations and regular access to food and time off, others reported having to sleep on the floor, food deprivation, and no days off for weeks on end. One young woman from Ethiopia described her experience quite vividly:

> We wake up before the sun comes up, and already work is starting. For me, I am tired even when I wake, because I have worked so hard for so long, but also because I am sleeping on the floor with no blankets. I work all day. Sometimes the kids screaming all day. Sometimes the madam yelling at me. Sometimes no money for me, no days to go to church, to see my friends. Sometimes no phone to call my family. Even many nights no food. But, sometimes money is coming, and I am sending home to my family. That keeps me here, working and hoping. Better than Ethiopia because here money. Here work. Here, I try to stay.

The tendency for some domestic workers to seek work in the sex industry prompts a closer look at the facilitating circumstances; largely, the difficult conditions of domestic work in the Gulf. Domestic workers who face instances of force, fraud, or coercion in their migratory journeys or in arranging their terms of employment can find little refuge in the UAE's incomplete or inapplicable labor laws. Paradoxically, the lack of protection afforded to domestic workers is a motivator for some to move into the sex industry, where they seek out increased autonomy and higher wages.

Global Women

Globalization and neoliberal economic policies have created push and pull forces across sections of societies and borders of nation-states. *Push forces* encouraging women to migrate in search of employment, survival, or safety include increasing poverty, development strategies in countries such as the Philippines and Indonesia that rely on remittances for strengthened economies, and postconflict settings such as those in Ethiopia and Somalia. The changing nature of demand for labor has resulted in the proliferation of a labor market that places women in roles traditionally considered female, such as caregivers, nurses, domestic workers, and entertainers. These are the new "global women," despite the charged international rhetoric on trafficking that highlights women in the sex industry to the exclusion of those outside of it.[11] Domestic workers, caregivers, and nurses working in the Gulf countries are not regarded as potential or actual trafficking victims, which impacts their access to this particular rights discourse as well as to certain social services.[12] Women migrating into these industries in the UAE, as in so many other countries across the globe, also fall outside the protection of labor laws and provisions, leaving them extremely vulnerable to abuse and with nowhere to turn for support.

Instead of viewing the increasing numbers of global female migrants as victims of globalization, it is perhaps more useful to look at the trajectories they follow to improve their lives. Without scripting these women solely as victims, we can look to the forces that shape their decisions, experiences, and challenges in order to compare their migration experiences to those of men. A rise in the number of migrating women has granted them greater autonomy and altered the socioeconomic status of both genders. The income they generate has allowed their families increased access to resources and additional educational opportunities for their children. While the lived experiences of female migrants encompass a vast spectrum of heterogeneity, a number of macro-social forces are at play—some at the policy level, others discursive, still others structural.

Structural forces include poverty, the threat or occurrence of war, and an imaging of labor that both assigns gender to certain forms of work and renders these forms invisible.[13] Structural *push forces* include the need to maintain dual-income households, for women with spouses, and the need to assume the role of sole provider, for women without spouses or other contributing family members. Male unemployment in home countries or abroad in turn compels many women to migrate. For women living in postconflict or war-torn nations, "home" offers neither viable economic opportunities nor the promise of stability, prompting them to migrate in search of safety and survival.

Structural *pull forces* include an increasing demand for female labor, predominantly in industries labeled as "care" industries.[14] These include domestic work, caregiving, nursing, and sex work, which, indeed, are not mutually exclusive. Women migrating into one of these industries often look to supplement their income by participation in a second or third industry. The care work that shapes the demand for female labor transnationally consists of work that typically occurs inside the home. Within the capitalist system, domestic work is not generally seen as "real" work, rendering the efforts of female migrants invisible. This invisibility is compounded by the stark lack of labor laws in place to protect women within these industries, and the hesitancy of law enforcement personnel within the UAE to intrude into what is seen as the private sphere of the home. When talking to police officers about mitigating conflicts between employers and domestic workers, they were emphatic about the notion that these disputes were private issues, not to be discussed outside the home out of respect for the families' privacy.

▮ ▮ ▮

The structural forces as outlined above affect and are affected by discourse and policy around the topic of female migration. Global policies on trafficking that seek to address and prevent sex trafficking have been enacted to the detriment of female migrants worldwide. The TIP recommends a heightened police force and a tightening of borders, measures designed to prevent the movement of women into the illegal space of sex work. Efforts to tighten borders typically result in a rise in the number of people migrating irregularly or through unofficial channels, as evidenced by the stories of Minia, Gloria, and Juju. While many do not seek to migrate into sex work, a variety of events can lead women to that industry. Laws that seek to prevent the migration of women without increasing job opportunities in home countries only make women more vulnerable to trafficking when they turn instead to middlemen brokers and recruiters. Enterprising migrants who have made the often wrenching decision to migrate will do so by any means necessary. When sending countries impose stricter regulations and added bureaucracy to discourage migration, or when receiving countries seek to tighten their borders, many migrants turn instead to informal channels that can be quicker and seem simpler, but that, sadly, are often abusive and exploitative and leave migrants mired in debt.

The TIP report, through its problematic ranking system, has accelerated the trend among sending countries such as Ethiopia, Indonesia, the Philippines, and Sri Lanka to increase restrictions on females who are leaving in search of employment elsewhere while maintaining economic development strategies that depend on their remittances. Countries that embrace both types of policies have created an environment that is rampant with contradictions and difficult for their citizens to navigate. When development strategies depend on remittances, women and men alike are increasingly reliant on jobs outside of home countries for income generation. In 1997 the remittances from just the Middle East to Sri Lanka totaled over $1 billion, which outweighed the country's trade deficit of $0.7 billion. In 1999, remittances to the Philippines totaled roughly $5 billion. As Ray Jureidini notes, "Asian governments pursued active policies for overseas employment, partly to alleviate unemployment and partly to generate foreign income."[15] This increasing dependence on the export of labor for national income generation works to limit citizens' employment options at home.

Alternatively, greater attention to development strategies that rely less on remittances and more on creating jobs at home would encourage migration based more on choice than on desperate need. It is often the case that sending countries are suffering from the aftershocks of structural adjustment programs and global economies in transition. Lacking the resources to create sustainable employment programs at home, these countries continue to rely on remittances. These economic dependencies should be acknowledged when crafting bilateral agreements that seek to prevent women's migration from home countries to receiving countries in the Gulf.

Thinking Globally, Acting Locally

Global policies that focus exclusively on ending sex trafficking ignore a large population of those entering the sex industry through the avenues of formal labor migration—for instance, legal female migrants in the domestic industry.

Domestic workers are among the most vulnerable populations within the UAE. Subject to abusive working conditions and a lack of supportive labor laws, some women are compelled to leave domestic work to seek work in informal and illegal spheres. International policies that induce governments to take specific measures to stop sex trafficking often result in redirecting government initiatives that might have been geared toward reforming labor laws, restructuring the *kefala* system, and strengthening civil society. These important issues take a back seat to far narrower, unproductive strategies such as increasing imported law enforcement and criminalizing sex workers through arrests and deportation.

Within the UAE, prime factors in female migrants' transition out of the domestic and caregiving industries include the structure of the *kefala* system, the lack of protection offered by labor laws, and the absence of social services or official civil society mechanisms that provide outreach. Indeed, the Emirati state apparatus has demonstrated its intent to mitigate the challenges experienced by undocumented workers by granting periods of amnesty during which migrants can regulate their work permits—though it is not entirely clear whether the state is motivated more by a genuine interest in improving migrant workers' conditions or by improving its public image by complying with the TIP. Yet global policies such as the TIP direct the state to concentrate on prosecution as a means to reduce sex trafficking, leading law enforcement personnel to focus time and energy on tactics such as brothel raids instead of assisting migrant workers who have been abused. The challenges presented by these structural and discursive forces, combined with the weight of larger global macro-social forces as outlined above, are leading increasing numbers of women to shift from the formal into the informal economy.

⋅ ⋅ ⋅

Virtually overnight, women in the UAE who flee from abusive employers become undocumented and subject to heavy fines, arrest, and deportation. Avenues for recourse or assistance—in the case of abuse or the withholding of wages, for example—are limited. Because domestic workers operate in the sphere of the home, they cannot look to friends or colleagues outside their work place for advice or assistance. Many do not have access to a phone, and if they do, the only help hotline currently in existence leads them to the police department. Several domestic workers with whom I spoke articulated their fear of the police, who had a reputation for calling employers and siding with employer-sponsors. Others expressed a desire for safe spaces or shelters run by nongovernmental groups. Such groups are in fact developing informally, but without official sanction from the state their options for fundraising and formal operation are limited.

The women whose stories were presented in this chapter highlight not only the disconnect between global policies on trafficking and the lived experience of migration, but also the ways in which these policies and discourses, and state responses to them, have added turmoil to migrants' already difficult lives. But migrant workers are not the only ones who feel the negative fallout of trafficking policy. Volunteers who have worked for over three decades to build a civil society in the UAE have also seen their work thwarted by policies such as those touted by the TIP report that nullify their efforts. Migrant workers are dependent on the crucial services volunteers provide, yet these organizations and efforts remain unrecognized and ignored by international policies and local governments alike.

6

AN (UN)CIVIL SOCIETY

IN A CAFÉ off of Sheikh Zayed Road, facing the soaring twin towers of the Dubai Financial Center, Sama sits at the table, takes a sip of her mint tea, and lets out an exhausted sigh before burying her face in her hands. She has brought a young woman named Meskit with her to the café this morning, and Meskit is accompanied by her son, a three-year-old boy named Karim. Karim tears around the café while his mother smiles at him and adjusts her head scarf.

"I am tired," Sama says. "Not just today, but tired because this work is taking its toll on me, and it feels like my job is getting harder and harder to do." She clenches her hennaed hands into fists. Meskit slides over to Sama and puts her arm around her. "This woman is the reason I'm alive," she says.

Meskit proceeds to tell her story, how she left Addis Ababa to work in Dubai as a domestic worker and was abused and raped by her employer. When her employer found out she was pregnant, he kicked her out of the house and she ended up in jail. After three weeks, Meskit found Sama's number and called for her assistance. Over the next three months Sama was able to persuade the authorities to let her out of jail and helped her to procure a new working visa. Today, Meskit is working as a nanny and lives in Dubai with her son. "She has helped so many Ethiopian women like me, but she is exhausted, it's getting harder and harder to do her kind of work."

Sama is tired from battling the global and local notions about human trafficking that combine to put undue pressure on female migrants in the UAE.

She is tired because international policies as championed in the Trafficking in Persons (TIP) report have hindered her efforts to create and mobilize a civil society in the UAE to meet the needs of migrant workers, trafficked or not.

Sama was born in Ethiopia and raised in refugee camps in Somalia and Italy. As an adult, she lived in Canada briefly before moving to Dubai in 2003. She says that it was her experience being a refugee and then a migrant worker in Italy and Canada that made her interested in forming an ad hoc social support group to help African women who have become migrant workers around the world. A tall woman with kind eyes, she speaks seven languages fluently and uses her linguistic skills to help translate for women who are facing legal troubles or are mired in court cases.

> The problem is that your George Bush and the Americans made trafficking so political. On top of that they made it so that all trafficking is sex trafficking, so what does that do? It makes people racist, it makes people think that any Ethiopian woman here is a sex worker, or has been trafficked, and is a criminal.

Every day Sama works with Ethiopian women who have been arrested for absconding from their jobs, overstaying their visas, accruing debt, or working as sex workers. She says that the pointed focus on sex trafficking within the TIP and in United Nations documents such as the UN Protocol to Prevent, Suppress, and Punish Trafficking in Persons (which operates under the umbrella of the UN Office on Drugs and Crime) has constructed the trafficking issue as a criminal matter in the minds of locals and UAE law enforcement. Sama is frustrated that members of law enforcement assume that women from certain nationalities must all be guilty. She is angered that local and international authorities articulate and reproduce local racialized and gendered hierarchies rather than approaching labor and migration issues within a human rights framework. She is also angered by international policies, such as those advocated in the TIP report, that consider all abused migrant women to be sex workers and, by default, criminals. Thus any migrant worker seeking assistance is first taken to jail for questioning.

> The worst part is that they don't even get good translators for these women. They, the police or the judges, they have made up their minds about Ethiopian women, and they get people to translate for them into words that they want to hear, that [the women] are guilty, that they are criminals. They don't even get a fair shot, that's why I insist on doing the translations, because it's just not fair.

Sama pulls out a photograph from her purse and hands it to me. In it, a frail Ethiopian woman not weighing more than ninety pounds is lying in a hospital bed. The woman is hooked up to an IV drip, but her arms are also handcuffed to the bed. I look up in confusion. Sama continues, raising her ordinarily soft voice for the first time:

> Yes, can you believe it? She is handcuffed to the bed! She ran away because her employer was abusing her, she was a housemaid. She ran away and as she was doing so she was hit by a car and was taken to the hospital. When she woke up, she was chained to the bed. They assume that because she ran away, and because she is an Ethiopian woman, she is a criminal. Now how do you handle that kind of racism?

Her voice once again becomes soft. Sama tells us that things weren't always this way; that people didn't used to be this harsh toward migrant women, and that doing her job used to be much easier. She acknowledges that there has been a long history of labor rights violations in the UAE, but stresses that in the late 1990s, migrant advocacy groups were beginning to make progress vis-à-vis the state; progress that was stunted, in her opinion, with the politicization of the trafficking issue. She emphasizes that it was only when the issue became political, when the UAE was put on the TIP watch list, that female migrant workers became synonymous with sex workers and, as sex workers, became labeled as trafficking victims—seen as a dangerous, politically damaging population that demanded what some would call protection in the form of observation and surveillance. While Sama was one of my first interviewees to name the negative effect of international policy mandates on building civil society, she was not the only one to do so. As a result of the TIP, the individuals and organizations providing public services and raising awareness about the circumstances of migrants in need have come under harsh scrutiny by the government.

Dubai Has No Civil Society?

"There are no NGOs here." "Dubai has NO civil society." "What do you mean 'NGO'?" These and other puzzling comments were commonplace among expatriates in Dubai as well as policymakers in Washington D.C. and were among the sentiments that left activists such as Sama feeling tired, unsupported, and unappreciated. On my first trip to Dubai these phrases echoed inside my head, and I even found myself reproducing them after a few weeks. I had searched high and low to find evidence of any social services or civil society, to no avail, until I realized I was going about it all wrong. I was looking through an American lens: searching for drop-in centers or billboard campaigns, organizations with websites and hotlines, or printed material distributed at airports and embassies. My radar was scanning for civil society as defined by American standards. It wasn't until I began spending more time with groups of migrant workers that doors were opened to reveal a large movement of informal and inconspicuous associations that had been quietly mobilizing civil society efforts since the 1980s to meet the needs of migrants in Dubai.

When I returned home from the field, excited to share stories about the evidence of civil society I had encountered, friends and colleagues in the United States responded skeptically. "No, there are no NGOs there because they don't care about human rights over there, they just want to make money," said one student when I introduced the title of my talk at her university as "Building Civil Society in the UAE." Others echoed this sentiment. "They don't even understand the concept of NGO, and they don't want or need to, it's just not in their culture," said one friend as I tried to cite examples of both state and informal civil society groups I had encountered. There was a pervasive idea among many people I met back in the United States that the UAE was just not interested in or capable of promoting civil society or human rights. UAE culture, defined uniformly as one entity without interrogation, was thought to be the culprit. Audience members emphasized their horror and shock at the trafficking situation and the rampant abuse of migrant laborers they had learned, through media reports, were taking place in Dubai. "Those people couldn't possibly care about promoting civil society, I don't think they even want to help the poor people within their borders," said one academic. I continued to present my data in order to show them just how wrong they were.

Among policymakers the skepticism continued. "There is no civil society in Dubai, that's part of why they are ranked so low on the TIP list," said one State Department official responsible for research informing the TIP report. One of the main criteria through which the TIP gauges compliance with international trafficking standards within a particular country is the presence of civil society organizations and the availability of social services to meet the needs of trafficked persons. If a country cannot demonstrate evidence of an active civil society, it is given a low ranking in the TIP report, yet such countries are not necessarily encouraged to focus their efforts or resources on creating such a presence. The TIP report unilaterally highlights what it interprets as a lack of civil society in the Gulf, disregarding and therefore invalidating the efforts of people like Sama, whose presence and contributions to civil society may not register on the State Department's tracking system.

Over the last three decades a number of informal groups have been organizing, with a nod and occasional support from the state, to strengthen civil society in the UAE. Such a movement both contradicts and challenges the Emirati law that prohibits the creation of labor unions and official NGOs (according to Laws 155 and 160 of UAE Federal Law no. 8 of 1980, also known as the "Labor Law"[16]). As Sama alluded to, many of the direct challenges to migrants' rights in the UAE stem from long-standing laws and conditions; moreover, progress in changing these laws was stunted by a larger moral panic on trafficking that manifests itself in the TIP report. While the TIP has emphasized this law's deficiency, it provides no inducement to rescind or rewrite such legislation. Report recommendations have instead focused on increased state-led initiatives in response to trafficking within UAE borders, rendering existing nongovernmental outreach efforts increasingly powerless.

Civil Society Reconsidered

What exactly IS civil society? And how is it measured? What are the consequences of ignoring both informal and state efforts to mobilize civil society? Generally accepted definitions of civil society revolve around the idea of a mediating body acting as an intermediary between the private sphere and the state.[1] According to Prof. Nawaf Salam, Harvard alumnus, American University of Beirut faculty member, and current Ambassador and Permanent Representative to the United Nations in New York:

> A classical definition of civil society in the history of ideas is nonexistent. Hegel's conception of it diverged from Locke's, and interpretations by Gramsci and Habermas as to what civil society is not only departed from earlier versions, but differed from each other as well. Likewise, there is no consensus among contemporary scholars on what constitutes civil society, what it precisely is and is not, and what elements it does include or should exclude.[2]

Thus, we begin with a concept not easily defined. The use of civil society as a universal measurement for the health and activity of civic life in a given state should make us uneasy at the very least. Attempting to define what civil society *is*, a far more difficult project than ascertaining what it is not, we can look at the following definition from Stanford Political Science professor Larry Diamond, at least as a start:

> The realm of organized social life that is voluntary, self-generating, (largely) self-supporting, autonomous from the state, and bound by a legal order or set of shared rules. It is distinct from "society" in general in that it involves citizens acting collectively in a public sphere to express their interests, passions, and ideas, exchange information, achieve mutual goals, make demands on the state and hold state officials accountable. "Civil Society" is an intermediary entity, standing between the private sphere and the state.[3]

We have seen an increase in scholarship that recognizes the many types of civil society gaining momentum in the Middle East, including Egypt, Jordan, Lebanon, Morocco, Palestine, Turkey, and most recently, parts of the Gulf.[4] This literature seeks not only to affirm the existence of civil society in the region, but also to critique mainstream discourses that claim an absence or incompatibility of civil society in the Muslim world (such as those manifested by policies seen in the TIP that eclipse the activism of these groups.

Any discourse on civil society must include the unique historical trajectories and demographic realities of the Arab Gulf states.[5] To discuss the relationship between citizen and state in the UAE, or any of the Arab Gulf countries, compels us to examine the shifting and unstable meanings of *nation*, *state*, and *citizen* in today's world, and the significant population that falls in uncomfortable in-between categories. The classical view of the nation-state and its citizen population must be modified to account for a state like the UAE in which large segments of the resident population are intentionally excluded from the full rights of citizenship.[6] If civil society is defined in terms of the state, we must ask, what is a state? And what is a likely profile of its citizens? In a country where 80 percent of the population is composed of noncitizens, often transitory, the creation of civil society faces the added challenge of building a movement for constituents who do not enjoy full rights of citizenship.

The relationship between civil society and the state is a two-way street. Those who champion a particularly EuroAmerican vision of civil society—namely, evidenced by the quantity of NGOs in a society—as a necessary foundation of democratization and who view the growth of civil society as an indication of major political change in the Arab world, would do well to remember that the link between civil society and the state is not necessarily defined by opposition and competition. Though civil society functions as a check on state power, it also depends on the legal protection of the state in order to survive. My fieldwork demonstrated and reinforced this point: the groups with the most promising, most developed networks of action and influence were those that remained on good terms with the state; they were the organizations that sought not to overtly criticize the government, but rather to work within the parameters of state power. While the efforts of these civil society pioneers remain, in a certain sense of the word, political, they strove to actively avoid the demonization of the state in their work and in public messaging campaigns.

It is of no small significance that many informal groups have had success in revising aspects of the UAE's approach to migration and rights. Their missions invariably centered on providing social services to persons in need rather than actively criticizing the government for its shortcomings; however, they have made great progress in changing state regulations and approaches to migrant labor (examples include the new UAE initiative to train members of law enforcement[7] as well as the law prohibiting construction laborers from working between the hours of 12:30 and 3 p.m., the hottest hours of the day[8]). While the political structure of the UAE is in no way democratic, and indeed the UAE shows fewer signs of moving toward any type of significant political change or liberalization than many of its Gulf neighbors, there are those who point to its unique political workings as the source of its almost unparalleled stability and prosperity, characteristics that individuals involved in civil society efforts have been utilizing to the best of their ability with increasing success.

While nongovernmental organizations can serve as valid indicators of growing civil society and progress along the path to democratization, they do not necessarily demonstrate either. Conversely, a lack of NGOs does not necessarily illustrate a lack of activity or development within the civil realm. In the United States, NGOs file for what is called 501c3 tax status. This delineation goes hand in hand with fundraising efforts by offering Americans the incentive to use their donations as tax write-offs. In the UAE, the religious tradition of *zakat* (the obligation to donate a fixed percentage of one's income) is widely practiced by Muslims and Muslim-owned businesses; taxes are thus conceptualized within the framework of religious duty and ethical obligation. Because *zakat* is seen as a pious duty not to be shirked, the concept of tax write-offs does not offer the same lure as in the West.

Because the dominant discourse on civil society takes the EuroAmerican concepts of the state, citizen, democracy, and social service provision as its cornerstone, the evolving civil society within the UAE is not noticed by policymakers such as the authors of the TIP. Informal efforts of groups of noncitizens seeking to provide outreach to other noncitizens, and groups whose main fundraising efforts stem from *zakat* funds, fall outside the standard paradigm and are thus not counted as civil society. The narrow framework presented by the dominant discourse has blinded policymakers to the efforts of a hard-working group of people who are building civil society in the UAE, have had some success in reforming and creating labor laws and protections, and are urgently in need of support. By ignoring their efforts, calling for state involvement in anti-trafficking efforts, and continuing to judge countries like the UAE for a purported lack of civil society, the work of people like Sama is made more difficult. The TIP has an unparalleled opportunity to encourage the UAE to formally register these informal groups, thereby giving them legitimacy in the eyes of the state, each other, and their constituents. For this to occur, policymakers and discourse producers must begin to grasp the magnitude of civil society efforts and challenges currently taking place in-country. I will begin here by chronicling the trajectory of this movement, how it began, major obstacles it has faced, and the direction in which it is now moving. Like the stories of the many migrants I interviewed, these stories highlight ways in which policies that ignore the existence of civil society in the UAE are not serving the needs of the target populations.

Early Efforts

As the UAE was developing rapidly after the discovery of oil and the emergence of Dubai as a major trading and financial hub in the Middle East, several informal groups began forming to address the needs of migrant workers in the UAE. In the late 1980s and early 1990s, expatriates from different ethnic, religious, and socioeconomic backgrounds came together with Emiratis to begin creating networks and building civil society initiatives to address labor standards and the lack of social services to meet the needs of non-Emiratis. These early gatherings laid the groundwork for four organizations, Valley of Love, Helping Hands, Villa 25, and City of Hope,[9] two of which continue to operate in the UAE to this day. These four groups have yet to receive official NGO status in the UAE, yet their members were among the first to pursue (and indeed create) avenues through civil society in order to address what they perceived as unmet needs in the UAE. They have each played an important role in interacting with the state on the issue of migrants' rights, and members of these organizations have been instrumental in lobbying the state to implement new labor laws and protections.[10]

Valley of Love

Valley of Love was created in an informal and spontaneous manner; eight volunteers—Indian, Pakistani, and British—united by their shared concern for a group of female laborers abandoned at a factory that closed down unexpectedly without providing any assistance to its workers, decided to organize and (re)act. Vasu, one of the directors of Valley of Love, is very vocal and animated about the aims of his group, which according to their mission statement, are as follows:

> A non-profit social and voluntary organization that is committed to humanity. Valley of Love was formed in the UAE in 1998, with the mission to offer assistance, solace and hope for anyone in need, irrespective of nationality, caste, creed or religion. Valley of Love volunteers regularly visit prison inmates, hospitals and labor camps, organize charity drives and blood donation camps, while coordinating with government agencies, hospital authorities and consulates to better the quality of human life for poor expatriate workers in the UAE.

Vasu works for the government of Dubai by day and engages in volunteer work in the evenings. He explained during an interview that he had taken the government job precisely because its flexible hours allowed him the time he needed to do volunteer work, his passion. In addition, he noted that being a government employee allowed him to lobby the government more easily for the types of migrants' rights that his organization supports. Vasu quickly became an important resource for us and provided us with stacks of literature about his organization and others with whom they had been working.

A handsome man in his early forties, Vasu wore a sharp suit and crisp blue shirt, his stylish short brown hair flecked with gray and complemented by a spot of facial hair on his chin. Born and raised in Calcutta, he said that his experience working in civil society in India, growing up in "the land of Mother Teresa," inspired him to pursue humanitarian work with Indian migrants in need in Dubai while fulfilling a teaching position. He sat down and was eager, albeit cautious, to tell the story of Valley of Love from the beginning.

> Ten years ago there was a company in Sharjah [another UAE emirate], that was closing down. And the women who were working the factory there, their

AN(UN)CIVIL SOCIETY   157

jobs were being affected because the owners just ran away and left all 250 of them, abandoned them. And so, a couple of friends got together and they mobilized support and they managed to find jobs for some of the women and they managed to arrange transportation back to their home countries. So this group of eight friends, after successfully doing this humanitarian work, they decided to carry on with it and that's how Valley of Love formed.

The organization started meeting informally in a living room in the mid-1990s. Its name, chosen from a Hindi proverb, came soon after in 1998. While originally formed to aid a group of unemployed women laborers, today, interestingly, they serve mostly men, mainly from Bangladesh, India, Pakistan, and Sri Lanka. But Vasu emphasized that they would like to work with women.

> It's a very sensitive thing to talk about or to recommend or bring out into the open typical domestic issues dealing with women, which are very private here. A labor issue is not something that is a household thing. It's more of a work-related thing. So, from that point of view, we have been luckier dealing with those topics and those issues.

Organizations that work with women perceived as victims of sex trafficking in the post-TIP era are under increased scrutiny from the state. At the same time, the very policies and TIP recommendations that largely exclude men and ignore abuses to migrants outside the sex industry make it easier to provide outreach to these populations, as organizations that do so escape notice by the state, now myopically vested in combating sex trafficking.

Valley of Love supports itself through private, individual donations, but because it is not an official organization, the members do not hold formal fundraising efforts for fear of financial complications or corruption. As Vasu explains:

> We help people who have faced abuse, absconded from their jobs, or not been paid, and people who have health problems or are in jail. We even take care of dead bodies and make sure their remains get home, we are mostly trying to help people who want to go home.

Today, Valley of Love counts over seventy on-call volunteers, but the organization operates day to day on a very informal, as-needed basis. "Okay, we don't have a very [laughs] . . . a very thought-out strategy or any kind of fancy thing like that. We operate on a crisis mode on a daily basis," says Vasu, running a hand through his salt-and-pepper hair.

> So, because we're operating this typical crisis mode on a day-to-day way, someone is in serious problem and needs help, we're just rushing around doing things like that. So, we haven't had a chance to, okay, find a way to become solidified and official, but we are doing the best we can to help as many people as possible.

Valley of Love's major mode of operating is to distribute its phone numbers at labor camps and to managers of construction sites. Migrants in need can then call VoL's hotline, and one of the volunteers will take their information, assess their needs, and then assemble a team of people to respond. Most often they raise money and provide transportation to local hospitals in the case of health emergencies. They also raise money to purchase return tickets for migrants who have become unemployed or who wish to return home. Several volunteers also provide legal services to help process visas, during court cases, or to negotiate withheld wages. On occasion, Valley of Love volunteers also provide housing and food outreach. In addition, members of the group have been active in lobbying the UAE government to implement new laws protecting migrant workers, such as the law that was passed preventing employers from withholding employee passports.[11] "We basically do everything that the laborers need us to do," explained Vasu.

> One day that might mean taking someone to a hospital, another day it might mean helping someone get a ticket to return home. We are very busy, as you can imagine. There are lots of laborers here with lots of needs, we just respond to their needs as best we can using our network.

Helping Hands

Helping Hands also developed out of a series of small informal gatherings that grew into a larger organization and which continues to function on an ad hoc basis today. Helping Hands was founded by a British husband and wife team, Richard and Elizabeth, and a few of their friends. Richard and Elizabeth are in their mid-sixties and have been living outside the United Kingdom since 1972. After living in Nigeria, the Republic of Niger, and Bahrain, they moved to the UAE in the early 1990s, where Richard took a position as a real estate manager. A fashionably dressed woman with shoulder-length blonde hair, Elizabeth emphasizes that she has long been dedicated to providing outreach to those in need, wherever she goes. In the early 1990s, Richard, Elizabeth, and some of their friends began having conversations about how they might provide outreach to migrants in Dubai to provide basic needs as well as assist those who wanted to return to their home countries. By October of 2006, Helping Hands became a formal group (registered in Europe), and today has over one hundred volunteers and receives support from international groups such as Hyder, Madinat Jumeriah, and other local and global financial organizations.

The work of Helping Hands focuses on matching interested donors with third parties who are in need. Volunteers use their social networks to raise money and also seek out migrant laborers who are in need of food, housing, or financial assistance. Sometimes the group provides housing by placing migrant workers in the homes of interested volunteers, other times money is raised to purchase a return ticket home. While the organization has been growing each year and helping more and more migrant workers in need, Elizabeth says that they worry how they will be able to survive the financial crisis. Additionally, while the state knows of their operations and on occasion calls on them for assistance, Helping Hands, like Valley of Love, does not hold official status as an NGO in the UAE, which hinders much of their activity; namely, their ability to officially fundraise on a global level, apply for grants, or publicize or promote awareness in Dubai.

Villa 25 and City of Hope

Villa 25 began in the living room of an American-born woman, Susannah, living in the southern part of Dubai. Susannah had married an Emirati citizen in the 1980s and moved to Dubai to join him. A decade later, she and eight other women all living in Jumeirah 1 (near the famed Jumeirah Beach) came together to address the needs of local and nonlocal women in the UAE facing domestic violence and other forms of abuse. They were interested in building civil society from the ground up.

While none of the founders had backgrounds in social work or psychological counseling, they resolved to set up a private shelter for "women and children who were victims of domestic violence or any kind of abuse," Susannah explained. They decided they would pool their funds and purchase a villa near Jumeirah Beach. This villa would serve as a safe house for abused women and would be staffed on a rotating basis by the volunteers. After purchasing a seven-bedroom home two miles from the beach, they named their informal group after their new property, Villa 25. When the villa immediately filled with women seeking assistance and refuge, the cofounders were ecstatic and began thinking of ways to expand their work and build a movement. Wary of what a confrontational approach might cost their cause, and wanting to be culturally sensitive to their environment, Susannah's eight women cofounders—three British, two South African, two Emirati, and one Australian—indicated that they did not wish to publicize their work, but rather to take the approach of their colleagues at Valley of Love and quietly solicit individual funding while lobbying the government from within and assisting as many women as possible.

Susannah disagreed. She felt that it was important to go beyond creating a shelter; that raising global awareness about injustices taking place locally should be a part of their mandate. "They want me to be quiet, they want me to shut up and be okay with the way things are here, and I can't do it. I want to get justice for my girls! I want vengeance!" she exclaimed when telling us the story of her split from the other group. This was the beginning of Susannah's crusade to attack the Emirati government and begin publicly campaigning against human rights abuses, which Susannah pinned on the state.

Her former cofounders did not approve of Susannah's tactics. "It's not the work I disagree with, it was her approach," explained Rania, one of the Emirati women and a former colleague of Susannah's who now works with the official government shelter in Abu Dhabi. "It was very American of her to throw her weight around and assume that because she was a white woman she knew best."

Another former colleague, a British woman named Sharon, echoed Rania's sentiment, "Yeah, Susannah was just too confrontational. That's what it was. She was the cause's worst enemy. She couldn't just quietly provide services to people, or try to work from within, she had to rock the boat, and that was what I didn't like, it's what ultimately made me stop working with her." Sharon noted that she agreed with Susannah's passion, but felt that her approach would not work in terms of achieving change vis-à-vis the state.

After a series of disagreements between Susannah and some of her colleagues, Susannah split off to start her own shelter, City of Hope, a completely distinct entity from Villa 25. Both shelters remained open until 2007, when the UAE government stepped in to close them down, accusing all the volunteers of harboring illegal immigrants, at best, and, at worst, running a brothel and "selling women."[12] Susannah's cofounders who stayed on at Villa 25 maintain

that it was because of Susannah's overly confrontational and accusatory de-
meanor and her campaign to mobilize against the state that the organizations
were disbanded. They pointed to the success of their friends at Valley of Love
and the more recent efforts of individuals like Sama who have managed to
call attention to the issues in a less offensive way. Susannah's colleagues now
express frustration at the dissolution of their organization, blaming her for
their failure.

Susannah was further marginalized within the informal efforts at civil
society building when she received sponsorship and funding through the
Middle East Partnership Initiative (MEPI). Initially supervised by members
of the Cheney family and operated by the U.S. State Department, MEPI began
a partnership with Susannah to support her endeavors and to instruct her
about anti-trafficking protocol (heavily influenced by Bush-era anti-prostitution approaches to trafficking). One of the major problems with this approach
was that many in the UAE felt that the United States was "meddling in our affairs," as Rania's assistant Safa told me. Susannah was also not trained to run
this kind of shelter, and over the years compromised the efficacy and safety
of her shelter by increasingly seeking out media exposure. Her vocal and in-
flammatory criticisms, exacerbated by her coupling with MEPI (the subject
of dubious scrutiny by many in the local population), directly contributed
to very public (and in the eyes of the local community, scandalous) confron-
tations with the UAE government and other members of the emerging civil
society. After several months of training by MEPI, Susannah had perfected
a rehearsed narrative describing her work, which she gave to us at least five
times in two months:

> I am, overall, a human rights activist. I look at cases of statelessness. I look
> after cases of human trafficking. I look after cases of abuse: housemaid abuse,
> labor problems. I look after cases of . . . any child abuse, domestic violence.
> Any kind of human suffering which is taking rights away. That is my man-
> date. There's a lot going on. Always. And, I moved here twenty-five years ago,
> and it was a very docile place. And from a very docile, sweet, innocent little
> neighborhood, it's become a target for exploitation, many times unbeknownst
> to its own citizens, unbeknownst to its own leaders. Because these people are
> doing this for the first time. They're inexperienced. Quite frankly, all of this
> [gestures to "Dubai"] can be purchased. All of this can be purchased! Social
> development takes a lot of expertise and a lot of grassroots information. And
> a lot of unity. Use the people who are down here working among the people in

trouble to get your information. If you're inexperienced, you're going to think that you can do the same thing that you did to do all this, build all this, create all this . . . you're gonna think, you're gonna imagine in your la-la land that you can actually do that same thing by making "human rights departments" and "social support centers," and the Dubai Foundation for Women and Children, and it's all bullshit. It has no . . . no knowledge. No foundation. Nothing. I don't know how they're going to do it without actually researching. Without talking to *me!* Without getting to know *me!* Without sitting me down and saying "What have you got here?" How are they gonna do it?! Magic wand?

In 2007, the government initiated efforts to shut down City of Hope, an action supported by many locals and nonlocals alike in the UAE. To be sure, Susannah was not aware of the ramifications of her desire to make gross human rights violations into a public action campaign. She was passionate about what she viewed as grave injustices and wanted to raise awareness by accusing the state, an action that was neither productive nor accurate. Her approach turned out to be very costly for her in that not only was she unable to achieve any gains in addressing the needs of abused women, but she was also marginalized by her community and then exiled from the UAE (she now lives in the United States and cannot return to the UAE under any condition). In response to what she referred to as a "defamation" campaign, Susannah told us:

The public is made up of the majority of investors and international community who get it, who love it. Who's opposed to me? A few police officers, with husbands, with a few people in the court. A few mullahs. Traffickers. That's my opposition. That's pretty big. That's where all the defamation is coming from. Because journalists, police, the CEO of the new foundation for women and children, the chairwoman of the new foundation are against me, because I know things. Because I know too much. Way too much. And because I've got information, they've got to destroy my credibility so that if I ever do come out with that information nobody's gonna take it. But, what I did is get a buffer of protection around me before they could actually do that. It's kind of like, okay, I've already been . . . it's already been covered by BBC and CNN and *al-Jazeera* and *al-Wabiya*, and it's already been in the *Washington Post, New York Times*, the *New Yorker, Time Magazine*. It's already been for years on the desk of Sheikh Khalifa. I've already worked with all of these people to bring an end to the camel jockeys. I've already earned the credibility, but it's been in international [arenas]. It hasn't been national. So these cronies don't realize what's out there, three million people following up on me at home. They don't realize. They live in a bubble. In this shitty little bubble. Their whole world is Dubai. It begins and it ends from Jebel Ali to the sands. That's it. So, if that's their entire world, they're going to stand up and they're going to make a lot of noise against me and against City of Hope. They're going to drag the country through the mud, not realizing what they're doing. When you think about it, you have an English newspaper and an Arabic newspaper. Simultaneously you have bullshit, bam bam bam, in two newspapers. Deh, deh deh deh, for one week! Simultaneously. Okay. The size of Dubai . . . *Emarat Al Youm* compared to the *New York Times, New Yorker, Time*, BBC . . . like I care. Like I give a shit. *Gulf News! Gulf News* compared to NYT, NY, BBC, *al-Jazeera, al-Wabiyah*. Now, what we've got. I've got an international cry for a boycott of *Gulf News*. I'm putting it out there to everybody, boycott *Gulf News*. You spread it! Don't click onto *Gulf News*. Don't buy it. Don't open it. Don't read it.

By 2009, City of Hope had been completely shut down, and Susannah and her codirector, an Ethiopian woman who lived in Dubai and the United States, had been banned from returning to the UAE. Several accusations were leveled against them, chiefly that they were not, in fact, trying to help the women they were sheltering, but rather using them to attract media attention. At least five of our interviews with other civil society activists reinforced this allegation. The public alliance between Susannah and MEPI led to increasingly widespread antagonism toward MEPI and the United States, in that many City of Hope volunteers as well as state officials felt that the United States was supporting the wrong woman for the job. Those committed to this civil society project expressed dismay at facing yet another hurdle, for which they felt America was largely responsible, one that uncontrollably sensationalized their cause, tarnished the validity of the campaign, and mired the grassroots type of movement they were trying to build in dirty political mudslinging.

▪ ▪ ▪

In the wake of the global moral panic about sex trafficking commencing in 2001, the UAE turned its efforts toward state involvement in fighting sex trafficking. An unfortunate side effect of these efforts was that organizations seeking to provide outreach to abused women came under harsher scrutiny. The result was that City of Hope and Villa 25 were shut down, Valley of Love changed its mandate to work exclusively with male laborers (stating that they felt it was safer and would be a more productive pursuit, as abused men and male migrants in need of services were not considered trafficked), and Helping Hands turned its efforts to hunger issues, providing food to the needy under the umbrella of church outreach. The larger civil society movement lost considerable momentum, significantly hindered by tensions between the different groups, and only began to regain its former pace in late 2007 and early 2008.

Local Responses to Global Policies

In response to the creation of the first TIP report in 2001 when the UAE was given a Tier 3 ranking, the UAE rushed to pass legislation theoretically aimed at preventing the forced movement of people within its borders. Practically, however, this meant that the state was obliged, on the defensive, to acknowledge its responsibility and to prove its ability to handle and respond to its classification as a trafficking hotspot. The TIP specifically recommends that the UAE "tighten borders" and "increase police" while curiously neglecting year after year to mention any existence of or merit to be found in civil society–centered approaches. The state has responded to the international community's call to take full control of the campaign against human trafficking (based on the presumption that it has the capacity to do so), while ignoring or co-opting the actions of informal groups that had been organizing around these issues and assimilating them within a national plan of action.

State involvement in curbing trafficking has been established through two official organizations: the Dubai Foundation for Women and Children, and a yet-unnamed shelter operated through the Red Crescent in Abu Dhabi. Simultaneously, the state has refused to grant official recognition to the informal groups already working on these issues. Many of my interviewees described frustration over the state responses to international policies and discourses around trafficking that have detracted from existing movements pushing for migrants' rights, and do not provide recognition for the efforts of informal activists in lobbying for reform. Randa, a Palestinian-American human rights lawyer and former volunteer for City of Hope who now lives in Dubai, had this to say:

> The problem is that the trafficking issue and sex trafficking got elevated to the political level. . . . the Bush Administration made all this stuff political, so anyone working on trafficking was under heightened scrutiny. I feel like they did more to harm this cause than anyone else. People here were trying to build

a movement, we were trying to do something about abuses to migrants, and trying to help women, but they stifled it.

When Randa stopped her work with City of Hope, she moved to an apartment south of the Marina to "be away from all the chaos of that drama," as she said one afternoon at a local Coffee Bean. She believes that global policies that mobilize moral panic over sex trafficking, such as those advanced by the TIP, are the greatest barrier to the establishment of a strong civil society response in the UAE. "I left City of Hope because I got tired," Randa said, scooping up her two-year-old son as she talked about her former work volunteering for the organization. The little boy was wearing a UC Berkeley bib that Randa told me she bought while in graduate school. His long brown hair flopped over his eyes, which were the same chocolate brown as his mother's, as he rubbed them. Randa gave him a kiss as he whispered, "I'm tired." Randa looked from her son to me, "I'm tired too, but in a different way," she said. "I got tired fighting the Americans and the Emiratis who made it so much harder to provide outreach."

Like Sama, who expressed fatigue at trying to continue outreach efforts for Ethiopian women who have been abused, Randa expressed fatigue and frustration at wanting to build a civil society momentum but being hindered by the policies espoused by the TIP embodying a discourse that continues to judge the UAE for inadequate civil society responses while ignoring the efforts of organizations such as hers. Sama had echoed Randa's sentiments: "Migration and trafficking, those were *the* issues that a lot of people were mobilizing around, and then they became political because of the Bush Administration, and it made it hard to come together around this. And also it became harder to have a healthy movement."

Randa and Sama both expressed feelings that the Bush Administration and sensationalism over sex trafficking, which they equated as synonymous, were responsible for damaging the emergent civil society–based approach to migration and trafficking in the UAE. According to Randa, Sama, and at least three other civil society activists, the political potency of migration and human trafficking poisoned civil society efforts in the UAE in three main ways: (1) through the pointed politicization of the issue that brought migrant women under unprecedented scrutiny; (2) through TIP rankings of the UAE and other Arab countries, which spurred unanticipated state involvement in the hitherto organic, resident-directed movement to address the egregious lack of social support systems; and (3) through the strategic use of scholarly

research on the presumed absence of civil society in the Gulf to demonstrate
the UAE's inability and noncompliance in dealing with the trafficking issue.

"What bothers me most about the TIP," sighed Randa, adjusting her
brown head scarf and smoothing down her matching brown *abaya*, "is that
the Bush Administration was after a bilateral trade agreement (the 123 Agreement referenced earlier) that would get them a better trading deal with the
UAE, so they manipulated the trafficking issue to negotiate a better deal."
Though the TVPA was signed into effect under President Clinton, and though
many of the challenges to migrants' rights predate the Bush Administration,
what Randa and others alluded to was that the moral panic around human
trafficking that was fueled and gained momentum under the Bush Administration, weakened the momentum for a process that many activists were
working hard to set into motion.

Chris and I sat with her for a few moments, processing her comments,
until the silence was pierced by the giggle of Randa's son as he poured his
orange juice almost in his mother's lap. Randa picked him up and moved him
to the corner of her living room before returning to continue. She took a deep
breath and, becoming more animated and agitated, added:

> Well, it also really bugs me that it seems like the TIP has an imperialist agenda.
> I mean it's a good thing to have human rights standards, but we must take into
> account how people come to those organically. In order for some feminists in
> the West to have their rhetoric, they must understand that some trafficking
> rhetoric is based on Western experiences and this rhetoric can be very conde-
> scending. I'm sorry, but that's how I feel!

Her son waddled over and dumped his crayons into Randa's teacup, which
punctuated her point.

Lila and Iman, two Emirati women who donate money to various informal groups working with migrants as well as to the current state-sponsored
efforts to combat trafficking, took Randa's sentiments one step further. When
I interviewed them at a café in Abu Dhabi, the conversation began quietly
enough; both spoke in low tones and Lila glanced over her shoulder every
few moments, partly to ensure that no one was listening but partly, as she
explained, "to make sure I'm not bothering people who are here trying to
enjoy a cup of tea." The quiet tones, however, dissipated once we began talking about civil society and the role of American policies such as those in the
TIP in helping or hindering a civil society movement in the UAE. Pushing

back the sleeves of her long black *abaya* so that she could gesture emphatically with her hands, Lila began talking about the reasons she believed that people in America react to Dubai the way they do:

> It's like this, like they couldn't conceptualize an Arab Muslim country do-
> ing so well, developing so rapidly and so successfully, and even having civil
> society, like it didn't fit into their little box that they had drawn about us.
> Now with things going a bit differently, they are so excited to point to us and
> our problems and say, "See, I knew they couldn't be doing that well, or if they
> were, they did it in a sneaky and backward way." Like it's because since *they*
> didn't anticipate it, and that it didn't fit into their box, they are doubly happy
> to see us struggle. They point to us and say that we have a trafficking problem,
> that we don't have civil society. They want to see us fail. They want to keep us
> down somehow.

Her friend Iman continued, also becoming very animated to the point where her head scarf actually began slipping off:

> They want to blame everything on Islam, they want to use something, to find
> something to point to the fact that [we] Muslims, there is something wrong
> with us, that we need to learn to be better, that we can't figure out our own
> way forward. I'm so tired of people trying to save us. Save us from whom? And
> from what? Oh the poor Muslim women. You know what? I feel sorry for the
> poor Western women who don't know anything. Tell them to get off our backs!

Certainly, the Emirati state apparatus is not blameless in tolerating the crippled status of civil society and the scarcity of outreach programs. However, before the trafficking issue took center stage, a number of organically sprung initiatives had been slowly strengthening civil society and building a labor and migrants' rights movement in the UAE. Not only was the government open to recognizing and working with these informal groups, but it was also considering a reform of the *kefala* system similar to Bahrain's. Randa, Lila, and Iman's comments reinforce the ways in which global discourse and policies have put the brakes on these initiatives while simultaneously casting the UAE in a negative light. Iman was passionate in conveying her frustration at how the UAE and Arab Muslim world in general had been tarnished in the academic and political discourse in EuroAmerica. She felt it was unfair that the UAE was accused of having a trafficking problem it could not grapple with when she knew from personal experience that various civil society attempts to address these issues had been squelched by the state precisely because of the rhetoric as laid out in the TIP.

● ● ●

One of the state responses to the TIP reports included opening a state-sponsored women's shelter, the Dubai Foundation for Women and Children (DFWAC). According to one official there, the reason they focus their energies on women, and primarily on women in the sex industry, is because "we modeled our organization on a series of groups in the U.S., and a bunch of people from the University of Texas who taught us combat skills in the war on trafficking." Several problems plagued the shelter, however, stemming from the stipulations that it serve only women who were "victims of sex trafficking" and that women had to be referred by the police in order to receive assistance. Consequently, law enforcement would sometimes resort to raiding brothels and rounding up sex workers in order to fill the halls of DFWAC's empty rooms. Moreover, the organization did not properly or effectively develop a caseworker system, neglecting to facilitate visa processing, passport retrieval, or legal counsel while favoring deportation as its principal strategy, a process aided by a well-documented and much-maligned lack of transparency. After repeated efforts to visit the DFWAC, I was only allowed to interview the officials by phone. Spokespersons indicated that the foundation was not yet ready (despite being three years old), to receive visitors.

Puzzled by the lack of access permitted by DFWAC, I decided to contact Rania, the Emirati cofounder of Villa 25 who now works with a government-sponsored shelter in Abu Dhabi. After talking with her, the DFWAC's no-visitor policy seemed justified:

> Look, the thing about the DFWAC, and even our shelter in Abu Dhabi is that we have all bitten off more than we can chew. This is a complicated situation, and they [the government] have put a lot in our laps, and we don't really know the best way to move forward, even though we want to help.

Later, Rania added that she relies on the informal network of ad hoc organizations that have sprung up in recent years to address the issue:

> We are a government organization, but at least on our end we rely on the people on the ground, the people who know how to do their work. I guess we are relying on the civil society. Even though we don't have official NGOs like in the U.S., I feel we do have civil society, and we rely on them.

The Campaign to Promote
Civil Society Perseveres

In 2001 the government began working toward state-level responses to the trafficking issue, as exemplified by the creation of the DFWAC. By 2007 it became apparent to a number of activists and volunteers that the government-run organizations were not adequately addressing the basic needs of certain vulnerable populations. The sheer visibility of this breakdown independently mobilized individuals and loosely bound groups to actively address the issues facing migrant men and women. This time, however, the mobilization would begin in an underground fashion, with a quiet, demure character that the typical evaluation criteria for civil society growth might fail to recognize. Since 2007, several informal networks of individuals or groups working to help migrants in a variety of capacities have reemerged within a very limited public sphere. Among their greatest challenges is their inability to become officially recognized NGOs and thus raise legal, legitimate voices to hold the government (and each other) accountable for their actions.

By late 2007 and early 2008, another wave of expatriates began organizing to address the unmet needs of various migrant communities. "When it became clear that the government wasn't delivering on what they promised, what they were supposed to be doing, we stepped up our work," explained Sama, whose activism increased in 2007. A new series of individuals and groups began assembling once more to create ad hoc organizations. They found creative ways to provide outreach to marginalized migrant populations and looked to building a civil society movement that could work with the state. Three years later, it is evident that they have had some success in lobbying state institutions; however, they remain unofficial.

Mustafa

The first time my students and I met Mustafa, founder of "Take My Junk UAE," we understood immediately what had earned him the nickname of the Robin Hood of Dubai. We walked into an alleyway between two towering apartment buildings to find a young Pakistani man with a long beard and slight eyes, who was simultaneously talking on the phone, carrying a chipped wooden table to his makeshift freight truck, and herding us in his direction.

"You see this stuff," he said, motioning to an IKEA bed frame in his truck and the coffee table in his hand. "The people who live in these buildings, the rich people, they think this stuff is junk, but to laborers, and the people who

PHOTO 6 Mustafa stands facing the "junk" in his truck. Courtesy of Abby DiCarlo.

built these buildings, this is luxury." He paused to answer a second phone that he fished out of his pocket. "Send me an SMS! Send me an e-mail! Tell me your address, I can't promise anything, but if I can, we'll get there," he shouted into the phone before hanging up to turn back to us.

We stood there quietly in the middle of the chaos that was his four-man operation as they slid past us carrying various household appliances and furniture. "Sorry," Mustafa said putting down the large table he was carrying. "There are about two hundred people a day leaving Dubai, and they just leave their stuff behind. And it's not just people, but companies, too! Come here, let me show you something," he said, shuffling toward his truck. He opened the rear door so we could get a better look. As we peered inside we saw over two hundred office chairs. I jerked my head back and looked at Mustafa.

"Yeah, those are from Microsoft," he said. He let out a booming laugh as he wiped the sweat from his brow. "All this stuff, there is so much money here, but so much is wasted, so I take from the rich and give to the poor." Robin Hood. With multiple cell phones.

In the ten minutes we had been there, Mustafa had already received ten phone calls. While on the phone this time, one of his Afghan colleagues asked for Mustafa's help in carrying a large dining room table. Mustafa transferred the phone to his left hand and took the other end of the table with his right. One hand on his phone and the other carrying the table, suddenly the second phone started ringing. Mustafa looked at his colleague, then at me. I caught the first phone while he fished out the second to answer it. "He-hello," I stammered, not sure what to do.

"Hello? Salam!" yelled a woman with a South African accent.

"Um, hi," I said, regaining my composure.

"Hey, what the . . . ? You're not the Take My Junk guy!" she barked.

I finally snapped out of it and responded, "No, I'm the Take My Junk girl, how can I help you?" I answered.

"Look, I don't have time for this, I'm leaving, moving out, bye-bye, today. I live in JBR, Amwaj 3, apartment 1605, the door's open, take what you like," she said quickly and hung up. I hurried to write down the address and handed it to Mustafa.

"This is what my life is like here," he sighed. "I can't take all the junk that people leave behind, but I do my best. Then I take all this and distribute it to the laborers in the camps. The nice stuff though I sell to make enough money, just enough, to keep our operation going and to pay these guys." He motioned to the three men who continued filling up the truck.

Mustafa was born to Pakistani parents in Dubai, but grew up in Canada; he moved back to Dubai in 2004 to be closer to his family who now lived in Karachi. He first had the idea to do this kind of work when he was distributing food to the migrant workers in labor camps during Ramadan. "I would go to the camps and see the really difficult conditions the men were living in, and I realized I had to do something to help," said Mustafa, between phone calls yet again.

Just then, a European-looking young man walked up to us carrying a camera. Mustafa turned his back. "No pictures of our faces!" he yelled. The journalist, who introduced himself as Thomas from Britain, put the camera down. "No pictures, and no recording my voice, but ask as many questions as you want," Mustafa told Thomas.

"It must be hard doing the work you do," I said to Mustafa, suddenly realizing that what he was doing was also probably sensitive in that the government was wary of public awareness campaigns to assist migrant workers. This must have been the reason he didn't want the journalist to take his picture.

"Yes, and no. It's rewarding, I love doing this, and you know, it makes sense. Everyone wins with the kind of work I'm doing here." He walked away from the journalist who was busy taking pictures of Mustafa's truck.

"But is the government OK with what you are doing?" I asked him, remembering that only a few months ago a Fulbright scholar from the United States had been removed from the UAE because the government found out she had visited a labor camp. Mustafa responded quietly:

> I'm not sure, I mean, I don't understand it; the locals think what I do is funny, like ridiculous, but why? It's not so different from the Salvation Army, and it's environmentally friendly, I mean you'd think everyone wins here, and it's improving the image of Dubai, which is what they are all about. But I don't know, I have to be careful, I can't take any chances. That's why I just work with men in labor camps whose supervisors I know from my local mosque. I can't take any chances, but I don't think what I'm doing is wrong.

Dr. Suparna

Across town in the part of Dubai sometimes affectionately referred to as Little Kerala, Dr. Suparna's office is located above a South Indian restaurant in Karama, Dubai's predominantly Indian neighborhood. The staircase leading to her office is filled with male laborers, many who are injured or ill like Ravi, some resting quietly in the shade, waiting for Dr. Suparna to find them a ticket to send them home. As we sit waiting in her office, several of the male laborers, such as Nitin, who have become volunteers at Dr. Suparna's clinic-turned-shelter invite us to view numerous albums filled with pictures of her helping to feed, treat, and provide outreach to various groups of male laborers over the years.

After a few minutes, Dr. Suparna walks in quietly with a smile on her face. She is wearing a bright green sari with gold trim over which she drapes a white lab coat. She radiates a quiet calmness about her that instantly fills the room.

"I moved here from Hyderabad a few years ago," she began. Her voice was so soft it hardly registered above a whisper, and we had to lean in to ensure that we caught every word. "When I came, well I am trained as a gynie [gynecologist], and I came to provide services to my gynie patients," she said, fighting the fatigue weighing down her eyelids. "Then I saw them, I met them, the homeless men, the laborers who come here, from my hometown and other places, and who have problems, who don't have food, who want to go home, and I knew I had to help."

Several times throughout our visit, various volunteers would walk into the room, greet us, and then return to the waiting room that had become a make-shift shelter as they awaited treatment or food or, for some, a ticket back to India.

"I began by preparing food for them. . . . What I do is I wake up every morning at 2 a.m., I feel that this is the nectar hour, the time when one can be closer to God. And I wake up then, that is when my day begins," she told us, closing her eyes and seemingly entering into a meditative trance for a few short moments before returning to our conversation. She then told us that after a few months of providing male laborers with needed food, she quickly realized that many needed medical attention as well. "They have all sorts of medical conditions, and sometimes accidents on the job. Some have diabetes, some break bones, some have depression and kill themselves," she said. She pulled out a photograph of a young man who was wearing casts on both of his legs while his arm was in a sling. This man, she explained, had been injured on the job and then lost his job when his employer decided he didn't want to pay for his treatment. He had sought out Dr. Suparna's help and she had provided him treatment before raising the necessary funds to send him back to India. The next picture was of Dr. Suparna cooking food and handing it out to seemingly endless lines of male migrant workers.

"How do you get your funding? How do you support yourself?" I asked her.

She told us that she also treats patients for money, and she uses the money from her wealthier patients to treat and provide food for the men who cannot afford it. "And many of my patients, they are good people," she explained. "They come to the clinic, they see the men, and they give us money to send them home."

Dr. Suparna then pulled out another binder filled with photographs of men she has sent home, accompanied by letters from their sponsors. She explains it as a matching service: she matches the willing donors with the laborers who need the money to go home.

> It is when they reach a point of desperation that they come to me, either mentally distraught or in a very sick state. I started helping these people by

providing food and medicines. But today, I also help them prepare their out-passes and get their tickets sponsored. When some of these laborers die, I make arrangements to send their bodies back home to their families.

Dr. Suparna pointed to a hand-drawn sketch of her ideas and explained that the problems of illegal migrants are all interconnected. Health problems can stem from and be the reason for employment tangles and the withholding of pay, which distresses migrant workers further.

> And I work on their cases. I try to help them in every way. Many want to go home so I do that, I help them. I believe in the WHO [World Health Organization] definition of health as a complete state of mental and physical well-being. I am doing this to get people to that state. If it means food, okay I give food. If it means counseling, okay I do that. If they want to go home, I send them home.

When asked if the government of the UAE is aware of her activities, she nodded and told us that they also call on her for assistance when they find sick laborers or when they need someone to claim a dead body to be sent home.

> But I need money. I am not an official organization, though I have been recognized and honored by being named woman of the year. But if I'm not official, I cannot get funding, and if I cannot get funding, I don't know how long we can go on.

Aleksander and Maria

Unlike Dr. Suparna and Mustafa, Aleksander and his wife Maria focus their work on female migrants in need, almost exclusively from Russian-speaking countries, who have either migrated or been trafficked into the service industry, domestic work, or sex work. A middle-aged man with long silvery hair that he ties back in a ponytail, Aleksander dotes on his wife, Maria, who has a permanently frustrated look on her face. It takes us two days before we can make her laugh, but when she does, her whole body lights up. The pair moved to the UAE in 2000 to work in managerial positions at an oil company located in Sharjah. After a few years of living there, they became heavily involved with their church. Maria eventually quit her job to work full time as a volunteer, helping to publicize church services, selling religious paraphernalia, and assisting the priests with various chores.

In early 2008, Aleksander and Maria became involved in helping Russian-speaking women who were suffering from monetary or health problems, as well as those who wanted to return to their countries of origin. Maria noted that she was dissatisfied with the lack of social services provided to migrants, especially migrant women in the UAE. She also expressed serious dissatisfaction in the way in which the official government shelters were "handling the problem of trafficked women." When we asked Aleksander how he and Maria came to work with these women, he answered casually:

> The answer is very easy. The people came to us, in the church, and said we have this and this problem. It's possible that our priest can help. And we said, okay, go see the priest. And the people went to the priest and told him about the problems they have there, and he said okay, let us pray. After that the people came to us and said, okay, they were praying together, but who is solving all my problems?! [laughs] And so we came into this . . . and after that when we solved the first problems we found out there were people in the jails, we were going to the jails . . . and we were creating there our connections, which are very necessary. And since now, one and a half years, mainline is the work with the victims of human trafficking.

One of the strengths of their approach is that, like Sama and Vasu of Valley of Love, they have built a relationship of trust with some of the immigration officials, as well as with high-ranking police officers and members of the government. We first heard about Aleksander and Maria through conversations with Rania, of the government-sponsored shelter in Abu Dhabi, who indicated that she relies on Aleksander for help with running the government shelter and for assisting her in working with the trafficked women at the shelter.

"I could not do the work I do without Aleksander," Rania had said, handing me a scrap of paper with his name and number scribbled on it. "This man is the real deal," she emphasized. "He is doing the real work, and we truly would be lost without him."

When we asked Aleksander how he operates, he explained that this relationship with the police and immigration officials is essential because it allows them to seek out women in need of services who are being held in the jails or immigration holding centers.

> Our first aim is to solve, to help people to solve their social problems. This is the first thing. The second thing is to identify and to help the victims of human trafficking. So, uh, that means the people knows our telephone numbers. They are calling us and telling us which problems they have. Then we decide

how to help them. And, uh, the second way to get them is, we are visiting regularly different jails in Dubai. That means especially immigration jail where the most, the biggest number of victims in trafficking [are] because they are often without visas. And that means [the police] abandon them in the immigration jails. Or in the police stations where we have also our connections to know.

He noted that much of their work was serving as moderators between Russian-speaking women and the police. He was emphatic that both personal experiences and the broader social histories of their home countries have instilled a profound fear of police forces. This, in the UAE, exacerbates the situations of abused migrants because, first, they are afraid to report abuse to the police, and second, if they are arrested and detained, they are unable to speak to the officers, which leads to severe anxiety.

The police, if they catch them, it's mostly all Russian speaking . . . they are not speaking with the police. They are seeing the police as they enemy. They are not seeing the police as helper because by their experience from the police in their own countries, they are thinking here the same. And sometimes so and sometimes not. And this is also our job to make them to understand they can speak to the police here. They have to go only to the right officer. Each police station you have now an officer, or an office for victims of crime. That's why we are working with them together. If they have some girls there and they cannot speak with them, they call us, and we speak together. In immigration jail also. They have the CID officers in the immigration jail in Jumeirah and they cannot speak Russian. Big problem. We are speaking with them, with the girls, if the CID officers have some questions for them. We are, every week, one or two times in the immigration jail . . . we know each other now. It's our second home! [laughs] No, they accept us because they know we are helping them . . . we are helping the girls. [It is in] their own interest that the girls are going faster through the process.

Aleksander explained that they have a good working relationship with the police and immigration department because the police "don't want to have to deal with these women, with identifying them, with providing them ladies clothing and everything, so we do that." He flashes a wide grin. Aleksander notes that he has had some success with many law enforcement personnel, as well as with the shelter in Abu Dhabi, in that his efforts have resulted in less immediate deportations of Russian-speaking women. "Instead of grabbing them, locking them up, and sending them home, now they call me," Aleksander explains. "Then I pick up the girls and put them with families where they will be safe while they decide what *they* want to do," he adds as Maria rushes to answer one of her three telephones. She looks at me, apologetic, then shrugs and answers the phone, speaking in rapid Russian.

"Our telephone number is famous," says Aleksander, in his thick Russian accent, lighting his fourth cigarette in the last hour. Their phones ring off the hook, and they rush around all day trying to help women solve legal cases or provide them with food or shelter. "When we don't do this, we are working with the government shelters," says Aleksander as Maria hangs up the phone.

At the mention of the government shelter a large scowl crosses her face. She speaks angrily in Russian to Aleksander who translates Maria's frustration to us. "She says she is frustrated with the way the government shelter in Dubai, the DFWAC, operates; they are not good, that they don't help the women, just hold them in cells and send them home without money," he says as she nods emphatically. "But soon we will have our own shelter," they both say. While Aleksander and Maria have had much success in working with the shelter in Abu Dhabi, they note that the DFWAC takes the much harsher stance of raiding, arresting, and deporting (similar to the raid-and-rescue tactics of anti-trafficking groups in the United States who presumably trained DFWAC personnel). Aleksander notes that he has tried to work with members of the DFWAC but has been turned away, as "they don't want to work with small fish or little groups."

Maria tells us she has already made a drawing of what her shelter will look like and how she will run the organization differently. Like Mustafa, Suparna, Vasu, Sama, and others, however, Aleksander and Maria, while working with the government, are not officially recognized and could therefore be punished or shut down at any time, a situation of which they are constantly aware.

"We have to be careful," Aleksander tells us. "We don't talk to journalists, and we have to realize we must do things the Arab way."

Aleksander and Maria are aware that they are working on a sensitive topic, and they do not want to overstep their bounds. But, as Maria reemphasizes, they are not happy with the way the government is approaching the issue, and thus have been quietly lobbying various government agencies from within. They also realize they do not have adequate training to address the many needs of the women they work with, but they feel that, given how much the government relies on them and the fragility of this relationship, they need to become official in order to continue to do their work. "This work is difficult and expensive," explains Aleksander. "Now we are tied to our church, for fundraising and for operating, because we can't have our own group because of the law that bans unions . . . so now we have to go through our church, but it's not easy. Someday we will have our own shelter, you will see."

Common Challenges, Collective Responses

None of the individuals discussed here came to the UAE expecting to be involved in any kind of civil society development efforts. Rather, each had migrated under the auspices of various industries but felt compelled to take action upon witnessing the challenges faced by migrant workers in various settings. No one was trained to do the work they are currently involved in, and almost all of them pointedly articulated a desire to receive further training and education, along with the desire to become "official." Though many work with the government, their presence known, their services utilized, and their suggestions sometimes taken to reform laws and training programs, they remain excluded from any official mechanisms that would allow them to press for accountability from the government or from one another. The same law that prohibits the creation of unions in the UAE has hindered the registration of NGOs as such in the country; while some of the groups have sidestepped this predicament by registering in other countries (such as India or Nepal), others operate on an informal basis, continuing their work in the hopes that the law will be reformed or overturned. The common desire to be officially recognized has emboldened the call for a more formalized civil society in the UAE. As Vasu told us:

> So, actually, we get called upon by government officials to help them with many of these issues. So it's strange because, at the top level we are not officially recognized, but, at an operational level they call upon us. You could say that they're using, misusing us. But, for us, at least we are able to help in some ways.

Indeed, many of these informal groups are called upon for assistance by government entities, without being granted NGO status or given official recognition of any sort. This allows the government to use, or misuse, as Vasu says, these groups, while dangling a carrot over their heads. Because of the intense politicization of the issues they address, many of our contacts face a constant threat of being shut down and have no power to prevent that from happening. Furthermore, the lack of official status bars them from legitimate avenues through which they may formally criticize the government or other institutions. The precariousness of being unsanctioned, ad hoc organizations also complicates fundraising efforts from both the campaigning side and the donating side. Potential donors may hesitate to risk their support due to the possibility of corruption or mismanagement of funds, as well as the potential legal ramifications of being linked to an organization not recognized as official.

All of our interviewees indicated an intense desire to receive training and become official in the eyes of the state. "I have a beautiful letter from DFWAC, a beautiful letter from Rashid Hospital, but I have never gotten official recognition for what I do . . . and I keep asking," said Sama. She explained that the government had called on her to help train law enforcement officials to better interact with migrant women. Though she is proud of her efforts thus far, she is also frustrated at not being able to register officially. "I mean, I want to have official identification, I want to be known; this gives me legal protection." Aleksander echoed her sentiments:

> They NEED us. The shelter in Abu Dhabi is calling us, how we can solve this problem? With who we have to deal with? Because we know. We are longer in the business than they. They have better connections with the ministry, but to the embassy, general consulates, the procedures which they have there, we know. The connections outside, we have . . . but the connections inside, they have. They are official, but we are not. We need to be.

Dr. Suparna and Vasu echoed this. When we asked each of them if they could change one thing about Dubai, they both individually responded that they wished they could make it easier for NGOs or community groups to be recognized so that many more volunteers can work together to build this movement. Formal acknowledgment by the government would convey legitimacy to these organizations and diminish the perceived risk of conducting their work. By refusing to do so, the state continues to evade any sort of relationship that would imply mutual accountability; by failing to "officialize" the organizations, the relationship maintains an exploitative one whose fragility the members of these organizations dare not jeopardize by criticizing the government in any way.

The relationship between the state and civil society is not merely one of aggressor and watchdog; it is a two-way street. Officializing the organizations currently in operation in the Emirates would hold them accountable to UAE law in transparent and standardized ways and allow these organizations to formally hold each other accountable to the same standards.

Perhaps one of the most frequent and disturbing accusations we heard were allegations and documentations of abuse occurring within one particular organization, City of Hope. These allegations, narrated by former volunteers and women who had sought refuge at City of Hope, extended beyond mismanagement or neglect to the actual exploitation (in the form of prostituting and physical abuse) of already traumatized, abused women after they had arrived within the walls of a supposed safe haven. The stories that emerged were like the shards of a shattered mirror that, when pieced slowly back together through overlapping and reinforcing conversations, reflected an ugly, harrowing reality. The populations being served by the organizations deserve the right to hold accountable the individuals and entities entrusted with advocating and supporting them. The state's transfer of the provision of social services to private entities does not absolve it of its duty to protect those individuals. In this case, if City of Hope had been an official organization, other members of civil society, as well as the state, would have been able to hold the responsible parties accountable for their actions. The only action taken by the state was to shut down City of Hope under the auspices of the TIP report, which encouraged a state takeover. The founders were never prosecuted, a fact that remains frustrating to many of the women who faced abuse within the organization.

Reaching Out

Beyond the desire for official status, another common theme that emerged from the fieldwork was the relative challenge of providing outreach to female laborers as compared with male laborers. Paradoxically, global policies that focus on women and exclude men from the trafficking narrative—such as the United Nations Protocol to Prevent, Suppress, and Punish Trafficking in Persons, *Especially Women and Children* (emphasis mine) and as disseminated in the TIP report—actually work to the advantage of the male migrant population in terms of civil society, in that those providing social services to men are under far less scrutiny than those providing services to women. This became apparent when comparing the experiences of Sama and Aleksander and Maria with those of Vasu, Mustafa, and Dr. Suparna. While the latter three were more open to speaking with journalists and more transparent about their work—articles about each of them had appeared in the various UAE newspapers, including *The National*, *Gulf News*, and *7Days*—Sama and Aleksander and Maria were not comfortable being recorded (even by us at first) and refused to speak with journalists. Throughout all our conversations, people pressed upon us the need for discretion and caution in their line of work, particularly regarding the relationship between their organizations and the state. The even more pronounced concern about the potential ramifications of working with female populations underscored the hypervigilance around issues perceived as belonging to the private realm of the family and the individual home.

Additionally, all of the informal groups we spoke with indicated that they operate purely in crisis mode. Perhaps Vasu, of Valley of Love, articulated this best:

> See, that's the thing with Valley of Love. There are so many things that we could actually specialize in, but because there are not enough organizations, we're just patching on this area, that area, trying our best . . . but actually each of these areas requires a specialist NGO to raise awareness, to lobby with the government . . . what you haven't realized is all of us have full-time jobs. So, because we're operating this typical crisis mode on a day-to-day way—someone is in serious problem and needs help—we're just rushing around doing things like that. So, we haven't had a chance to, okay, find out who's doing what, where, because it involves meeting up with them and they also have the same problems that we have.

Most of these volunteers are doing this work in their spare time, without being trained to do so. Because they spend all of their available time responding to immediate needs, they are unable to develop a long-term vision, build organizational infrastructure, or pursue relationships with other organizations, though they all indicated a desire to do so.

Civil society is seen as an integral part of democratization, a process frequently construed by policies reflected in the TIP report as absent within the Gulf countries. As can be seen throughout this chapter, contrary to popular opinion, civil society in informal or formative phases has emerged in full force within the GCC countries. Although these groups face significant challenges, the work they have done, not only in terms of outreach, but in impacting state policies on labor laws, training programs, and assisting with government sponsored agencies such as the Abu Dhabi shelter, must be underscored.

Many of my interviewees were adamant that a migrant labor rights movement *is* the beginning of an official civil society, and that their efforts were
sure to bring about change not only in terms of labor laws and rights provisions (which they have been active in), but also in the structure of civil society
as a whole within the region. Indeed, in the few years during which I conducted my fieldwork, many things changed and improvements could be seen
and felt. Sama's and Randa's efforts to educate and train law enforcement and
judicial personnel had been approved, and many of the policemen and judges
with whom I spoke reflected positively on the training programs and manuals
compiled by the two women. In addition, Valley of Love had succeeded in
working with the state to push for increased numbers of labor inspectors and
to mandate that companies enforce the law intended to protect workers from
working outdoors between 12:30 and 3 p.m. Ironically, these successes are over-
looked by the condemnatory discourse among policymakers and researchers
(such as those who have authored the TIP), who have been quick to judge the
Gulf countries as lacking in civil society.

￼ ￼ ￼

Many people feel that the UAE is genuinely interested in meeting the needs of
citizens and noncitizens within its borders. "I don't believe that in their hearts
they want to create a place where people are exploited and want to leave. That's
not in Dubai's long-term self interest," explained Randa. Sama echoed this
sentiment:

> I really don't think that the UAE wants to be known as a place where human
> rights are violated; I believe they want to do something, they want to make the
> situation better. All of us here want to do something, it's just a matter of figur-
> ing out how to do it by ourselves.

Sama and Randa both reiterated that they were hopeful about the future of
civil society efforts in the UAE. Though both women had faced blockages by
the state in their efforts to advocate for the rights of migrant women, both
indicated that these would fade away once the trafficking issue was no longer
politically charged.

Several state officials with whom I spoke supported this. "People think
that we don't care about rights violations, that we are just this capitalistic society interested in making money, but that's not the case," said a government
worker. He highlighted the fact that he and his team were vested in being

compliant with the recommendations in the TIP report, but were also interested in promoting the aims of the UAE's little-known civil society. "The TIP has put us in a tough situation," he continued. "We want to listen to their recommendations, but we also need to work with our informal on-the-ground groups. We are a small country, with a lot of interests, it's hard to figure out what to do first," he said. One of his colleagues, a government official responsible for drafting reports on trafficking added:

> It's also really frustrating because people, people in America, keep thinking that we don't care, that we don't mind human rights abuses and that we aren't doing anything. We do care, we do want to have civil society, we do want rights to be respected, but we also want to comply with the American international laws. It's hard to know what to do. Tighten borders, increase police, or support NGOs. I just wish everyone wasn't so critical, we are working hard.

During a conversation I had with a U.S. State Department official residing in Dubai, she agreed with this sentiment, noting, "I think that's what makes the UAE special, that's what makes it different from Iran, for example, that they want to make a change, but they just don't know how to do it." Yet the consensus in my interviews seemed to be that the government is not equipped to address the issues and thus relies on informal groups of mainly noncitizens to do the work instead. I concur with the many individuals we spoke with in ad hoc outreach organizations who stress the importance of being supported in their efforts to build a civil society, as they may be the best, most sustainable long-term mechanism for addressing the unmet needs of migrants and trafficked persons living in the UAE.

As Sama told us that morning when we were sitting in a café on Sheikh Zayed Road: "There is a lot of possibility here, and most important, the desire to change is here, and the people who can change and want to help make the change, we are all here. It's just a matter of removing the obstacles in our way." Though the UAE is accused of stunting the growth of civil society within its borders, the very existence of even an embryonic campaign to address the needs of migrants and trafficked persons is itself evidence of a fledgling civil society in this Gulf nation-state. Interestingly, the biggest roadblocks arise not from the state, initially, but from the global rhetoric about the presumed lack of civil society in the region, as well as the heightened scrutiny on sex trafficking, which is ultimately only one aspect of a much more complex issue.

The international community would do well to recognize and support the efforts of informal civil society groups operating in the UAE. Moreover, the Office to Monitor and Combat Trafficking in Persons would do well to utilize the potency of the TIP report to press nations to do the same, rather than to encourage, in the case of the UAE, a heightening of imported police forces and tighter border controls. People who work at the grassroots level are best suited to provide hands-on, practical solutions for migrants and trafficked persons. The history of this movement over the past two decades suggests that formal recognition of these organizations is the most far-reaching strategy for supporting the needs and rights of migrants in the UAE. With state sanction, these groups will be better able to push forward, conduct business, and hold the state and one another accountable for their actions.

The challenges to migrant workers and those who provide outreach and social services to them are many, chief among them the paradigms and binds brought on by global policies and the moralized, melodramatic rhetoric around sex trafficking. Migrants in Dubai, though transient, have been hard at work building not just skyscrapers and malls, but also the infrastructure for civil society and social support for their communities. Their efforts deserve recognition.

7

BUILDING TOWERS,
BUILDING STRUCTURES

"I MISS MY MOM AND DAD," says the woman on my right. "I miss my children," says the man sitting to my left. The man next to him stands up and says, "I can't figure out how to renew my visa, and it's running out and I don't know what to do!" The three women sitting in front of me all begin to talk at once, all sharing their visa horror stories, a topic that leads nearly every participant to start talking at once, the noise level swelling quickly. Jorge, the exuberant young man who is leading the session stands on a coffee table and motions for everyone to quiet down and be seated. "We can't make too much noise or we will be asked to leave, it's a small room, please work with me," he begs his audience.

It is 10 p.m. on a Tuesday in July of 2009, and it is one of my last nights in Dubai. I am sitting in an overcrowded hotel room near the Mall of the Emirates. Jorge and his friends rent out a hotel room twice a month to provide a space where he and his fellow Overseas Filipino Workers (OFWs) can meet to talk about their experiences and problems. "It's something between group therapy and Sunday night dinner at your grandmother's house," Jorge told me earlier that evening.

They have created this informal group to foster a sense of community among the migrant Filipinos and Filipinas living and working in Dubai. "It's great, we can go there and meet other people who are having the same problems like us," Marie told me earlier that summer when I first heard about the group. She explained that the group functioned as a space for making friends as well as a valuable resource for migrant Filipinos transitioning to life in Dubai. At these group meetings, some OFWs share experiences in resolving problems such as visa issues or other legal obstacles, while others air their feelings of homesickness or loneliness or being overwhelmed.

Marie and her friends told me that when they first moved to Dubai the biggest struggle was dealing with the loneliness they felt. "I mean, we had just moved to a different country, and we didn't know *anyone!*" Marie's colleague, Lisa, said. Then one evening a group of OFWs came to the complex where Marie and Lisa were living.

> They just knocked on the door one night and said *"mabuhay!*" [welcome!].
> Then they asked me if I was okay, if I needed anything, or if I wanted some
> friends. I started crying. Hearing my language and having someone just know
> what I was feeling in my heart, it was more than I could bear. I felt my heart
> was exploding.

Lisa's eyes welled with tears as she recounted her story. After that evening, the group invited her to the bimonthly informal gatherings hosted by Jorge. "But," Jorge notes, "we aren't supposed to be meeting. If the authorities find out about us, we are in trouble." Apparently, any kind of informal gathering could be seen as a violation of the UAE's strict laws prohibiting labor unions. For this reason, Jorge changes location every month and rents out a hotel room for the gatherings. "It's not comfortable, I know. And the room is small, and it gets packed with Pinoys. But, it keeps us more undercover."

"But I don't mind the heat and the crowd. I like it," Marie interjected as Lisa nodded in agreement. "It feels like home. It feels like for these few hours, I'm okay. I'm with my people, my family, and I am okay."

Two nights prior to my visit to Jorge's hotel room gathering, I had decided to visit a friend of mine, Saara, who lived in a part of Dubai that was north of the city, closer to the emirate of Sharjah. On my way there I took a wrong turn, as usual, and ended up on a back road that was still, thankfully, heading north. At first it seemed like I had entered the less developed part of town, sprawling desert as far as the eye could see. Then suddenly, the dull beige hues of the desert were interrupted by a burst of color. After a few miles of driving on this road I had entered a neighborhood that I later understood to be "Little Kerala," named after the state in India that was home to most of the migrants who formed the community. As I entered this little town I saw dozens of clothing stands featuring brightly colored pink, orange, and green shawls, accompanied by shoe stands showcasing beaded ballet slippers, bright sandals, and handbags. Food shops displayed fruits and vegetables that I hadn't seen in the grocery stores in town, as well as spices that I had only seen in the spice market; here, however, they were much more affordable. The food and clothing stands were interspersed with multiple makeshift housing complexes. Below some of them were small rooms with signs advertising "visa advice," "legal advice," "fax services," or "phone services." It looked similar to many of the villages or shantytowns that one might expect to see outside of major urban cities, but this one was populated by a group of migrants who had presumably come to live in Dubai temporarily yet were clearly in the process of establishing roots and building a community in this village-type setting.

When I told Saara, who was also originally from India but raised in Dubai and the UK, what I had seen on my way over to her house, she smiled and nodded. "Yes, Little Kerala, we love it there," referring to herself and her teenage daughter. "This is why we love Dubai, because here we have the best of both worlds. We have all the opportunities that are here in this country, opportunities to really work and learn, but we also don't have to miss home, because it's

PHOTO 7 A merchant selling goods in Little Kerala. Courtesy of Abby DiCarlo.

like home is right here." Given my enthusiasm, we decided to spend the evening wandering around the streets of the vibrant and treasure-filled little town.

When we arrived, I had the chance to speak to several of the area's residents. Many of the people with whom I spoke indicated that they particularly valued living in this community because it helped them transition to life in another country. "It's also good because she is saying that since she doesn't speak Arabic or English, she can come here and find someone who can answer her questions," Saara told me, translating for the woman working in a clothing stand with whom we were speaking.

It was interesting to note the way in which an informal economy had sprung up in this village-like setting outside of Dubai. Many of the people who were operating food or clothing stands were doing so illegally, but indicated that they had entered into this type of work (chosen from among a limited set of options) in order to be able to support themselves while they tried to attain work permits or legal employment. The perverse integration of this informal economy was impressive.[1] The village provided social support and social capital for community members, as well as income-generating activities for many migrants in transition. Though legally chartered, the community was working to the benefit of those who had constructed it, a classic example of perverse integration. "Dubai is not easy," said another young man in Little Kerala as my friend continued to translate. "But at least here we feel like it's home. We feel like we have a chance, and we feel like tomorrow will bring opportunities. And this is a good feeling."

Many of the challenges migrant workers face fall outside the realm of force, fraud, or coercion, ranging from homesickness to legal difficulties to compromised health and more. In recent years migrant groups have organized to provide informal resolutions to such problems through religious or ethnic organizations and small, industry-based support groups.[2] Understanding the challenges migrants face is integral to knowing what kinds of programming are needed in order to ultimately reshape macro-social and political economic policies on a transnational scale. A look at some informal resolutions constructed by migrants to meet their own needs points to the types of programs we should be supporting. In what follows, I begin with some of the most pressing issues narrated by many of my interviewees, experiences that fall outside the narrow realm of force, fraud, or coercion but that can be equally insurmountable when encountered by migrants in the absence of a support network.

Dubai Blues

Global structural forces such as the bilateral agreements mentioned in earlier chapters form the parameters affecting migrants' options and their decision-making processes. Their challenges cover a series of themes, including navigating complex bureaucratic systems, feelings of disconnect and homesickness, and health issues.

Navigating the Ropes

By far, navigating the legal channels of the UAE proved to be the most trying challenge that migrants were up against. Whether it was facing visa issues, absconding from their jobs and breaking their work contracts, trying to reclaim wages owed by employers, or being arrested on false charges, virtually every one of the workers I spoke with recounted experiencing a traumatic legal problem while living in the UAE. They felt unequipped to navigate the channels of the legal system or communicate with members of the police force or judicial system, which only compounded the inherent stress of finding oneself on the wrong side of the law.

Aid workers who have advocated for migrants in criminal court were unanimous in their opinion that judges and other courtroom authorities interpreted the law and passed judgments based on racist and misogynistic prejudices. Such bias, coupled with a lack of transparency on the part of the UAE government about its infrastructure, produced significant obstacles that put many migrants in a cycle of legal-structural violence. Keeping pace with the cost of living, not to mention legal costs incurred while trying to sort through their cases and unable to work in the formal economy, put many interviewees at a disadvantage and exposed them to the risks of working in the informal economy.

For some, the challenges began at the airport. Many migrants arrive in Dubai only to find that their visas are fraudulent. Having paid exorbitant amounts for these fake visas, they feel that they cannot return home empty-handed. Thus they remain in Dubai, sometimes working in the informal economy and living at the airport or in bus stations for weeks on end. Their presence in the informal economy leaves them vulnerable to abuse and to rights violations, setting into motion the cycle of violence that can begin with a single systemic infraction. The story of one Nigerian man, Tokes, exemplifies this issue well:

> So it was a long flight, and I had to go from Lagos to Addis Ababa and then to Dubai. I got here; I'm like whoa, I'm finally in Dubai! Because it's very very

hot and sunny here. I got to Dubai and it's like, damn, is it that hot here? Okay. And I came down, and I was walking toward the counter where you check in. I brought out my passport and the moment I bring out the green passport, man, all eyes on you. You know, Nigerian passport, trouble. Brought out my passport. "You're Nigerian?" I said yes. "Okay, can I see your visa?" and I brought out a printed copy. I give it to him, and the guy looked at it and checked his screen. It was a fake visa.

Tokes explained that he was shocked to find out that his visa was fake because a good friend in Nigeria had sold it to him. He indicated that this friend, a young man he had "trusted and known my whole life," had made all his travel arrangements, and he was particularly hurt that his friend would have cheated him. When he arrived in Dubai and realized his visa was fraudulent he felt that he could not return to Nigeria given the amount of money he had spent getting to Dubai.

You know what it is to sell what you have, just to make a trip? You don't know where you are going to stay there. I got here [to the airport], and I was like, "I have a fake visa. I have a fake visa?!" He said yes. I said, "Just give me a few time, let me try and clarify some things." And I left me at the airport thinking, thinking of how I was going to go through. I tried getting tough, we tried having talk, I was caught up, what am I going to do?! And I called up the guy that makes the visa, and he said sorry, the sponsor who actually gave me a visa gave me a fake visa. Which means you have to go back to Nigeria. I was like, damn! Go back home to Nigeria? Impossible! And you know, one thing about Nigerians who are kind of desperate, who want something, we go for it. We're like that. So I'm like, what am I going to do about this? And I'm stuck at the airport for weeks thinking about my problem.

Tokes spent the next two months living at the airport. He could not afford to return home, but finding work in Dubai without a visa was very difficult. He finally became involved in the informal economy, selling alcohol illegally to private homes, in an attempt to make enough money to support himself and leave the airport. When we met him, he was living in a small, one-room apartment with five other men from Nigeria, Cameroon, and Ethiopia. He was still working in the informal economy and trying to make enough money to procure a legal working visa. He said that the hardest part for him was figuring out how to get a proper work permit. "If you ask me what I would change about Dubai? I would make it easier to get a visa. Once you are here, you are here to work and you want to work hard. It shouldn't be so hard to get a visa!" he said.

Tokes was not the only person to feel that he had been cheated by a friend or agent back in his home country. While only three other migrants reported being sold fake visas, at least fifteen indicated having to pay exorbitant visa fees that left them so deeply in debt that they would have to work for many months, sometimes years, to pay back what they owed. Natalie, a former government employee of the Philippines who was working at a beauty salon in the Dubai Mall, explained:

> The problem is we have to pay a lot of money just to come here, so like it or not, we have to stay here to work to pay back our debt. But the setup is that you have to pay the . . . somebody else who is recruiting us from the Philippines. And there is a lot of times no receipt, so you pay the money and then it's gone.

This particular young woman from the Philippines reported having to pay 4,000 Dhs ($1,000 USD) in order to procure a work visa for the UAE. Over a dozen other interviewees lamented the fact that they had had to pay a lot of money, money that they did not have and often borrowed from friends or family, in order to migrate. A Nepalese security officer indicated his frustration at having to pay his agent, as he told us when he was off duty one evening in the summer of 2009:

> Actually, my agent cheated me, the agent took me too much money. It's only when I came here that after I understand. The agent cheated me, and at that time I can't do anything. Because my money . . . not back. This money I have to recover after working six months, but no way for me to get back.

For this man and many others, having a system of legal recourse, perhaps in their home countries or perhaps transnationally, would have assisted them in recovering their money or prevented such financial exploitation in the first place.

Several interviewees reported problems that arose when their visas expired or when they absconded from their jobs. Transferring visas, retrieving old visas, and renewing visas proved challenging for many migrants, some of whom ended up in jail due to fines for expired or nullified visas (in the UAE people who overstay their visas are fined roughly $30 USD per day). One young woman named Jeanette had migrated from Cameroon to work in the newly opened Dubai Mall, but after nine months her visa expired and her boss would not rehire her. Jeanette was not ready to return to Cameroon and wanted to renew her visa in order to continue working in the UAE.

> It's really terrible. And if Dubai can eliminate this visa change, everything, I think Dubai would be a better place. Because even after two months I have to spend five thousand [Dhs; about $1,300 USD], only for visa change. You know? It's too much money. Because you pay visa one time, you pay extension one time, and the flight ticket maybe 800 dirhams, and then the hotel bills for one month, it's too much. And I know many girls, when they come in, they realize that they cannot cope with the visa change. Spending this amount of money every two months. What they do is they will run away and hide. And that way the sponsors cannot find them, so the card is blocked. So then they will hide for like one month, and then after that time, they will come back and just start. You don't have papers, that's why they will call you *calli-walli* because you don't . . . now you are an illegal immigrant.

Jeanette paused and looked up, drawing in her breath before completing her last sentence. As she repeated the last two words I saw her fight a shiver going down her spine. "Illegal immigrant. Without papers, that is what you are, just because you can't renew, it isn't right."

Being an illegal or undocumented worker renders migrants vulnerable to exploitation and subject to situations of trafficking. Furthermore, the current legal structures offer no protections for undocumented migrants who want to formalize their in-country status. Though not restricted to the UAE or Gulf Countries, the unique structure of the *kefala* system renders significant numbers of migrants undocumented in the event of disputes with employer-sponsors, who sometimes operate with impunity and shift all blame to the workers.

ı ı ı

Some migrants felt compelled to abscond because they were not getting paid the wages they were owed, and reclaiming these lost wages proved to be nearly impossible. During an interview I conducted with a migrant advocacy group in Dubai that had its headquarters in the Philippines, the director told me that one of their main duties was helping migrants retrieve the money they were owed.

> One thing we have started doing, exploring for OFWs, is how to run after their claims. Money that they deserved to get but didn't get. They have this, what we call a revolving-door policy, the companies I mean. They keep tak-

ing in migrant workers even if they know there are plenty of undocumented workers there. And we believe that it's because they know it's an income-generating thing.

One of his colleagues picked up where the director had left off and indicated his frustration at the ways in which many migrants in the UAE and elsewhere were not being paid.

> They don't pay them, that's not right. Then the OFWs abscond, because they aren't being paid. But then they are there without a legal visa, and they become undocumented workers and it's even harder to get the money back. So there is this system where the Middle East recruits, deports, recruits, deports. They recruit them, use them for a while and then send them back.

The consequences for absconding deter many from attempting to do so. For some, the fear of legal repercussions dissuade abused or cheated migrants from ever going to the police to file a report or claim, a situation that only perpetuates the structural violence. Because many know that if they admit to absconding they will be imprisoned or deported immediately with no chance of returning, they choose to either suffer in their workplaces or run away and become illegal immigrants. Given the debts they have frequently incurred to migrate and the often extreme poverty in their home countries, returning home without money is not an option for many. Knowing they will be punished for attempting to reclaim their wages or report abuse, migrants frequently turn to the informal economy, where they face even more challenges and are vulnerable to further rights violations with even less of a possibility for formal recourse.

Ineffectual labor laws and the opaque nature of changing visa standards in the UAE lead migrants to feel helpless and frustrated when trying to navigate the legal system. Embassies, often severely understaffed, slow to respond, or simply closed, seem to offer little to no assistance, a fact we can personally confirm based on our futile attempts to contact embassy officials or visit consular offices. The confusion, silence, and dismissal we encountered was emotionally exhausting for us, without the added impetus of exigency experienced by migrants.

Migrants who end up in jail for reporting abuse or problems with employers can languish for months, their cases ignored. Some are arrested on false charges and face imprisonment and harsh penal sentences without transparent trials. As Sama and Randa highlighted, the judicial system in the UAE can be uneven and sometimes tainted by racist perceptions of the judges and police interacting with migrant workers from different ethnic or class backgrounds.[3]

"Sometimes a woman will go to the police saying my employer raped me, and the police call her employer to pick her up," explained Randa. "Sometimes they will yell at the woman and tell her not to talk like this, but sometimes they will lock her up."

Shari, an informal social worker who used to work with Villa 25, echoed these sentiments. "The cops think all runaways are prostitutes and criminals. If you run away, you're not going to go to the cops for protection because they might lock you up, or even rape you, so it's hard because you have nowhere to go."

Sama was quite frustrated because she felt that judges and policemen "have bad impressions about Ethiopia, about Africans, so they generalize." She further explained that the judges see Ethiopian women and automatically define them as sex workers or criminals. She said that women who have been abused are held in jail until their scars heal and then are brought to the judge who asks for evidence of the abuse. "Then the judge will say 'why didn't you find a way to jump out the window?' They come to the decision that [the women] agreed to be in prostitution." Sama was referring to a case where she had tried to defend an Ethiopian domestic worker who had been abused by her employer but was accused of prostitution.

Perhaps the most harrowing tale that demonstrates the ways in which race, class, and gender play a role in the application of Emirati law was recounted by Sama. She told us of a case in which she was trying to defend an Ethiopian domestic worker who had been repeatedly raped by her employer. The judge presiding over the case decided that "If there are no bruises, it is not rape. How could you open your legs easily [unless you wanted to]?" Glaring cases of racism and sexism such as this one form the moments in which migrants face their most difficult challenges.

Gender plays a significant role in how migrants experience different types of challenges. Women are subject to acute scrutiny in addition to the abuse, false imprisonment, visa problems and other obstacles encountered by both genders. Before even leaving their home countries, women are often exploited by illegal recruiters, sexually harassed in exchange for migration assistance, and subject to harsher immigration regulations such as higher age limits or the requirement of being married. Women migrants working in the domestic sphere and in sex work also have to face the reality that their work is not seen as labor. Racism and sexism, evident in both criminality allegations and the prosecution, and persecution, that women face in the legal system, are daily realities for many female migrants.

Beyond the larger structural challenges outlined above, many migrants also face individual and interpersonal obstacles during migration. Below, I outline some of the most common personal difficulties migrants workers narrated to me that colored their experiences in Dubai. While some of these speak to both individual and structural issues, they are all aspects of what migrant workers contend with on a daily basis.

Homesickness

PM: Did you like Dubai? Before you returned home to the Philippines?

Angela: Well, ma'am, it wasn't really what I was liking. It was good money, which made me feel good, but I didn't like it there, that's why I came back, came back to Manila.

PM: Can you tell me more about why you didn't like it there?

A: Well [looks around the room at her children, smiles], I was missing my three children back here. These guys [motions to two boys and a girl sitting in the corner playing a game], you know? My husband was working a night shift so he could be with them a lot, but I was very worried about him. And I was very worried about my children, I would think of them all night every night and I would cry. I knew I needed to come back to be with them.

PM: I see.

A: And also, I wasn't making as much money as I thought, you know? I thought, well they tell us we make more money, and I think dollars to pesos, it's a lot of money. But then we didn't make that much, and I had to use a lot of the money for myself so it was really hard. And then I realized that no amount of money is worth for me to be away from them [motions to children]. I couldn't take it, just crying, crying every night. It wasn't worth it.

The one topic that virtually everyone mentioned at least once was homesickness. Many migrants would tear up when talking about their home countries or their families. Several missed the comforts of home and the feeling of belonging in the country where they were living. Some lamented the fact that they could no longer go back home because home had been destroyed by war, or it contained no opportunities for a better life. Others narrated difficulties in adjusting to their new environment but were determined to "tough it out," as one person told me, in order to make their families proud.

Gina, a young woman with whom we spent a lot of time in 2008 and 2009, migrated to Dubai in 2007 from the Philippines to work as a driver for an Emirati family. She was upbeat, always enthusiastic about her job, and eager to learn more about her surroundings. Gina almost always had a smile on her face.

Shortly after moving in with her Emirati family, Gina converted to Islam. "It was amazing, one day I saw Gina in her usual attire of jeans and a T-shirt, and then the next, she was all covered up," said a mutual friend.

Gina was very enthusiastic about her conversion to Islam and said, "I have found so much peace since I have embraced Islam." We would often talk about religion together, and she said she hoped to be able to quit her job as a driver (which required her to work very long hours) and move to Egypt to attend a Muslim theological school to learn more about Islam and dedicate her life to understanding her religion and educating others about it.

One afternoon, however, Gina became very emotional when talking about her conversion. I had only seen Gina smiling throughout the two years I had known her, but that day, for the first time, I sat with her as she cried for a very long time and spoke of her family.

> Ever since I embraced Islam, though, my family, well my parents mostly, they don't want to talk to me. I have a problem with my parents actually. They wanted me to go [migrate to Dubai], but now they aren't happy with how I've changed. And I'm supporting my sister. And *insha'allah* [God willing] everything's going to be okay. I miss my mom. I saw her picture online in my cousin's Facebook profile . . . and . . . and . . .

Gina stopped as she burst into tears. She sobbed quietly for a while as I asked her if she spoke to them or wanted to visit them. "I'm, I'm sending them cards . . . I want to visit them . . . I told my madam [boss] about it, maybe she'll let me go. Maybe she'll come with me, *insha'allah*. . . . " Gina said, catching her breath between sobs. She told me later that afternoon that while she was transitioning to her life in Dubai and learning to love it, that the most difficult part was missing her family. She said she wished she could go home to smooth things over with her parents and just spend time with them. "I just want to go home and hug my mom. And be able to sit at dinner with her and my sister. I just want to be with my family."

Another young man from Nepal, Neom, who worked at a clothing store in the Dubai Mall, also talked about missing his family. When I asked him if he liked Dubai, he was hesitant before answering, "It's okay." When I didn't say anything, he sat down and said, "Sometimes, I miss my family too much."

As he said the word *family*, his voice dropped and his eyes filled with tears. "Like . . . in my shop . . . when a daughter, mom come to the shop, I feel 'my God,' my eyes is full of tears. I am thinking too much my mom," he explained.

Neom said that his living conditions in Dubai were not ideal, and that he didn't like the weather because it was "much hotter than Nepal," but he added that he was grateful to have a job at all. He said that the most difficult part of living and working in Dubai was not the long hours he worked in the mall, nor the cramped living conditions with ten men to a room, but rather how much he missed his family back home. "It's something you can't say money better, money not better than family. My mom most better."

Trish, a sex worker from the Philippines, echoed these sentiments:

> Sometimes people think that the hardest part about my work is that I have to have sex with strangers all day, but isn't it. The hardest part is when I'm alone, when I go back to my home, well, back to my bed [in Dubai], and I think about my family. And I know I'm not the only one, all the girls I work with, everyone talks about families back home and what's happening there.

Trish said she had made the decision to work in Dubai as a sex worker so that she could make a lot of money to send home to her family. She explained that she felt a sense of familial obligation. When things would become difficult for her at work she just thought of her family, how happy and proud they were that she was sending money home. "So I think of them, and it keeps me going, but it also makes me miss them and miss home," she explained. When I interviewed her, she was on a visit back to the Philippines, but indicated that she would be returning to Dubai soon in order to earn more money.

One of her friends, Juba, also a sex worker in Dubai who was on a visit back home to the Philippines, indicated that the hardest part of her decision to migrate into sex work in Dubai was leaving behind her children. "Um, you know it's hard, because I'm doing this so they can have a better life you know," she told me, motioning to her children. Juba's husband was a seafarer and worked on a ship that traveled around the world. When his salary was not enough to support the family, Juba had made the difficult decision to move to

Dubai to engage in sex work. But she said she often worried about the effect of her and her husband's absence on their children:

> Well, let's just say that, you know, family structures have changed a lot [laughs] since the . . . kids have to grow up with one, sometimes both, parents gone. And an extended family that takes care of it. And I know that parents tend to overcompensate actually. So like the kids get whatever toys and . . . you know; someone told me a funny story once that said that women when they buy appliances for their families . . . they buy the practical stuff. Like if you're a woman OFW and you're gonna send your money home for them to buy something, or you buy something there and send it to them, it's gonna be practical stuff . . . but the guys, the men, like my husband, they'll buy like the toy TV. [laughs] So even though the women are abroad, they still think of practicality.

While feelings of homesickness often centered around families, some migrant workers I spoke with indicated they also missed their countries and the comforts of familiar surroundings. Nigel, a young man from Cameroon who was working in the informal economy selling handbags on street corners stated that while his transition to life in Dubai was difficult, he felt that it ultimately made him a stronger person:

> I, for one, it's my first time traveling abroad, going out of my country to anywhere, so all the way to another country! So many things were different. So many things I didn't know, I had to learn. When I first came, I thought, I can't do this. But then I stayed and I made myself. And now it's different. Even socially, the way I used to think about things while back home is different now. I have a lot of experience now, I can tackle a lot of situations in front of me. Just because of the hard things I went through here. I guess it's good, but I still miss Cameroon.

Nigel repeatedly returned to his last sentence and spoke of missing Cameroon. He said that while life in Dubai was different and that he was happy he was "making it," he missed the comforts and familiarity of his home country.

For some, returning home was no longer an option, and this impossibility intensified their emotional dilemmas. One young woman, Shoma, an Eritrean domestic worker who engaged in sex work on the side, indicated that she could no longer return to Eritrea due to the violence in her home country. "My husband is killed, for the war," she explained as I asked her about her reasons for not being able to return home. "Her husband helped Ethiopia, so they're after her," explained my translator. "So to punish the family because her husband was helping Ethiopian projects, now the Eritrean government wants to punish anyone related to him. So she's under a lot of danger, a lot of threat. So she cannot go back to Eritrea." Not being able to go back made Shoma feel even more homesick; in fact, she indicated that this was the worst feeling she could possibly imagine. Later, her translator told me that Shoma had been abused during her time in Dubai but that her feelings of not being able to return home hurt her more—"make her ache," as she said—more than the abuse she had endured during her time abroad.

This woman was not alone in expressing her heartache at not being able to return home. Several Iranian women also indicated that they could no longer return to Iran due to legal problems they had incurred there, and this feeling of "living in exile" made them miss Iran even more. "The worst part about being here is that I miss Iran, my family, my country, the place where everyone speaks my language," explained Ezhat, an Iranian woman we met at City of Hope. She had married an Emirati man and had a son with him. After her son was born, her husband had left them. When Ezhat phoned her family to tell them she wanted to return home with her son, her family said she would not be welcome, that everyone assumed she had gone to Dubai to engage in sex work. Thus she faced the possibility of arrest if she returned home to the Islamic Republic of Iran.[4] Two other Iranian women I met who were engaged in sex work indicated that they also could no longer return to Iran for fear of arrest. This feeling of living in exile, they told me, increased their longing to return to the country in which they were born.

For women like Ezhat and Shoma, the threat of deportation represents a greater danger than for their counterparts who are reluctant to return home in debt and empty-handed. For people like them, being sent home evokes a fear that weighs on them and affects their daily experiences.

Health

Many migrant workers experienced major health issues due to poor housing and working conditions. It is well acknowledged within public health circles that cramped and substandard housing is a breeding ground for the transmission of diseases. For many, malnutrition exacerbated the intensity of symptoms they experienced. Difficult working conditions, on-site accidents, and lack of access to health promotion/disease prevention services compounded these problems.

A nurse and volunteer labor camp outreach worker talked about the conditions in a labor camp that housed female hospital cleaners. The camp had a scabies problem, and hospital administrators worried about it spreading. On one visit to the labor camp, she and a hospital administrator found "filthy conditions," as she explained. "There were four to six women in a room, not clean, no amenities." The hospital administrator decided then and there that they would have to "pull the bedding out and sterilize everything," she elaborated. She noted that the hospital administrators had no idea about the living conditions of the employees and that their investigation was motivated by concerns about possible disease transmission between these female laborers and the patients in the hospital. After her experience, this woman, an Emirati nurse who trained in the United States, decided to volunteer her time at women's labor camps. "But they are bad places, and they are breeding grounds for disease."

A Nepalese nun who also does outreach in the labor camps echoed the Emirati nurse's sentiments when describing her own visits to the labor camps. "They were all staying in one room, twenty of them. They were sleeping close to each other, and sanitary was not there. It smelled bad, and you had to walk on your toes to enter. But I always covered my nose," she explained. This woman said that the close quarters of the labor camps coupled with the fact that sanitation was not properly enforced led to the transmission of many diseases. Without the assistance of physicians, many times diseases will go undiagnosed and are easily spread. She was insistent upon the pressing need to improve living conditions and make regular doctors' visits a part of the routine for migrants living at labor camps.

One Nigerian man who had been working in a mall but had recently switched to driving a taxi spoke of his experience with malnutrition during the time he was waiting for his visa renewal and living at the airport during the summer of 2007. "I was just eating bread. I just feed on bread and Pepsi alone," he said.

> After three days though, when I go to the toilet I poo blood, Jesus, I was like, God, I'm gone, what's happened to me? I have to call my family back home and tell them what I was going through. What my dad said was "Son, come back home. Come back home." I was like, I came very far, I came very far, this is not the end here. But I was stranded, left with not a dime on me.

For this man, the malnutrition he suffered took a heavy toll on his health. He was unable to see a physician and thus his intestinal illness continued for about nine months until he was able to return to Nigeria and receive medical attention in his hometown before returning to Dubai to seek new employment.

Migrants' health problems are made critical by lack of access to medical treatment. Most of the male construction workers I met at Dr. Suparna's clinic had experienced significant injuries on the job or faced advanced health problems such as diabetes, lice, or staph infections. Because their employers would not pay for their medical treatment, their conditions deteriorated to the point where they could no longer work. They would have no choice but to abscond, and the lucky ones would find their way to Dr. Suparna's clinic for assistance. While she was able to help some of her patients, many had serious conditions that required long-term treatments that she could not provide due to the limitations of her small center. For these men, the best she could offer was to send them home to India in the hope that they would receive adequate medical attention there.

One security guard from Nepal noted that it was difficult to obtain medical attention, as his employer would not pay for services beyond first aid. "If I am sick, I come, there is a doctor. But this is only first aid, you know? More problems, not good. Doctor not help."

Another young man from Nepal who worked at the Dubai Mall echoed these sentiments. "Some health care is free. But only like a headache or something like this. If you have internal problems, like my cousin had, the company will not pay, it's yourself." He was referring to a cousin of his who had been sent home to Nepal due to serious gastrointestinal complications.

A Kenyan employee of the Mall of the Emirates added, "if I want to go for any health care here, now I'm solely on my responsibility, now I'm working. And again, if locals got to go to this government hospital here, I've got to go to a private hospital, which is much more expensive." This young woman had wanted to access family planning resources and reproductive health care but was unable to do so. She became pregnant a few months later and had to return to Kenya because her boss fired her. She said she had wanted to have an abortion, but had not found an avenue to do so.

Soraya, an Emirati gynecologist whom we interviewed in 2008, spoke of the stringent rules on pregnancy outside of marriage. When I asked her about options for women who were pregnant outside of marriage, she said:

> It is illegal. But it's not that we don't see her. You know, actually we see pregnant women who are single and we try to solve the issue before, you know, it

gets very complicated. Because once she delivers . . . so we try to solve the issue before it gets complicated.

Soraya noted that women who were pregnant out of wedlock were encouraged to marry as soon as possible (this is what she meant when she referred to trying to "solve the problem"). When I asked her what to do if a woman could not find the man who had impregnated her, Soraya fell silent. "You know, I saw one single nonlocal who got pregnant. And I discussed her options and told her she could go to her own country before it gets too late and she gets . . . legal problems." Soraya was referring to the fact that an unmarried woman who is found to be pregnant will be arrested.

Abortion is illegal in the UAE, and evidence of a positive HIV test leads to immediate deportation for noncitizens and quarantine for Emirati citizens. Interestingly, nonlocals are tested regularly when they apply for visa renewals, while Emiratis are not required to test. Through this logic, an Emirati could carry and spread the virus unaware of his or her condition. When I asked Soraya about this, she was once again silent as she thought through a response. "I guess you are right," she said. "Maybe in this part of health we need to change things."

Dr. Vishnu, a midwife and gynecologist from India, spoke of the difficulties in treating patients from diverse ethnic and socioeconomic backgrounds. "There is a huge, diverse population. Teachers, nurses, doctors, maids all need health care, and it's hard for us to be giving everyone everything at the same time," she said. Dr. Vishnu indicated that treating patients with such an array of health problems was challenging because their facilities were not equipped to do so. Beyond that, she said, many doctors were not trained to diagnose and treat diseases from different parts of the world. "We do our best, but it isn't easy," she added, noting that she wished she could increase the staff and budget at her hospital.

Many doctors articulated the desire to provide more services to these different populations. One social worker I spoke with in 2008 and 2009 expressed her concern that prison inmates were not able to access psychological services or even basic health care. She noted that she had tried to work to reform this rule, but had been frustrated by the bureaucracy she encountered. Another physician, Dr. Saeed, originally a refugee from Iraq, also expressed his heartfelt desire to provide health care to all regardless of socioeconomic or ethnic background. He was working at a free health center in the northern emirate of Ajman and was adamant that "we cannot have separate medicine for the rich, separate for the poor. Food, clothes, yes. But medicine, no." Dr. Saeed's clinic appeared to have all the latest in technology, and his pharmacy boasted a wide array of medicines, thanks to donations by way of the Islamic tradition of *zakat* that induced religious followers to donate a percentage of their income to charity. "We want the poor to come here and feel rich," he emphasized. "The psychological aspect is very important. They must feel good about their hospital to be cured." Dr. Saeed was committed to fostering a sense of dignity and respect for working-class migrants visiting his center, a goal he seemed quite successful in achieving, given the enthusiasm that emanated from his patients.

▪ ▪ ▪

The types of challenges and injustices highlighted in this chapter are not unique to Dubai or the UAE. I present these stories to underscore some of the trials migrants face that are not often discussed in larger studies on trafficking, migration, and global labor flows. While these issues are truly global in nature, what makes migrants' experiences in the UAE unique is the combination of discourse and law enforcement that reinforces racial hierarchies and the glaring lack of formal structures to address the needs of the majority of the UAE's population. Moreover, the structure of the *kefala* system, by favoring employers, further ingrains patterns of structural violence. There is perhaps no other place in the world where migrants make up an astounding 80 percent of the population of the country. Given the high numbers, multiple needs, and unmet rights of these migrants, it is crucial for the UAE government—as well as the governments of sending countries and countries involved in international policymaking, such as the United States—to confront the issues surrounding migrants' living and working conditions.

Though the challenges are many and may seem insurmountable, migrant communities have come up with many creative and informal types of resolutions to address the issues. These innovations provide rays of hope, and as such, should be recognized and supported.

Resolutions Outside Law

Informal migrants' networks based on religion, ethnic group, or employment sector present excellent models of programming that should be supported and emulated in policymaking. These networks function as social support groups, providing a sense of kinship and belonging. "It's a place to go when you are feeling lonely, or sad, or have questions about your environment," said a Pakistani domestic worker, referring to her religious group. Many informal groups organize to raise money and conduct outreach projects geared toward different populations. Most important, however, are the social capital and support they provide to migrant communities in Dubai.

Social Networks

"When you go to a new place, especially a place that is so different, like Dubai, it's not easy," explained Alice, a former domestic worker from the Philippines. "You have this new job, it's a new country, and no one has told you anything about where you are going, so you need help." Alice said that forging a type of fictive kinship bond by spending time with other migrant Filipinos in Dubai made her time there survivable.

> We import [the equivalent of] the kinship system. The equivalent, they, we, import the kinship system. It's so necessary and convenient for us to survive. We invent relatives. If you have a close group, they meet regularly. They get together, tell their master [referring to employer or sponsor] that they are going to spend time with relatives, and then these relatives become our major network. Sometimes there is an elder, sometimes not, but these people, they become your family, and you would do anything to be with them.

Alice spoke to an issue that many others referred to, namely the creation of close networks as a survival strategy. Several sex workers reported relying on these fictive kinship networks for safety, guidance, and assistance in their employment sector. One Iranian woman who works in the sex industry stated:

> I came to Dubai because a friend of mine was working here as a working girl and she told me about it. Because she was how I came, I came to rely on her for advice and direction. I had never been in this business before, but she showed me around. That's why I call her my sister.

Sammy, a nanny from Bangladesh, also spoke to the importance of fictive kinship structures. I had met her on several occasions when I visited her employers who were friends of mine from Iran, and I had occasionally talked to her about her experiences in Dubai. She said that overall, she was happy, but that she missed Bangladesh and her family very much. One afternoon I told my friends I would watch their daughters, ages five and seven, and they could give Sammy the afternoon off. When I arrived to pick up the little girls, I asked them where they wanted to go. They told me they wanted to go to the playground near their house, and I obliged. When I arrived at the playground I was overwhelmed by not only the number and heterogeneity of the children, but also the diversity of their caregivers. Children from Iran, Iraq, Japan, Sudan, Nigeria, Poland, France, Russia and other parts of the world ran laps around each other and the swing set, while caregivers from India, Sri Lanka, Bangladesh, Morocco, Iran, China, Thailand, and Ethiopia looked on.

A scene that I would later discover was common to playgrounds around the world, the visual kaleidoscope of that day has always stayed with me. As I pushed my friends' daughter on the swing, I caught Sammy's eye who was watching the little girl as she talked with her friends. I later asked her why, on her day off, she had come to the playground. She laughed a little. "I come because here is my family," she said, pointing to a group of Bangladeshi caregivers who lined the benches around the sandbox. "These women are my sisters, they are my friends, they are who I love." Sammy led me back to the benches where they were sitting. As she introduced me to her fictive kinship network, they all reiterated her point about the importance of their visits at the playground in helping them overcome feelings of loneliness and homesickness, and because it provided a venue where "we can just speak each other's language and trade stories," as one of them said. "It's a place we come and talk about our lives and we feel that someone cares," explained another woman.

Fictive kinship networks are just one type of coping mechanism. Informal support groups such as the one described at the beginning of this chapter provide another networking outlet. Workers who do not live with their employers or at mandatory labor camps populate the various ethnic communities and enclaves that have sprouted up in and around Dubai. Little Kerala (described earlier), Little Ethiopia, Little Pakistan, and a part of town near Sharjah where a Russian-speaking community has developed were among the most substantial ethnic communities I encountered in the UAE. In these neighborhoods, people said they felt like they were "coming home." Some noted that these venues provided employment opportunities for those in the informal economy and for migrants who were between visas or jobs, while others emphasized their importance when in need of legal advice and other services. Some of the sex workers I spoke with indicated that these were areas where "we feel safe," as one of them told me in 2008, noting that they often returned to these neighborhoods after long periods of work or for leads about other possible job sources.

"I didn't know how to go about my work," said one Ethiopian sex worker. "But I had heard there was good money to be made here doing this, and I was told that here I would find people who could tell me about how to do it." She later added that upon arriving in Dubai she had come to Little Ethiopia and met a slightly older Ethiopian woman who had been a sex worker, but was then functioning as more of a madam. "She took me under her wing and told me what to do and how to do it. I am most grateful to her," she said.

Though migrant workers may not be permanent settlers in Dubai, this has not deterred them from creating informal networks and spaces to meet and provide one another with support. Carving out physical, geographical neighborhoods has gone a long way toward addressing their needs. Offering everything from legal advice to phone and fax services and money wiring, these ethnic enclaves played an important part in the lives of most of the people I met.

Religious Networks

Another source of solidarity and support for migrants from all backgrounds was the church. Like the neighborhoods that served the various ethnic populations, churches filled a similar role of providing an informal venue for networking and for exchanging information and services ranging from legal advice and counseling to food and shelter. Some groups used church settings to come together under the auspices of religion to organize and mobilize efforts pushing for reform. "No one can object to us wanting to go to pray, so we use that as a space to organize," explained a Nepali security guard. He and at least four others emphasized that churches offered the best avenue for organizing a migrants' rights movement, as the state would not be suspicious of their activities.

Whether for the purpose of organizing, exchanging information, or just finding friends and social support, church was a big draw for over half of my interviewees. Though not all migrants are religious, nor do they subscribe to the same religion, many indicated visiting one of the three large religious complexes located in the Bur Dubai neighborhood of Dubai on a regular basis as a way to meet other overseas workers and access the wide array of services offered by these venues.

The first time I visited St. Mary's, one of the large religious complexes that housed many of the protestant sects of Christianity as well as a few rooms for Hindu and Buddhist worship, I was struck by the diversity of the crowd and the different types of services offered. It was a hot Thursday afternoon, a popular day for attending church as it is a day that many migrants are released from their work duties owing to the weekend in Dubai being on Thursday and Friday. When we arrived, I was amazed to see migrants from a wide variety of ethnic, religious, and socioeconomic backgrounds. Nigerian women wearing colorful, loose, traditional dress and matching head wraps mingled with Chinese women passing out fliers in Mandarin. I sat with a group of Indian women wearing elaborate saris, who explained that their church was open to people of all denominations, and met a group of Pakistani migrants who were collecting money for aid relief in their hometowns.

The St. Mary's complex consisted of a series of buildings, each housing four to five spaces, which were used by different religious groups at different times. The buildings were arranged in a circular manner, with a large, open courtyard in the center where people tended to congregate and set up booths to raise money or advertise services and outreach. At the entrance to the courtyard was a revolving sign that advertised the times and locations of that day's services. Literally hundreds of people of all backgrounds and ages scurried across the courtyard seeking out their specific service.

On that particular day, we had come to this complex to meet with the minister of a Pentecostal church who provided outreach to male migrant workers living in the labor camps near Sharjah. As we waited for him outside the building where his service was supposed to be held, I felt myself growing weak from the heat. As I leaned back, trying desperately to fan myself with my notebook, a Sri Lankan woman who was also waiting for the Pentecostal service turned to me and said, "You'd better get ready, this particular service doesn't have air-conditioning inside, so it's even hotter in there." My eyes must have widened because the woman began laughing. "I know, it's so hot I've sometimes thought about switching denominations because that service over there, the Evangelicals who are singing, they have a/c." She pointed across the courtyard.

I decided that air-conditioning was at this point more important than my interview with the minister, so I thanked the woman and walked across the courtyard into the room she had been pointing to. When I walked in, the cool air of the room gave me the relief I needed. Members of the lively congregation, including Filipinos, Indians, Sri Lankans, and Thai, were on their feet singing and dancing as I walked toward the back of the room and slumped down in a chair, trying to catch my breath and cool down. A soft-spoken Indian woman walked up and sat down next to me.

"Welcome to our church, is it your first time?" she asked. I nodded. "I saw you waiting outside the other building," she said, smiling. "Why did you decide to come in here?" she asked. I admitted that I was waiting to interview the minister of the other service but that I had become overwhelmed by the heat and decided to come into this service instead to cool off. I half expected her to be offended and angry, and I was ready to leave now that I had been discovered, but instead she just laughed. "That's why I first started coming here too," she admitted. "But then I was filled with the Holy Spirit and met many wonderful people, so I decided to stay. Maybe you will too."

Throughout my time visiting these religious centers, I met many people who offered informal types of support and outreach to migrants and fellow congregation members. "People turn to God when they have nowhere else to turn, and to share their grief and see if they can get something when they need," said a Nepalese nun we met at one of the services. This woman provides free counseling to all the members of her congregation and also specializes in family counseling for migrants who have come with their families or are having trouble with family relations back home. "They are strangers in this place, and our goal is to provide a place to worship," explained a Pentecostal priest who worked St. Mary's. "In these places, people can get to know people from their own land."

Some services were dominated by one ethnic group, while others featured a heterogeneity of worshippers. According to an Evangelical minister, "all nationalities—Indian, Pakistani, Filipino—all coming to the church." When we visited his congregation, I could see that he was right, and that people from all types of backgrounds were gathered there worshipping together. The minister added proudly: "Also some Arabic peoples here, Iraqi, Lebanon, Latin, all together they are praying. Here, everyone like one country, everybody is happy because they have the church, that is our common language."

Garage sales, alms collections, and food drives organized by ministers, pastors, and nuns help fund outreach efforts to migrants in labor camps and social support for prison inmates in the various jails throughout the UAE. One Indian woman noted that she and her group of nuns made weekly trips to the prisons to visit inmates from a wide variety of ethnic backgrounds and provide them with bibles and "spiritual nourishment." She noted that these visits were an important part of the work of her church and said that the inmates appreciate their efforts.

> We work with the prisoners, we try to help them. We tell them God loves them, that we love them, that God is a forgiving God, and we care. This helps them. I used to visit mostly the Asian prisoners, but now I visit with the Africans, too.

They are all open to us, and I think they like when we bring them bibles and other gifts.

Another minister who does outreach in the prisons and labor camps noted that the core of his mission was to provide the migrants with a sense of hope. He said he would continue working so that they would know that people care about them. A poster hung outside the room where he presented his services, which the pastor said summed up his feelings about his work. It read:

> Time is short and the need is immediate. Meeting the needs of a hundred men is like a drop in the ocean when thousands of them are being made redundant every day. The Bible Society is preparing itself now with its "feet fitted with the readiness that comes from the gospel of peace" (Ephesians 6:15). The entire ministry scene in the labor camps has changed drastically. People need the Word of God and the assurance that someone besides God still cares for them. They need to see again that the God of Hope is with them in spite of all the uncertainties of the economic depression. Pray with the Bible Society in the Gulf, as its staff in partnership with churches do their best to meet some of the needs of some of the migrant workers at least by providing them with the message of the Gospel that gives them eternal hope. . . . As reported in a newspaper in India last year, forty men who were returned home in similar circumstances committed suicide after returning to India. . . . Can we do something to prevent such tragedies?

Many of the ministers offered a variety of services for their congregations. The minister of a popular Episcopalian service explained:

> Our churches, we are doing a great help. We are not caring financial side, like who are the people coming with various problems. They come here with problems, they are delivered from their problems. Job problems people are coming, when they come and pray they are getting a job. Visa problem people are coming and they are getting their visa. That is help isn't it?

He later clarified that he did not ask about the socioeconomic background of the members of his congregation. When asked about how he and others who ran his church supported themselves, and how they were able to finance the work they do, he thoughtfully responded:

> It is a great help we are doing, not by the financial side, but through the power of God. Through the power of God we are doing everything. Without salary, without expectation from anyone, we are doing free of cost for everything, for

God's good. A lot of different denominations, a lot of different languages, you are free. Here when they come, they are receiving everything . . . all the problems met by the power of God.

Indeed, it seemed that several of the congregations we met with were intent on providing a variety of outreach to all types of migrants. While some accompanied their outreach with sermons, others did not, choosing instead to provide food, clothing, or counseling without any religious propaganda.

During our time in the field we encountered Christians, Hindus, and Buddhists involved in outreach work with migrants. When we asked if the mosques provide these same services, one of our interviewees told us that the mosques in the UAE did not function in the same way as the churches or like mosques in other countries that served as community centers. Rather, their principal involvement was in funding charity centers like Al-Ihsan, an umbrella organization that provided food, housing, and health care free of charge through its different arms of service.

For migrants, the church provided a venue to come together and to seek out the emotional, social, and sometimes financial support they sought. One man noted that while he never attended church services at home in India, he had become very involved with his congregation in the UAE, to the point where he tried to participate on a daily basis. "When I am going every day, praying there, I feel, I can feel relieved from my mental agony, from the prayer. I am free from all these things . . . and I am energizing my soul." A domestic worker from Ethiopia echoed these sentiments. I asked her how she felt when she attended church, to which she responded, "I am happy." After a few moments of silence she added, "I am happy. I find my community, my brothers and sisters, I like pray. I am at peace."

Despite their unofficial nature and lack of recognition as NGOs, it is useful to look to these religious organizations and the types of outreach they provide in order to delineate the types of services migrant workers in the UAE need and the methods of outreach that seem to work best. It is important to recognize the work that these religious groups are doing and for policymakers to support, not punish, their efforts to prevent or address instances of force, fraud, or coercion that migrant workers face.

 ▪ ▪ ▪

In order to help migrants, we must look at the challenges they are up against, the hardships they endure, and the ways in which they have sought to tackle these obstacles. While it is tempting, within policy or academic circles, to become fixated on labels such as *migrant, illegal alien, sex worker, trafficked victim, tourist,* and *smuggler,* none of these words or concepts sum up the lived experiences of migrants in the UAE. To truly address their problems, we must follow migrants of all backgrounds and in all employment sectors through the labyrinthine pathways they traverse. We must observe how they find ways of procuring visas, temporary work, food, and housing in the informal economy. And we must strive to understand the passages of perverse integration they rely on to survive and take the next step. It is in these winding roads and pathways that the most interesting stories can be found and that solutions can be observed. Policy recommendations that glean wisdom from migrants' own experiences are a first step toward reshaping our perceptions of human trafficking and toward reconstructing policy and discourse within a human rights framework.

8

BUILDING CASTLES IN THE SAND

ON DECEMBER 1, 2009, the ever-popular late-night comedy/news host Jon Stewart focused a segment of his show on Dubai. In keeping with the show's satirical nature, Stewart targeted Dubai's fledgling economy amid needling remarks about why a nation-state built on a real estate bubble thought it could even survive. The title of the segment was "United Arab Emirage," sealed by the punch line, "Maybe they should change their name to Du-sell." While the piece was humorous and witty, Stewart had put his finger on two important and interrelated issues: the rapidly declining economy of the Emirates, and the even more rapidly declining image of Dubai.

In the decade leading up to the economic crisis of 2009, the image of Dubai put forth by celebrities, magazines, commercials, and films was one of glamour and glitz. Dubai was seen as a major hotspot and destination for the rich and famous and those aspiring to be in that category. Viewed as the ultimate luxury destination for an extended vacation or a second or third home, Dubai attracted increasing numbers of American and European tourists, many of whom decided to settle in the emirate and start businesses. Inspired by the popular discourse on Dubai and its reputation as a bastion of stability and modernity in the Middle East, several American universities even decided to set up satellite campuses in the Gulf. Seen as more progressive than neighboring Iran and Iraq, for example, and as potentially important allies for the West, the UAE and like-minded Gulf nations seemed to be on track for success.

Lurking beneath the excitement about Dubai, however, was this issue of trafficking within the region. The Emirates only once managed to achieve the coveted Tier 1 ranking granted by the U.S.-created TIP report (in 2003). For most of the past decade, like many of its GCC neighbors, the UAE hovered in the liminal space of Tier 2, not entirely demonized but still reminded of its inadequacy in the eyes of the international community. Frustration over the issue came to a head when the UAE was bumped to Tier 3 in 2005 and then a slight notch up to the watch list in 2006.

With the burgeoning economic crisis across the globe, the image of Dubai began to slowly shift. Instead of magazine spreads featuring the latest celebrity in one of Dubai's new restaurants or clubs in modern high-rises growing out of the sand, the attention shifted to the "dark side" of Dubai.[1] Media depictions of the emirate as a nest of corruption portrayed Dubai as a hotbed of sex work and human trafficking, with many people drawing comparisons to Las Vegas, highlighting the presence of organized crime and pointing to the irony of the evolution of a "sin city" in the Middle East.

Discourse and policy began to change almost simultaneously. Before long, the UAE was placed on the Tier 2 watch list, raising ire throughout the Emirates. What the U.S. State Department officers responsible for writing the TIP report did not realize, however, was that trafficking discourse and policies that spotlighted women in the sex industry, while ignoring abuses taking place in other industries, were only exacerbating the situation for migrants. Though the 2009 TIP acknowledged the problem of forced labor outside sex work, the focus of the recommendations remained tied to the sex industry in many ways. The TIP recommendations for the UAE were clear: increase law enforcement, increase numbers of raids and arrests of sex trafficking offenders, and tighten borders.

As I have shown throughout this book, these three recommendations had negative repercussions for migrant workers throughout the Gulf. In the UAE, given the extraordinary ratio of citizens to noncitizens and hence a lack of sufficient candidates, increasing law enforcement necessitated importing officers from neighboring countries, often without any extra training. The potential for increased abuse of sex workers and other migrants by this contingent of culturally unsensitized officials was great, and did occur. In addition, the contours offered by this framework of increasing law enforcement furthered the problem of arrests and criminalization of workers perceived to be illegal.

In practice, increasing raids and arrests of "sex traffickers" translates to the often indiscriminate arrest and deportation of sex workers, regardless of whether they were actually trafficked. Through this process, women can be sent back to unstable and even dangerous situations in home countries. Finally, requiring the UAE to restrict the number of migrants permitted to enter the country has the unintended effect of making migrants rely increasingly on unethical and exploitative middlemen recruiters.

Given the abstract ranking system that has placed increasing numbers of Muslim countries on Tier 3 or the Tier 2 watch list, the TIP report seems to draw from a set of assumptions about these nations based on unstated criteria. The resulting lack of transparency has undermined the report's authority and credibility in the region and contributed to its being perceived as yet another implementation of U.S. hegemony. The United States is further perceived as trying to force its values, morality, and system of law enforcement onto other countries, and the arbitrariness of the TIP ranking system is seen to favor friends of the United States while penalizing its foes, and is perceived to have Islamophobic undertones. This inherent inequality is consequently weakening the power of the report as well as the potential for cooperation with the United States and Europe.

The power of discourse and policy is apparent in the ripple effects of even minor adjustments to the TIP rankings. Imagine, then, the possibilities and potential good these tools would hold if reframed within a broader context of migrants' rights, as opposed to the current framework of criminalization and prostitution. Though the TIP and UN policies are now finally moving away from a hyperscrutiny on sex trafficking, the interpretation and implementation of these policies at the local level remains focused on sex workers. This situation allows local officials to ignore the issue of forced labor and exacerbates the desperate need to reform *kefala* and legalize social service providers. I acknowledge that gross violations can and do accompany sex work and migrant labor, and I acknowledge that trafficking is indeed a real and present phenomenon. It begins at the point where migrants experience force, fraud, or coercion, yet its contours are not as rigid as the discourses would suggest.

Migrants' experiences take on a range of shapes, forms, and narratives involving the interplay of individual and macro-social factors and decision making. Some migrants are seeking better employment opportunities, others are fleeing violent situations in their home countries. Some are exploited and become trafficked at the time they elect to migrate, others face abuse when they are arrested in the host country and forcefully detained or deported. Still others migrate in search of love, adventure, or a chance at a better life. Many are willing to risk violence, abuse, and possible detainment in the hope of making money to send home to their families.

Yet what stands out as key in the trafficking phenomenon are labor conditions and migrants' status as legal or illegal workers. Surely, the *kefala* system and racialized hierarchies in place in the UAE influence these conditions, and policies crafted to respond to the extraordinarily complex phenomenon of migration must address this dimension.

Policies and discourses on trafficking are in desperate need of reform. Currently, all transnational sex work is imagined as trafficked, and the functional definition of trafficking as outlined especially within discourse ignores abuses to migrants outside the sex industry. Thus the implementation of policies must be both broadened and narrowed—broadened to *include* all instances of force, fraud, or coercion regardless of industry or migrants' perceived complicity in their circumstances, and narrowed to *exclude* instances of sex work outside of force, fraud, or coercion.

Gulf Migration in Context

Discussions and policies about trafficking must deal with the complexities of real life. Reflecting on stories and narratives of migrant workers in the UAE, it became apparent to me that people draw upon a number of different paradigms when talking about their reasons for migration as well as why they migrate into sex work. I argue that rather than focus on the question of consent regarding the decision to migrate, it is more productive to advocate for the need to improve migrants' living and working conditions once migration has occurred. Addressing restrictive immigration policies and decriminalizing sex work would encourage a discourse on universal rights for all laborers in Gulf countries, while improving migrants' agentive access.

Developed countries have directly affected economic conditions in the developing world through restructuring programs, aid policies, and economic sanctions, all of which act as "push" factors in emigration from the developing to the developed world. The economies of developed countries benefit from mass influxes of informal, unregulated labor, regardless of whether the migrants providing it are legal, illegal, or "trafficked"; capital makes no distinction. Unfortunately, the focus on sex trafficking eclipses the root causes of all trafficking along with the complicity of the developed world in igniting the need/desire to migrate. Economic reforms and international debt forgiveness are among the most potentially effective, long-term, and comprehensive measures that can be taken against trafficking. Many developing and underdeveloped countries are currently subject to structural adjustment programs by the IMF. Implementation of such measures result in open-market policies that do not encourage domestic state spending, job creation, or infrastructural solutions at home. Populations in these countries feel the brunt of reduced state spending on welfare, nutrition, and health programs and are often compelled to consider migration as an economic alternative. We must recognize that people may choose to migrate illegally if they feel they have no other choice for economic survival or for other personal reasons; still, consent to the migratory process is not synonymous with consent to exploitation or abuse. The development in home countries of alternative choices that ensure access to a sustainable flow of income, basic necessities, possibility of upward mobility, and the improvement of personal and communal levels of human development are the only truly effective "combat" strategies against trafficking.

Migration is a global reality that will continue to occur through innumerable channels and means, regardless of the categories we create or policies we construct. The resilience of the individual with the will and necessity, created out of severe global inequalities, to migrate has proven that migration cannot be stopped. Consequently, a more open, visible, regulated (but not restrictive) migration process remains one of the most promising venues for improving the lives of future migrants. Safeguarding rights, providing education and information to migrants as well as sponsors, and dismantling the culture of prosecution coloring the implementation of most migration policies will be important steps in addressing the challenges that have risen out of contemporary migratory patterns.

Recommendations

Though I have problematized the term *trafficking* throughout this book, it is important to note that the trafficking framework can be a useful tool in shaping the contours of policy about migrants' rights, both locally (in the Gulf) and globally. While the interpretation of trafficking has varied, policies have room for a positive construction of the discourse that can be used to help migrants worldwide.

From broad global policy recommendations to narrow, specific changes that can be implemented immediately, a number of measures can be taken to address the needs of migrants and people who are vulnerable to instances of trafficking, recommendations that have been noted by many migration scholars for several years but bear repeating in the context of this research. This work acknowledges the global scope of trafficking and is not intended to contribute to a sense of Gulf exceptionalism, of which I am critical. Rather, I hope that the data presented here will help contextualize the issues within a larger global framework.

One important, albeit ambitious, goal for policymakers is the restructuring of structural adjustment programs so that developing and underdeveloped countries can focus on the creation of jobs at home. This would help discourage development policies that rely on remittances and ultimately make migration an option for some rather than a desperate alternative. Second, migration policies that seek to restrict the out-migration of certain population segments (women under thirty or single women, for example[2]) must be reformed to permit the movement of these migrant workers through regulated channels. Thus women who are making the decision to migrate would not have to rely on middlemen or irregular avenues of migration where the potential for abuse is elevated. Third, the TIP report should be reformed in an effort to approach trafficking in the broader context of migration and human rights rather than its current emphasis on prosecution and sex work. In this vein, recommendations should align more closely with the region- and country-specific needs of the ranked nations, and TIP officers should work more closely with researchers in order to better grasp the scope and contours of the in-country trafficking debate. Finally, the ranking system itself must be revamped to reflect the actual gradations of efforts and successes/failures of the countries being assessed, rather than echoing the whims of U.S. foreign policy.

More specific to the UAE, there are also a number of focused recommendations that should be encouraged and implemented to meet the needs of migrants and trafficked persons more immediately. One of the reasons cited for the UAE's low rankings on the TIP report is its purported lack of civil society. This blind spot is part of the problem. To address the needs of trafficked individuals, migrant workers, and other needy populations in the UAE, the best policies will take stock of the social systems already in place and those currently developing. Finding often low-key and inconspicuous outreach efforts among migrant communities in host countries involves abandoning the American yardstick used heretofore by the international community and making a genuine assessment of ongoing efforts. Disregarding the existence of civil society in the UAE ultimately functions as a self-fulfilling prophecy, denying the activity and agency of the individuals and groups that advocate on behalf of change and social development. TIP officers need to see the value of exerting pressure on nations to recognize these groups. The current arrangement in the UAE of tacit state acknowledgment being offered to unofficial civil society groups in exchange for the freedom to operate places all the power on the side of the state and leaves fledgling outreach programs underfunded, unrecognized, and without a voice. The TIP, as an instrument, has the power to make a specific recommendation to encourage the state to officialize the civil society, on whose work it depends. The state benefits greatly from the work of these informal groups, often relying on them and their ties to various ethnic communities to address and alleviate migrants' issues within the UAE's borders. But the fact that they are not official or legal in the eyes of the state hinders the scope of their work.

Beyond encouraging the implementation and sanctioning of civil society, the TIP should also recommend a larger reform of the *kefala* system, a goal that activists had been moving toward before the trafficking issue usurped the government's attention. Reforming the *kefala* system involves instituting a series of employee rights that reflect the needs and hardships of migrant workers and that dismantle the one-sidedness that currently favors employers. By doing so, many migrant workers who abscond from work in the formal labor market in search of increased autonomy and mobility in the informal economy might opt to stay at jobs that can be regulated and monitored. To that end, there is a need to increase both the number and the authority of labor inspectors. Though the UAE has acknowledged this need, in 2008 the state was compelled by TIP recommendations to turn its attention toward importing more law enforcement personnel, rather than increasing the numbers of labor inspectors. This trade-off has been costly for the many migrants who face abuse daily without any avenue for recourse.

Instead of calling for increased numbers of imported law enforcement officials, the existing police officers, as well as judges and members of the legal system in Dubai, need to be trained. A number of the actors introduced throughout this book, including Sama, Randa, and Vasu, have been working to create training manuals to inform members of law enforcement on best practices for dealing with migrant workers and trafficked persons. If these or similar training programs were mandated by the TIP, the UAE would be obliged to take the efforts of these informal actors more seriously.

Finally, on a more basic level, migrant workers need drop-in centers, hotlines, and avenues of assistance for difficulties they encounter while in the host country. A number of groups have formed to meet these needs informally, and their work must be recognized and supported by the UAE government and the international community in order to gain strength, momentum, and legitimacy.

Rethinking Trafficking in the Gulf

Assigning blame for the social ills of trafficking and sex work to the UAE is neither productive nor wholly accurate. The UAE developed rapidly into a booming financial hub almost overnight. It is now moving to develop a social infrastructure to catch up to its uneven economic development. Discussions at the state level about how to address the large migrant population (over 80 percent) residing within the Emirates have been overshadowed in recent years by a global hysteria that points to Dubai as a hotbed of sex trafficking and rights violations. This alarm from international quarters has been instrumental in creating policies such as those advanced in the TIP report that have castigated the UAE for its inability to handle the sex trafficking taking place within its borders.

It is important to note that while the TIP is not an ideal mechanism, it is one that has some teeth in the Gulf. While many of the GCC countries (the UAE included) have signed or ratified UN or ILO conventions on labor and migrants' rights, they do not always abide by the recommendations in these documents. In-country officials are, however, concerned about and responsive to the TIP report because of the possibility of sanctions (upon presidential order) and the desire to remain in good standing with the United States. The report is thus a powerful tool in need of reharnessing. While some of the recommendations I offer cannot be accomplished by pressure from the U.S. government alone, and a more global framework on trafficking—perhaps led by the United Nations—might be ideal, TIP recommendations carry sufficient weight to affect change in the Gulf. Incorporating even some of the suggestions outlined here into the TIP and the broader trafficking discourse would produce international reverberations that would benefit those it is designed to protect.

∎ ∎ ∎

The selectivity of first-person narratives is the Achilles heel of the trafficking debate. Thus far, only certain voices have been privileged within the discourse, and those are the narratives of people who fit the current paradigm of sex trafficking through kidnapping. These first-person narratives are not representative or based on broad-reaching research; they are highly biased and rescripted so as to convey a simple victim narrative. Preventing the complexity of personal experiences from factoring into the trafficking discourse and resulting policies denies agency, intelligence, and value to the individuals who have lived them. Focusing obsessively on the question of choice as the qualifying condition for sex workers to receive services (as articulated by some members of international NGOs) merely reinforces the idea that the only type of trafficking in which migrants merit protection is sex trafficking. Sex work must be approached within a context of labor, regardless of personal views toward sex work as a profession. Furthermore, abuses outside the sex industry are many and deserve attention.

In the months and years I have spent working on this book, much has changed in the world. In the United States, we have elected a new president and installed a new ambassador on Trafficking, Luis C. deBaca, who is changing policy and discourse on trafficking as we speak. After spending eight months in Washington D.C. in 2009 and 2010 talking with State Department officials and other policymakers, I am much more hopeful about the future of trafficking policy than I was when I began this project a few years ago. Ambassador deBaca is committed to reframing trafficking within a context of migrants' rights, and TIP officers in his office were very open to criticisms of the TIP report and eager to incorporate necessary changes; if and how they do so remains to be seen. While policymakers are open to viewing trafficking in a new context, however, the discourse remains fixated on the issue of sex trafficking. Each time I presented my study at the many universities and research venues I was invited to speak at around the country, the focus of the questions inevitably came back to sex work and sex trafficking.

As the study of human trafficking progresses, research projects need to become increasingly interdisciplinary in analysis and interorganizational in their approach. Unfortunately, trafficking has been relegated to certain, specific research domains such as "women's studies," "sexuality studies," and "discourse analysis." The problem then becomes that the issues are segregated and contextualizing trafficking within a broader framework of migration is less manageable. The difficulties plaguing the development of an effective response to trafficking stem in large part from this compartmentalization. Trafficking is an incredibly complex phenomenon shaped by a convergence of the most powerful forces influencing the twentieth and twenty-first centuries. Policies and discourses must be reinterpreted to provide rights protections, rather than an excuse to arrest and prosecute perceived irregular migrants. Furthermore, the exclusion of men and certain forms of labor outside the sex industry from the arena of human trafficking will impede any and all measures taken to combat the phenomenon as a whole.

The gridlock that has resulted from the conflation of gender, sexuality, labor, migration, and trafficking has confused all of the aforementioned concepts. This fusion must be deconstructed. Sex workers and trafficked persons are not synonymous, though the categories may overlap. A misconception regarding sex work and sex workers affects the discourse surrounding trafficked peoples and migrant laborers in general.[3] Trafficking must be viewed in the context of globalization, political economy, and the individual and macro-social forces structuring people's decisions to move across borders. Understanding human trafficking calls on us to examine the lived experiences of those that engage in all forms of migration across the globe, from forced labor to voluntary relocation.

REFERENCE MATTER

ACKNOWLEDGMENTS

The research for this book would not have been possible without the generous support of the American Council of Learned Societies, the Woodrow Wilson International Center for Scholars, the Asia Society, and the Pomona College Faculty Research program. I benefited greatly from the monetary and infrastructural support of all four of these groups, and I am deeply indebted to each of them. I feel incredibly lucky to count myself among the faculty of Pomona College, an institution that supports its faculty not only in the form of monetary assistance, but in granting a leave before tenure, terrific students to work with, and fantastic colleagues who have been supportive throughout this process. The faculty are too many to name, but I am particularly grateful to Debby Burke, Jennifer Perry, Larissa Rudova, and Cynthia Selassie for their support of this project.

While in the field, I was lucky enough to have three incredibly gifted students accompany me at various points in the research. In 2008 Christine Sargent and Abby DiCarlo came with me to Dubai and were crucial in making contacts in the field and conducting in-depth research during their short stay. In 2009, Sarah Burgess joined us and was very helpful in adding new dimensions to the research. In between ethnographic visits, and after my return from the field, I was also able to benefit from the assistance of several strong research assistants including Samah Choudhury, Alexandra Fries, Ratna Kamath, and Christine Sargent. Christine, in particular, was more than an assistant to me but a friend, colleague, and co-conspirator. Chapters 1 and 6 draw on articles that she and I have cowritten, and she has been an integral part of not only the book, but the larger project as well. I am also indebted to Abby DiCarlo for taking such fantastic photographs when the rest of us couldn't think to pick up a camera. Her pictures can be found throughout the book.

Many people read various drafts of chapters and provided very useful feedback on the manuscript in its different forms. I wish to thank especially Andrew Gardner, Rhacel Parrenas, and an anonymous reviewer at Stanford University Press for their detailed comments on the manuscript as a whole and for helping to shape an ultimately stronger book. The following people also read and provided helpful feedback on various chapters: Dovelyn Aguinas, Zahra Babar, Rodney Collins, Lara Deeb, Sara Friedman, Paasha Mahdavi, and Karsten Parregard. Joan Dempsey did a fantastic final read through of the manuscript when I couldn't bear to look at it anymore.

I presented my work at a number of conferences and seminars and benefited greatly from comments and feedback from colleagues at these venues. In particular, the Migrant Studies working group at Georgetown University in Qatar, and the fellows and staff at the Woodrow Wilson Center, especially Denise Brennan, Haleh Esfandiari, and Sonya Michel, provided excellent support and comments on the project in various stages of its formation. In addition, working with Attiya Ahmed, Andrew Gardner, and Neha Vora on organizing and presenting panels at the American Anthropological Association and the Middle East Studies Association afforded me the opportunity to benefit from their insights, and I am most grateful to these amazing Gulf scholars.

I would never have embarked on a study of human trafficking and migration if not for the inspirational work of my graduate school advisor, Carole Vance, and the many folks at Columbia University who shaped my thinking on this topic, including Elizabeth Bernstein, Alice Miller, and Alicia Peters. I continue to be inspired by their work and thinking on this complex issue.

The team at Stanford University Press, especially my wonderful editor, Kate Wahl, never ceases to amaze me. The speed and efficiency with which they work and the detailed and thoughtful comments Kate has given me on the manuscript have been truly unparalleled. Joa Suorez and others at the Press worked diligently and quickly to expedite the production of the book, and for all their efforts I am eternally indebted to them.

I would not have been able to persevere in this project without the unconditional love and support of my family and close friends. My brothers, Paymohn and Paasha, provide an endless supply of jokes and smiles that keep me going throughout the most difficult times. My husband, Ahmad Kiarostami, not only read many drafts of the book but also has been a great source of strength to me while in the field and upon my return. My parents,

Mahmood and Fereshteh, to whom this book is dedicated, were the first migrants whose stories I ever heard, and I have carried them in my heart throughout this process. This book is really inspired by their journey and is dedicated to all migrants who have had to make the difficult choice to leave their homes in search of a better life. Finally, I am eternally grateful to all the people who opened their hearts and homes to me while in the field. Each of you has touched me more deeply than you know.

NOTES

PROLOGUE

1. Claudia Aradau, "The Perverse Politics of Four-Letter Words: Risk and Pity in the Securitisation of Human Trafficking," *Millennium Journal of International Studies* 33, no. 2 (2004): 251–27.

CHAPTER 1

Parts of this chapter draw on an article cowritten with Christine Sargent that is forthcoming in 2011: "Trafficked Voices: Re-Thinking Discourses on 'Human Trafficking' in Dubai."

1. Denise Brennan (lecture, Woodrow Wilson Center, 2010).

2. This study of human trafficking in the Gulf received Institutional Review Board (IRB) approval from the Pomona College Human Subjects Board.

3. For an in-depth discussion of anthropological research methods such as participant observation and in-depth interviews, see Russell Bernard, *Social Research Methods: Qualitative and Quantitative Approaches* (Thousand Oaks, CA: Sage, 2001).

4. Carole Vance (lecture, Society for Medical Anthropology Annual Conference, Yale University, 2009). I recognize that neither the term *trafficking* nor the concept are new phenomena, but rather have deep historical roots dating back to the white slave trade, hysteria about immigration at the turn of the nineteenth century, and a broader discussion of labor and the migration of bodies. A full discussion of the historical roots of this issue is, however, beyond the scope of this book. For an in-depth description of the panic over the white slave trade, see Bernstein (2007). For further references about hysteria over migrants and immigrants at the turn of the nineteenth century, see Benton-Cohen (2009) or Frydl (2008).

5. Attiya Ahmad; Jane Bristol-Rays (lectures, Georgetown University conference on Gulf Migration, Doha, Qatar, January 2010).

6. Some scholars have argued, and I agree, that it is not useful to dichotomize structure and agency, but rather to note that they may operate on a continuum; that is, structures can limit or enable choices made to exert agency. For an in-depth discussion of this point, see Constable (2003), Bourgois (1996), or Duneier (1999).

7. Feminist activist Carol Leigh was among the first to use the term *sex work*. For an in-depth explanation of the term and its uses, see Leigh (1998).

8. Michel Foucault, *The Archaeology of Knowledge* (London: Routledge, 1972).

9. Though conversations about these issues have a long history dating back to debates about the White-Slave Traffic Act of 1910, better known as the Mann Act, the term *trafficking* has become popularized in EuroAmerican discourse mainly since the passing of the TVPA. Some scholars have astutely noted, however, that there is a continuum between the terms *slavery* and *trafficking*, and the former continues to be used in trafficking discourse today. For examples, see Bales (1999), Bernstein (2007), and Saunders (2005).

10. Trafficking Victims Protection Act 1466.

11. TVPA article 1477.

12. Denise Brennan, "Re-thinking Trafficking" (lecture, Woodrow Wilson Center, March 1, 2010).

13. Denise Brennan (lecture, University of California, Los Angeles, May 14, 2010).

14. TVPA Article 1423.

15. For examples of scholars' thinking about this disconnect, see the writings of Laura Agustín, Elizabeth Bernstein, Denise Brennan, Kemala Kempadoo, Rhacel Parrenas, and Carole Vance.

16. At the time this manuscript was submitted, the United States had never been ranked by the TIP. However, the newly appointed ambassador to combat trafficking, Lou C. deBaca, had announced that the United States would be included in the 2010 report.

17. Such as the "123 Agreement" or Bilateral Agreement for Peaceful Nuclear Energy Cooperation; see uaeembassy.org.

18. Rhacel Parrenas (forthcoming); Sealing Cheng (2010).

19. Kathleen Frydl (lecture, Woodrow Wilson Center, 2010); Mahdavi and Frydl, "List of Moral Wrongs" (forthcoming).

20. Samuel Huntington, *The Clash of Civilizations and the Remaking of World Order* (New York: Simon & Schuster, 1997).

21. Parrenas (2010); Agustin (2010).

22. For an in-depth discussion of the effects of French immigration policy on Muslim immigrants in particular, see Joan Scott, *The Politics of the Veil* (Princeton, NJ: Princeton University Press, 2007).

23. For an example, see Minister Gargash's response to the UAE TIP ranking in 2009: http://www.wam.ae/servlet/Satellite?c=WamLocEnews&cid=1241072976464&pagename=WAM/WAM_E_Layout.

24. www.uae-embassy.org.

25. Gargash, http://www.wam.ae/servlet/Satellite?c=WamLocEnews&cid=12410729 76464&pagename=WAM/WAM_E_Layout.

26. Ibid.

27. See "Bahrain Commended for Sponsorship Reforms," *Gulf Daily News* (Bahrain; April 30, 2010); "Bahrain Introduces Job Switch Visa Rules," *The National* (United Arab Emirates; August 1, 2009); "Bahrain Scraps Foreign Labour Sponsorship Scheme," www .arabianbusiness.com (May 5, 2009).

28. Moshoula C. Desyllas, "A Critique of the Global Trafficking: Discourse and U.S. Policy," *Journal of Sociology and Social Welfare* 34, no. 4 (2007): 59.

29. Jo Doezema, "Now You See Her, Now You Don't: Sex Workers at the UN Trafficking Protocol Negotiation," *Social Legal Studies* 14, no. 1 (2005): 73.

30. Desyllas, "Global Trafficking," 58.

31. Harm reduction is the catch-all phrase used to refer to a public health practice that allows individuals to engage in high-risk behaviors with a lower level of risk. Examples include the provision of clean needles for heroin users, safer cigarettes, or condoms for sexually active individuals.

32. Desyllas, "Global Trafficking," 59.

33. Pinar Ilkkaracan, *Deconstructing Sexuality in the Middle East: Challenges and Discourse* (London: Ashgate, 2008), 202.

34. Wijers, "Women, Labor and Migration: The Position of Trafficked Women and Strategies for Support," in *Global Sex Workers: Rights, Resistance and Redefinition*, ed. K. Kempadoo and J. Doezema (New York: Routledge, 1998).

35. Siddharth Kara (lecture, Scripps College, February 2008).

36. Kempadoo, *Global Sex Workers*, 10.

37. Kathleen Barry, *The Prostitution of Sexuality: The Global Exploitation of Women* (New York: New York University Press, 1996).

38. Kempadoo, *Global Sex Workers*, 11.

39. Chacon (2006) also extensively documents ways in which the anti-trafficking campaign in the United States has focused more on prosecution than protection or prevention.

40. Desyllas, "Global Trafficking," 64.

41. Gretchen Soderlund, "Running from the Rescuers: New U.S. Crusades Against Sex Trafficking and the Rhetoric of Abolition," *NWSA Journal* 17, no. 3 (2005).

42. A. Wooditch, M. A. DuPont-Moralis, and D. Hummer, "Traffick Jam: A Policy Review of the United States Trafficking Victims Protection Act 2000," *Trends in Organized Crime* 12, no. 3–4 (2009): 235–50.

43. Elizabeth Bernstein (lecture, Woodrow Wilson International Center for Scholars, March 1, 2010).

44. Mohan Dutta, *Communicating Health: A Culture Centered Approach* (Cambridge, UK: Polity Press, 2008), 11.

45. Kevin Bales (2007) blames trafficking "on the perversion of organized crime," 331.

46. Desyllas, "Global Trafficking," 72.

CHAPTER 2

1. J. Hari (2009), http://www.independent.co.uk/opinion/commentators/johann-hari/the-dark-side-of-dubai-1664368.html.

2. *Abaya*: traditional cloak covering bodily curves and skin up to the wrists and ankles; *hejab*: head covering or head scarf worn by many Muslim women in the region.

3. "The Dark Side of Dubai," *Independent* (April 7, 2009), http://www.independent.co.uk/opinion/commentators/johann-hari/the-dark-side-of-dubai-1664368.html.

4. Dubai Statistical Center, 2009.

5. Economist Intelligence Unit (EIU) and Western Union, "Global Migration Barometer" (online survey, 2008): 24, http://www.un.org/esa/population/meetings/seventh coord2008/GMB_ExecSumEIU.pdf.

6. Christopher M. Davidson, *Dubai: The Vulnerability of Success* (New York: Columbia University Press, 2008), 10.

7. Karen Leonard, "South Asians in the Indian Ocean World: Language, Policing, and Gender Practices in Kuwait and the United Arab Emirates," *Comparative Studies of South Asia, Africa and the Middle East* 25, no. 3 (2005): 677.

8. Davidson, *Vulnerability of Success*, 21, 24.

9. According to UAE archaeologist Peter Helleyer as cited in Jim Krane, *Dubai: City of Gold* (London: St. Martin's Press, 2009).

10. Fatma Al-Sayegh, "The Merchant's Role in Changing Society: The Case of Dubai, 1990–90," *Middle Eastern Studies* 34, no. 1 (1998): 87.

11. Ibid., 90.

12. Krane, *Dubai*, 24.

13. Davidson, *Vulnerability of Success*, 29, 31.

14. EIU, "Global Migration Barometer."

15. Al-Sayegh, "Merchant's Role," 99.

16. Bureau of Democracy, Human Rights and Labor (BDHRL).

17. Leonard, "South Asians in the Indian Ocean World," 678.

18. Martin Baldwin-Edwards, "Migration in the Middle East and Mediterranean," University Research Institute for Urban Environment and Human Resources, Athens (2005): 5.

19. Davidson, *Vulnerability of Success*, 190.

20. BDHRL.

21. Baldwin-Edwards, "Migration in the Middle East and Mediterranean," 17.

22. Rima Sabban, "Women Migrant Domestic Workers in the United Arab Emirates," in *Gender and Migration in Arab States: The Case of Domestic Workers* (Geneva: International Labour Organization, 2004), 9.

23. Nisha Varia, "Globalization Comes Home: Protecting Migrant Domestic Workers' Rights," *Human Rights Watch World Report* (2007): 4.

24. Baldwin-Edwards, "Migration in the Middle East and Mediterranean," 30.

25. Andrew Gardner, *City of Strangers: Gulf Migration and the Indian Community in Bahrain* (Ithaca: ILR Press, 2010).

26. Longva, "Keeping Migrant Workers in Check: The Kafala System in the Gulf," *Middle East Report* no. 211, 29 no. 2 (1999): 21.

27. Ibid., 22.

28. Ibid.

29. Ibid., 21.

30. United Arab Emirates, Department of Labour, Labour Law, Article 2; General Provisions.

31. Silvey, "Power, Difference and Mobility: Feminist Advances in Migration Studies," *Progress in Human Geography* 28, no. 4 (2004): 490–506.

32. United Arab Emirates, Department of Labour, *Labour Law*. Article 3, sections C and D.

33. Human Rights Watch Report on the UAE 2009.

34. Baldwin-Edwards, "Migration in the Middle East and Mediterranean," 35.

35. Longva, "Keeping Migrant Workers in Check," 22.

36. http://www.wam.ae/servlet/Satellite?c=WamLocEnews&cid=1241072976464& pagename=WAM/WAM_E_Layout. One official within this NCCHT task force empha-sized that anti-prostitution activists from the United States had played a large role in refocusing the UAE's efforts on sex trafficking. Responses to the TIP have included the establishment of the NCCHT (which is made up primarily of public prosecutors and law enforcement officials), as well as a human rights task force within the police sec-tor whose mandate is to arrest people deemed as trafficked persons. In addition, the NCCHT has worked to create the Dubai Foundation for Women and Children, which has admitted 43 cases of trafficking (all women), and a shelter in Abu Dhabi which has admitted 15 women since its inception in 2009. In 2009 there were 20 registered cases of trafficking (all related to the sex industry), up from 10 in 2008, and in 2008 6 persons were convicted. While these are important and impressive measures of progress, one activist who has been working to reform the *kefala* system expressed frustration and felt that some officials were using the hyperscrutiny on women in the sex industry to get away from the larger issue of labor laws in need of reform.

37. Chandra Mohanty, "Women Workers and Capitalist Scripts: Ideologies of Dom-ination, Common Interests and the Politics of Solidarity," in *Feminist Genealogies, Co-lonial Legacies, Democratic Futures*, ed. C. T. Mohanty and M. J. Alexander (New York: Routledge, 1997).

38. Jane Bristol-Rays (lecture on migrant work in the UAE, Georgetown School of Foreign Service, Qatar, January 2010).

CHAPTER 3

Parts of this chapter appear in Pardis Mahdavi, "Race, Space, Place: Notes on the Racial-ization and Spatialisation of Commercial Sex Work in Dubai, UAE," in *Culture, Health and Sexuality* 12, no. 8 (November 2010), 943–54, and will appear in "The Traffic in Per-sians," in *Comparative Studies of South Asia and the Middle East* (forthcoming).

1. For an in-depth discussion about equating trafficking with sex work, see Laura Agustín (2007) or Jane Scoular (2004).

2. Mario Pechemy (lecture, "Rethinking Sexuality" conference, Rockefeller Estates, Bellagio, Italy, September 2008).

3. Jo Doezema, "Now You See Her, Now You Don't: Sex Workers at the UN Traffick-ing Protocol Negotiation," *Social Legal Studies* 14, no. 1 (2005).

4. Siddarth Kara, *Sex Trafficking: Inside the Business of Modern Slavery* (New York: Columbia University Press, 2009). This rhetoric is espoused by first-wave feminists and policymakers such as Laura Lederer, Norma Ramos, Swanee Hunt, and Mark Lagon.

5. It is important to note here that "trafficking" into sex work, even by UN esti-mates, makes up only a small percentage (less than 5 percent) of global trafficking. Many

scholars (see Shah 2006, Cheng, Brennan) have noted that an overfocus on sex trafficking detracts attention from the large numbers of migrant laborers who face abuse in work settings outside the sex industry globally.

6. Wendy Chapkis, "Trafficking, Migration, and the Law: Protecting Innocents, Punishing Immigrants," *Gender and Women* 17, no. 6 (2003); Soderlund, "Running from the Rescuers."

7. These sentiments are not unique to Dubai; for an excellent discussion of similar experiences in the Dominican Republic, see Denise Brennan, *What's Love Got to Do With It? Transnational Desires and Sex Tourism in the Dominican Republic* (Durham, NC: Duke University Press, 2004).

8. Throughout this book I use the term *informal economy* to refer to labor that takes place outside of formal structures such as taxation, or in the case of the UAE, outside of the *kefala* or sponsorship system that structures labor laws and regulations in the Emirates. The work conducted in the informal economy is not always illegal, yet the nature in which it is conducted ("off the books") makes it informal and unregulated. Some work in the informal economy is illegal (such as buying and selling drugs, or in some countries, commercial sex work), much is not (domestic work, childcare, and so on). The distinction made between the formal and informal economies is along the lines of regulation. Some people work in the informal economy because they do not have legal permits in the countries in which they reside; others are conducting illegal work. For more on the informal economy, see Bourgois (1996) or Duneier (1999).

9. I do not deny that trafficked persons are often subjected to unscrupulous and criminal figures or that migrants, trafficked or not, are often victims of macro and micro instances of violence and exploitation. I am wary, however, of the term *victim*, because of the unequal power dynamic that is implied. By positioning trafficked women as victims, the attention and power is then shifted to *rescuers*, who set the terms for who counts as victims and what they are understood to be victims of. For an in-depth explication of the politics of the rescue industry, see Soderlund, "Running from the Rescuers."

10. Examples of media representations include films such as *Taken* or *Body of Lies*, journalistic books such as Jim Krane, *Dubai: City of Gold*, and a BBC documentary that is being made about commercial sex work in bars in Dubai.

11. For examples of this relationship in other contexts, see Bernstein (2007), Chapkis (1997), Soderlund (2005), and Vance and Miller (2004).

12. For an in-depth discussion of this phenomenon, see Bernstein (2007), Cheng (2010), or Vance and Miller (2004).

13. Penelope Saunders, "Traffic Violations: Determining the Meaning of Violence in Sexual Trafficking Versus Sex Work," *Journal of Interpersonal Violence* 20, no. 3 (2005); Jo Doezema, "Forced to Choose: Beyond the Free v. Forced Prostitution Dichotomy," in *Global Sex Workers: Rights, Resistance and Redefinition*, ed. Kemala Kempadoo and Jo Doezema (New York: Routledge, 1998).

14. Elizabeth Bernstein and L. Schaffner, eds., *Regulating Sex: The Politics of Intimacy and Identity* (New York: Routledge, 2005).

15. Parrenas (lecture, Scripps College, 2008); Wendy Chapkis, "Trafficking, Migration, and the Law: Protecting Innocents, Punishing Immigrants," *Gender and Women* 17, no. 6 (2003); Gretchen Soderlund, "Running from the Rescuers: New U.S. Crusades Against Sex Trafficking and the Rhetoric of Abolition," *NWSA Journal* 17, no. 3 (2005): 64–87.

16. Scholars such as Wendy Chapkis, Jo Doezema, Kemala Kempadoo, and Gretchen Soderlund have written about the artificial dichotomy drawn between "innocent migrants" and "guilty sex workers" in other contexts as well, and it is important to recognize that this phenomenon is not unique to the UAE or GCC countries.

17. For an excellent discussion of the flaws inherent in the "rescue industry," see Soderlund, "Running from the Rescuers."

18. NGOs are prohibited in the UAE based on a law that bans the formation of labor unions (according to Articles 155 and 166 of UAE Federal Law no. 8 of 1980, also referred to as the "Labor Law"; Human Rights Watch Report on the UAE 2007). Additionally, an NGO in the American sense of an organization, with a 510c3 tax status, does not carry the same weight in a country where banking and tax structures are governed by Islamic financial principles. In the UAE, *zakat* (the Muslim tradition of giving a certain percentage of one's income to charity) is widely practiced among citizens and noncitizens alike, who donate to various informal groups, mosques, and loosely formed associations. For more on the types of civil society in the Gulf, see Norton (1995/1996) or Mahdavi and Sargent (forthcoming).

19. The overemphasis on trafficking within the commercial sex industry (in which trafficking is often presented as accounting for all participants in the industry), and the overreliance on criminalization-based, narrowly focused responses against the sex industry as the most effective anti-trafficking initiatives, have dominated and distorted the nature and aims of a movement based initially on the principles of socioeconomic justice and migrant laborers' rights. The obsessive focus on violence within the sex industry obscures the widespread existence of labor rights abuses against migrants in all industries, and collapses the motivations of female migrants, both those seeking to enter the sex industry as well as those seeking to enter other labor sectors, into a homogenous tale of victimization.

20. Gayatri Chakravorty Spivak, "Diasporas Old and New: Women in the Transnational World, *Textual Practice* 10, no. 2 (1996): 245–69.

21. Lila Abu-Lughod, ed., 1998. *Remaking Women: Feminism and Modernity in the Middle East* (Princeton, NJ: Princeton University Press, 1998); Carole S. Vance (lecture, Society for Medical Anthropology, Yale University, 2009).

22. Kamala Kempadoo and Jo Doezema, *Global Sex Workers: Rights, Resistance, and Redefinition* (New York: Routledge, 1998), 54.

CHAPTER 4

1. Note that it is against UAE labor laws to confiscate passports (http://www.uae
-embassy.org/uae/human-rights/labor-rights).

2. While many laborers do report accidents and carelessness on the part of managers at construction sites, it is important to note that at least three male construction

workers we spoke to indicated that their employers paid careful attention to avoid accidents and permitted their employees to take off the hours between noon and 4 p.m. (the hottest time of the day, especially during summer) in order to rest in the shade. It is also important to note that it is neither the case that all Emirati-owned work sites abide by labor laws, nor that all nonlocal companies throw caution to the wind; rather, migrant laborers report a range of experiences within their work in the construction industry, and the variability in their experiences is tied to the variability in their employers and managers.

3. Denise Brennan, "Re-thinking Trafficking" (paper presented at Woodrow Wilson International Center for Scholars, March 1, 2010).

4. Paul Farmer, *Infections and Inequalities: The Modern Plagues* (Berkeley and LA: University of California Press, 2000); Nancy Scheper-Hughes and Carolyn Sargent, eds., *Small Wars: The Cultural Politics of Childhood* (Berkeley and LA: University of California Press, 1998); Philippe Bourgois, *In Search of Respect: Selling Crack in El Barrio* (Cambridge: Cambridge University Press, 1996).

5. Gardner, *City of Strangers*.

6. Technically, according to an official at the Ministry of Health with whom I spoke, if an unmarried woman gives birth to a child, she will go to jail and her child will be taken to an orphanage.

7. *Jaan* is a Persian term of endearment or respect roughly translating to *dear*.

8. According to UAE law, those who are in debt may not leave the country until their debts have been repaid or their cases settled.

9. Other migration scholars have noted the phenomenon of informal employment networks; see Ehrenreich and Hochschild (2002), Parrenas (2001, 2008), Strobl (2008).

10. Other scholars have written about the challenges inherent in sending home remittances and the difficulty of saving money for families back home; see Osella and Osella (2000), Gamburd (2000).

CHAPTER 5

1. Rima Sabban, "Women Migrant Domestic Workers in the United Arab Emirates," in *Gender and Migration in Arab States: The Case of Domestic Workers* (Geneva: International Labour Organization, 2004).

2. Rhacel Parrenas (lecture, Woodrow Wilson Center, March 2010).

3. Paul Farmer, *Infections and Inequalities: The Modern Plagues* (Berkeley and LA: University of California Press, 2000).

4. For excellent examples of research about migration in the Gulf, see Gardner (2010), Vora (2008), Silvey (2004), and Osella and Osella (2000). Some have studied the issue of domestic work in countries such as Kuwait (Longva 1999), Saudi Arabia (Silvey 2004) and Sri Lanka (Gamburd 2000), while others have assessed migrant demographics and communities in the UAE (Vora 2008, Kapiszewski 2001).

5. See chapter 3, note 8.

6. Manuel Castells, "Information Technology, Globalization and Social Development" (Geneva: United Nations Research Institute, 1999).

7. Mitchell Duneier, *Sidewalk* (New York: Farrar, Straus and Giroux, 1999).

8. For further reading on perverse integration and organized crime, see Bourgois, *In Search of Respect.*

9. De Regt, "Migrant Domestic Workers in the Middle East."

10. Due to a lack of local population to fill all needed government jobs, the UAE often imports members of its law enforcement.

11. Barbara Ehrenreich and Arlie R. Hochschild, *Global Woman: Nannies, Maids, and Sex Workers in the New Economy* (New York: Henry Holt, 2002).

12. While in some areas of the TIP report domestic workers are considered trafficked persons (such as the sections on Hong Kong or Singapore), in the Gulf context they are not.

13. Ehrenreich and Hochschild, "Global Woman"; Rhacel Parrenas, *Servants of Globalization: Women, Migration, and Domestic Work* (Stanford: Stanford University Press, 2001).

14. Ibid.; Rhacel Parrenas, "Migrant Mothering in Philippines" (lecture, Scripps College, Claremont, California, 2008).

15. Ray Jureidini, "Migrant Workers and Xenophobia in the Middle East" (Geneva: United Nations Research Institute for Social Development, 2003), iii.

16. Human Rights Watch Report on the UAE 2007.

CHAPTER 6

This chapter draws from an article coauthored with Christine Sargent that is forthcoming in 2011, "The Campaign to Address Forced Labor and Human Trafficking in Dubai."

1. Larry Diamond, "Rethinking Civil Society: Toward Democratic Consolidation," *Journal of Democracy* 5, no. 3 (July 1994): 5.

2. Nawaf Salam, "Civil Society in the Arab World: The Historical and Political Dimensions," Islamic Legal Studies Program, Harvard Law School, Occasional Publications (October 2002): 2.

3. Diamond, "Rethinking Civil Society," 3.

4. For examples, see A. R. Norton, *Civil Society in the Middle East*, vols. 1 and 2. London: Brill, 1995, 1996.

5. For a thorough and in-depth discussion of the alternative types of civil society found in the Gulf and, more broadly, in the Middle East, see ibid.

6. Note that over 80 percent of the population of the UAE are non-nationals (Davidson, *Vulnerability of Success*, 2008).

7. See http://www.uae-embassy.org/uae/human-rights/human-trafficking.

8. See http://www.uae-embassy.org/uae/human-rights/labor-rights.

9. For examples of these new provisions, see http://www.uae-embassy.org/uae/human-rights/labor-rights.

10. See http://www.uae-embassy.org/uae/human-rights/labor-rights.

11. As stated in chapter 1, I have changed the names of all the individuals I interviewed while retaining, at the request of my interviewees, the names of organizations. Though many interviewees asked that I also retain their actual names, I felt that it was in

their best interest to provide anonymity, due to the sensitive nature of the research topic and because, despite consenting to participate in the study, interviewees may not have been aware of my framework of analysis.

12. For full details of this case, refer to www.uaelawdirectory.com.

CHAPTER 7

1. The concept of perverse integration has been introduced in the previous chapter. For an in-depth discussion, see Bourgois (1996), Dunier (1999).

2. For further discussion of the ways in which various ethnic enclaves in the Gulf organize to meet their needs, see Nagy (2006) or Longva (1999).

3. For an in-depth discussion of xenophobia within labor sectors in the Gulf, see Jureidini (2003). Also, for information on interactions between members of the police in Bahrain and migrant workers accused of various crimes, see Strobl (2008).

4. Under Sharia law (which governs Iran today), sex work is illegal, thus anyone suspected of engaging in it could be arrested and detained.

CHAPTER 8

1. Johann Hari, "The Dark Side of Dubai," in *The Independent* (April 7, 2009), http://www.independent.co.uk/opinion/commentators/johann-hari/the-dark-side-of -dubai-1664368.html.

2. These policies have been adopted and implemented by countries such as Indonesia, Pakistan, and the Philippines.

3. Svati P. Shah, "Producing the Spectacle of Kamathipura: The Politics of Red Light Visibility in Mumbai," *Cultural Dynamics* 18, no. 3 (2006).

BIBLIOGRAPHY

Abu-Lughod, Lila (ed.). 1998. *Remaking Women: Feminism and Modernity in the Middle East*. Princeton, NJ: Princeton University Press.

Agustín, Laura Maria. 2010. Rescue, Rights, and Trafficking (lecture, Woodrow Wilson Center, March 1).

———. 2007. *Sex at the Margins: Migration, Labour Markets and the Rescue Industry*. New York: Palgrave Macmillan.

Al-Sayegh, Fatma. 1998. The Merchant's Role in Changing Society: The Case of Dubai, 1900–90. *Middle Eastern Studies* 34 (1):87–102.

Aradau, Claudia. 2004. The Perverse Politics of Four-Letter Words: Risk and Pity in the Securitisation of Human Trafficking. *Millennium Journal of International Studies* 33 (2):251–77.

"Bahrain Commended for Sponsorship Reforms." 2010. *Gulf Daily News* (Bahrain, April 30).

"Bahrain Introduces Job Switch Visa Rules." 2009. *The National* (United Arab Emirates, August 1).

"Bahrain Scraps Foreign Labour Sponsorship Scheme." 2009. www.arabianbusiness.com (May 5).

Baldwin-Edwards, Martin. 2005. Migration in the Middle East and Mediterranean. University Research Institute for Urban Environment and Human Resources, Athens.

Bales, Kevin. 2007. *Ending Slavery: How We Free Today's Slaves*. Berkeley and Los Angeles: University of California Press.

———. 1999. *Disposable People: New Slavery in the Global Economy*. Berkeley and Los Angeles: University of California Press.

Barry, Kathleen. 1996. *The Prostitution of Sexuality: The Global Exploitation of Women*. New York: New York University Press.

———. 1979. *Female Sexual Slavery*. Englewood Cliffs, NJ: Prentice-Hall.

Benton-Cohen, Katie. 2009. *Borderline Americans: Racial Division and Labor War in the Arizona Borderlands*. Cambridge, MA: Harvard University Press.

Bernard, R. 2001. *Social Research Methods: Qualitative and Quantitative Approaches*. Thousand Oaks, CA: Sage.

Bernstein, E. 2007. *Temporarily Yours: Intimacy, Authenticity and the Commerce of Sex*. Chicago: University of Chicago Press.

————, and L. Schaffner (eds.). 2005. *Regulating Sex: The Politics of Intimacy and Identity.* New York: Routledge.

Bourgois, Philippe. 1996. *In Search of Respect: Selling Crack in El Barrio.* Cambridge: Cambridge University Press.

Brennan, D. 2010. Re-Thinking Trafficking (lecture, Woodrow Wilson Center, March 1).

————. 2008. Competing Claims of Victimhood? Foreign and Domestic Victims of Trafficking in the United States. *Sexuality Research and Social Policy* 5 (4).

————. 2004. *What's Love Got to Do With It? Transnational Desires and Sex Tourism in the Dominican Republic.* Durham, NC: Duke University Press.

Castells, Manuel. 2008. The Rise of the Fourth World: Informational Capitalism, Poverty, and Social Exclusion. In *The Information Age: Economy, Society and Culture,* vol. 3: *End of Millennium.* Oxford: Blackwell.

————. 1999. Information Technology, Globalization and Social Development. Geneva: United Nations Research Institute.

Chacon, Jennifer M. 2006. Misery and Myopia: Understanding the Failures of U.S. Efforts to Stop Human Trafficking. *Fordham Law Review,* vol. 74, p. 2977.

Chang, Grace, and Kathleen Kim. 2007. Reconceptualizing Approaches to Human Trafficking: New Directions and Perspectives from the Field(s). *Stanford Journal of Civil Rights and Civil Liberties* 3 (2).

Chapkis, Wendy. 2003. Trafficking, Migration, and the Law: Protecting Innocents, Punishing Immigrants. *Gender and Women* 17 (6).

————. 1997. *Live Sex Act: Women Performing Erotic Labor.* New York: Routledge.

Cheng, Sealing. 2010. *On the Move for Love: Migrant Entertainers and the U.S. Military in South Korea.* Philadelphia: University of Pennsylvania Press.

Constable, N. 2003. *Romance on a Global Stage: Pen Pals, Virtual Ethnography, and "Mail Order Marriages."* Berkeley and Los Angeles: University of California Press.

Davidson, Christopher M. 2008. *Dubai: The Vulnerability of Success.* New York: Columbia University Press.

De Regt, Marina, and Annelies Moors. 2008. Migrant Domestic Workers in the Middle East. In *Illegal Migration and Gender in a Global and Historical Perspective,* edited by M. Schrover, J. Van der Leun, L. Lucassen, and C. Quispel. Amsterdam: International Migration Integration Social Cohesion.

Desyllas, Moshoula C. 2007. A Critique of the Global Trafficking: Discourse and U.S. Policy. *Journal of Sociology and Social Welfare* 34 (4).

Diamond, L. 1994. Rethinking Civil Society: Toward Democratic Consolidation. *Journal of Democracy* 5 (3):5.

Doezema, Jo. 2005. Now You See Her, Now You Don't: Sex Workers at the UN Trafficking Protocol Negotiation. *Social Legal Studies* 14 (1).

Doezema, Jo. 1998. Forced to Choose. In *Global Sex Workers: Rights, Resistance, and Redefinition,* edited by Kamala Kempadoo and Jo Doezema. New York: Routledge.

Duneier, Mitchell. 1999. *Sidewalk.* New York: Farrar, Straus and Giroux.

Dutta, M. 2008. *Communicating Health: A Culture Centered Approach.* Cambridge: Polity Press.

Economist Intelligence Unit (EIU). 2008. Global Migration Barometer. Western Union. http://www.un.org/esa/population/meetings/seventhcoord2008/GMB_ExecSum EIU.pdf.

Ehrenreich, Barbara, and Arlie R. Hochschild. 2002. *Global Woman: Nannies, Maids, and Sex Workers in the New Economy.* New York: Henry Holt.

Emirates, United Arab. *Labour Law*, edited by Dept. of Labour.

Farmer, Paul. 2000. *Infections and Inequalities: The Modern Plagues.* Berkeley and Los Angeles: University of California Press.

Foucault, M. 1972. *The Archaeology of Knowledge.* London: Routledge.

Frydl, Kathleen. 2009. *The GI Bill.* Cambridge: Cambridge University Press.

Gamburd, Michele Ruth. 2000. *The Kitchen Spoon's Handle: Transnationalism and Sri Lanka's Migrant Housemaids.* New York: Cornell University Press.

Gardner, Andrew. 2010. *City of Strangers: Gulf Migration and the Indian Community in Bahrain.* Ithaca: ILR Press.

Goodey, Jo. 2003. Migration, Crime and Victimhood: Responses to Sex Trafficking in the EU. *Punishment Society* 5 (4).

Hari, J. 2009. The Dark Side of Dubai. *The Independent.* http://www.independent.co.uk/opinion/commentators/johann-hari/the-dark-side-of-dubai-1664368.html.

Human Rights Watch. 2006. Building Towers, Cheating Workers: Exploitation of Migrant Construction Workers in the United Arab Emirates. Report.

Huntington, S. 1997. *The Clash of Civilizations and the Remaking of World Order.* New York: Simon & Schuster.

Ilkkaracan, Pinar. 2008. *Deconstructing Sexuality in the Middle East: Challenges and Discourse.* London: Ashgate.

Jureidini, Ray. 2003. Migrant Workers and Xenophobia in the Middle East. Geneva: United Nations Research Institute for Social Development.

Kapiszewski, Andrzej. 2001. *Nationals and Expatriates: Population and Labour Dilemmas of the Gulf.* Berkshire: Garnet.

Kara, Siddarth. 2009. Sex Trafficking: Inside the Business of Modern Slavery (lecture, Claremont, Feb. 18).

———. 2009. *Sex Trafficking: Inside the Business of Modern Slavery.* New York: Columbia University Press.

Krane, Jim. 2009. *Dubai: City of Gold.* London: St. Martin's.

Leigh, Carol. 1998. Inventing Sex Work. In *Whores and Other Feminists*, edited by Jill Nagle. New York: Routledge.

Leonard, Karen. 2005. South Asians in the Indian Ocean World: Language, Policing, and Gender Practices in Kuwait and the United Arab Emirates. *Comparative Studies of South Asia, Africa and the Middle East* 25 (3):677–86.

Longva, Anh Nga. 1999. Keeping Migrant Workers in Check: The Kafala System in the Gulf. *Middle East Report* no. 211, 29 (2).

Mahdavi, Pardis. 2008. *Passionate Uprisings: Iran's Sexual Revolution.* Stanford: Stanford University Press.

———, and Kathleen Frydl. Forthcoming. "List of Moral Wrongs" (article manuscript).

————, and C. Sargent. Forthcoming. "Trafficked Voices: Questioning the Discursive Construction of 'Trafficked' Persons in Dubai." *Journal of Middle East Women's Studies.*

————, and C. Sargent. Forthcoming. "The Campaign to Address Forced Labor and Human Trafficking in Dubai" (article manuscript).

Mohanty, Chandra Talpade. 1997. Women Workers and Capitalist Scripts: Ideologies of Domination, Common Interests and the Politics of Solidarity. In *Feminist Genealogies, Colonial Legacies, Democratic Futures*, edited by C. T. Mohanty and M. J. Alexander. New York: Routledge.

————. 1991. *Third World Women and the Politics of Feminism*, edited by C. T. Mohanty, A. Russo, and L. Torres. Bloomington: Indiana University Press.

Nagy, S. 2006. Making Room for Migrants, Making Sense of Difference: Spatial and Ideological Expressions of Social Diversity in Urban Qatar. *Urban Studies* 43 (1):119–37.

Norton, A. R. (ed.). 1995 and 1996. *Civil Society in the Middle East.* London: Brill.

Osella, Filippo, and Caroline Osella. 2000. Migration, Money and Masculinity in Kerala. *Royal Anthropological Institute of Great Britain and Ireland* 6 (1).

Parrenas, Rhacel. 2010. Re-Thinking Trafficking: Filipina Migrant Hostesses in Japan (lecture, Woodrow Wilson Center, March 1).

————. 2008. Migrant Mothering in Philippines (lecture, Scripps College).

————. 2001. *Servants of Globalization: Women, Migration, and Domestic Work.* Stanford: Stanford University Press.

Peters, Alicia. 2009. Things that Involve Sex are Just Different (lecture, Society for Medical Anthropology, Yale University).

Sabban, Rima. 2004. Women Migrant Domestic Workers in the United Arab Emirates. In *Gender and Migration in Arab States: The Case of Domestic Workers*, edited by S. Esmin and M. Smith. Geneva: International Labour Organization.

Salam, N. 2002. Civil Society in the Arab World: The Historical and Political Dimensions. Islamic Legal Studies Program, Harvard Law School, Occasional Publications.

Saunders, Penelope. 2005. Traffic Violations: Determining the Meaning of Violence in Sexual Trafficking Versus Sex Work. *Journal of Interpersonal Violence* 20 (3).

Scheper-Hughes, Nancy, and Carolyn Sargent (eds.). 1998. *Small Wars: The Cultural Politics of Childhood.* Berkeley and Los Angeles: University of California Press.

Scott, J. 2007. *The Politics of the Veil.* Princeton, NJ: Princeton University Press.

Scoular, Jane. 2004. The "Subject" of Prostitution: Interpreting the Discursive, Symbolic and Material Position of Sex/Work in Feminist Theory. *Feminist Theory* 5 (3):343–55.

Shah, Svati P. 2006. Producing the Spectacle of Kamathipura: The Politics of Red Light Visibility in Mumbai. *Cultural Dynamics* 18 (3):269–92.

Silvey, Rachel. 2004. Power, Difference and Mobility: Feminist Advances in Migration Studies. *Progress in Human Geography* 28 (4):490–506.

Soderlund, Gretchen. 2005. Running from the Rescuers: New U.S. Crusades Against Sex Trafficking and the Rhetoric of Abolition. *NWSA Journal* 17 (3):64–87.

Spivak, Gayatri Chakravorty. 1996. Diasporas Old and New: Women in the Transnational World. *Textual Practice* 10 (2):245–69.

Strobl, Staci. 2008. Policing Housemaids: The Criminalization of Domestic Workers in Bahrain. *British Journal of Criminology* 29 (2).

U.S. Department of State. 2008. Trafficking in Persons Report 2008.

Vance, Carole. 2009. Criminal Conversations: The Traffic between Criminal Law and Melodrama (lecture, Society for Medical Anthropology, Yale University).

———, and A. M. Miller. 2004. Sexuality, Human Rights, and Health. *Health and Human Rights* 7 (2):5–15.

Varia, Nisha. 2007. Globalization Comes Home: Protecting Migrant Domestic Workers' Rights. *Human Rights Watch World Report.*

Vora, Neha. 2008. Producing Diasporas and Globalization: Indian Middle-Class Migrants in Dubai. *Anthropological Quarterly* 81 (2).

Wijers, Marianne. 1998. Women, Labor and Migration: The Position of Trafficked Women and Strategies for Support. In *Global Sex Workers: Rights, Resistance and Redefinition,* edited by K. Kempadoo and J. Doezema. New York: Routledge.

Wooditch, A., M. A. Dupont-Moralis, and D. Hummer. 2009. Traffick Jam: A Policy Review of the United States Trafficking Victims Protection Act 2000." *Trends in Organized Crime* 12 (3–4): 235–50.

INDEX